ADVANCING CRITICAL CALL ACROSS AND BORDERS

Reimagining Possibilities for Languages, Literacies, and Cultures

Edited by Emma R. Britton, Angelika Kraemer, Theresa Austin, Hengyi Liu, and Xinyue Zuo

Since the Advances in CALL Research and Practice book series was launched in 2016, the field of computer-assisted language learning (CALL) has seen rapid pedagogical developments, as learners across all grade levels have benefited from online learning. During the recent COVID-19 pandemic, abrupt and extensive migrations to emergency online teaching exposed social trauma, isolation, and inequities emerging with CALL. While teachers and learners with access to computer-based technologies will continue to use them extensively to support language learning moving forward, the need to recast CALL as a humanitarian project which amplifies diversity, equity, inclusion, and access (DEIA) seems greater now than ever before.

This volume reimagines CALL as a vehicle for elevating the DEIA practices of language teachers and their students. It proposes that interinstitutional partnerships (i.e., those that involve knowledge and resource sharing across more than one institution) and transnational collaborations (i.e., those that include stakeholders located across national borders) are crucial for this purpose. It highlights a variety of CALL projects that have been collaboratively developed by stakeholders who are located at different institutions across the world, working with different languages. While the featured projects have varied aims, including curriculum development, virtual exchange, software development, and teacher professional development, collectively they advance our understanding of the ways that CALL and accessibility (DEIA) are purposefully and inextricably linked.

(Advances in CALL Research and Practice)

EMMA R. BRITTON is an applied linguist whose research centres on applications of critical linguistic, post-humanist, sociocultural, and multimodal theories in a variety of digitally-mediated second and world language settings.

ANGELIKA KRAEMER is an applied linguist and the director of the Language Resource Center at Cornell University.

THERESA AUSTIN is a critical sociolinguist in education and a professor of language, literacy, and culture at UMass Amherst.

HENGYI LIU recently completed PhD studies in language, literacy, and culture at UMass Amherst.

XINYUE ZUO recently earned a PhD from the Department of Teacher Education and Curriculum Studies at UMass Amherst.

Advances in CALL Research and Practice

Series Editor: Stephanie Link, Oklahoma State University

The *Advances in CALL Research and Practice* book series is published in partnership between the Computer Assisted Language Instruction Consortium (CALICO) and the University of Toronto Press. While the series will typically include a single volume published annually, it is possible that two books are published in a year or that the series goes a year without a volume, depending on the response to calls for papers.

Founding Series Editor: Greg Kessler, Ohio University

Published

2016
Landmarks in CALL Research
Edited by Greg Kessler

2017
Learner Autonomy and Web 2.0
Edited by Marco Cappellini, Tim Lewis, and Annick Rivens Mompean

2018
Assessment Across Online Language Education
Edited by Stephanie Link and Jinrong Li

2019
Engaging Language Learners through CALL
Edited by Nike Arnold and Lara Ducate

2020
Understanding Attitude in Intercultural Virtual Communication
Edited by Ana Oskoz and Margarita Vinagre

2021
Project-Based Language Learning and CALL: From Virtual Exchange to Social Justice
Edited by Michael Thomas and Kasumi Yamazaki

2022
Identity, Multilingualism and CALL: Responding to New Global Realities
Edited by Liudmila Klimanova

2024
Technology-Mediated Crisis Response in Language Studies
Edited by Senta Goertler and Jesse Gleason

Advancing Critical CALL across Institutions and Borders

Reimagining Possibilities for Languages, Literacies, and Cultures

EDITED BY EMMA R. BRITTON, ANGELIKA KRAEMER, THERESA AUSTIN, HENGYI LIU, AND XINYUE ZUO

UNIVERSITY OF TORONTO PRESS
Toronto Buffalo London

Published by the University of Toronto Press
Toronto Buffalo London
utppublishing.com
Printed in Canada

© Emma R. Britton, Angelika Kraemer, Theresa Austin, Hengyi Liu, and Xinyue Zuo 2025

ISBN 978-1-4875-6724-8 (paper)   ISBN 978-1-4875-6726-2 (EPUB)
                                    ISBN 978-1-4875-6725-5 (PDF)

Advances in CALL Research and Practice

Library and Archives Canada Cataloguing in Publication
Title: Advancing critical CALL across institutions and borders: Reimagining
    possibilities for languages, literacies, and cultures / edited by Emma R. Britton,
    Angelika Kraemer, Theresa Austin, Hengyi Liu, and Xinyue Zuo.
Names: Britton, Emma R., editor. | Kraemer, Angelika, editor. | Austin, Theresa Y.,
    editor | Liu, Hengyi, editor. | Zuo, Xinyue, editor.
Description: Series statement: Advances in CALL research and practice | Includes
    bibliographical references and index.
Identifiers: Canadiana (print) 20250155338 | Canadiana (ebook) 20250155370 |
    ISBN 9781487567248 (paper) | ISBN 9781487567262 (EPUB) |
    ISBN 9781487567255 (PDF)
Subjects: LCSH: Language and languages – Computer-assisted instruction. | LCSH:
    Multilingual education. | LCSH: Transnational education. | LCSH: Sociolinguistics.
Classification: LCC P53.38 .A38 2025 | DDC 418/.00285 – dc23

Cover design: John Beadle

We wish to acknowledge the land on which the University of Toronto Press
operates. This land is the traditional territory of the Wendat, the Anishnaabeg, the
Haudenosaunee, the Métis, and the Mississaugas of the Credit First Nation.

University of Toronto Press acknowledges the financial support of the Government
of Canada, the Canada Council for the Arts, and the Ontario Arts Council, an
agency of the Government of Ontario, for its publishing activities.

 Canada Council for the Arts / Conseil des Arts du Canada    ONTARIO ARTS COUNCIL / CONSEIL DES ARTS DE L'ONTARIO
an Ontario government agency
un organisme du gouvernement de l'Ontario

Funded by the Government of Canada   Financé par le gouvernement du Canada   Canadä

 MIX Paper | Supporting responsible forestry FSC® C103567

Contents

List of Figures and Tables vii

Acknowledgments ix

Abbreviations xi

1 Introduction to Critical CALL across Institutions and Borders   1
   EMMA R. BRITTON, ANGELIKA KRAEMER, THERESA AUSTIN,
   HENGYI LIU, AND XINYUE ZUO

**Part One: CALL In/Through Transnational and
Community-Oriented Learner Exchange**

2 Critical Virtual Exchange: At the Interface of Critical CALL,
   Critical Digital Literacy, and Critical Global Citizenship
   Education   29
   MIRJAM HAUCK

3 Advancing Inclusion through Pre-Mobility Virtual Exchange   55
   ÁNGELA M. ALONSO MORAIS

4 COILing Discrimination Narratives across Continents:
   A Virtual Exchange Project between a Community College
   in New York City and a Four-Year College in Jordan   75
   DENIZ GOKCORA AND RAYMOND OENBRING

5 Using Technology and Art in a Middle School Exploratory
   Heritage Language Program: Diversity Matters   90
   LULU EKIERT AND THERESA AUSTIN

Part Two: CALL In/Through Less Commonly Taught Languages

6 Indigenizing Language Pedagogies with Technology: Entangling Human and Non-Human Affordances for Indigenous Language and Culture Maintenance, Revitalization, and Reclamation — 121
SABINE SIEKMANN, JOAN PARKER WEBSTER, AND STEVEN L. THORNE

7 Developing an Interactive AI-Based Spoken Dialogue System for Improving Oral Proficiency in Indonesian and Burmese — 145
RAHMI H. AOYAMA, MAW MAW TUN, AND REZA NEIRIZ

Part Three: CALL In/Through Teacher Professional Development

8 Technology-Enabled Interinstitutional Professional Development for Less Commonly Taught Languages — 171
EMILY HEIDRICH UEBEL, LUCA GIUPPONI, KOEN VAN GORP, AND THOMAS JESÚS GARZA

9 Interinstitutional and Transnational Language Teacher Professional Development: Teachers' Critical Reflections and Future Directions — 191
AN NGUYEN SAKACH AND TRANG PHAN

10 Advancing Arabic Language Education: Empowering Teachers and Promoting Critical CALL through the Arabic Teachers' Council — 217
KAMILIA RAHMOUNI

Index — 241

Figures and Tables

Figures

2.1	Internet World Penetration Rates	36
2.2	Critical Virtual Exchange	37
2.3	Critical Virtual Exchange – Expanded Framework	38
6.1	Map of Alaska Native Languages	122
6.2	The Design Cycle	128
6.3	Our Redesigned Conceptual Framework	139
7.1	Task Description for Ordering Coffee	154
7.2	First Screen of the Indonesian SDS	154
7.3	Second Screen of the Indonesian SDS	155
8.1	The PIC-RAT Matrix	182
9.1	Several Phases in the Reading Assessment Design Workshop	197
9.2	Different Types of Feedback One Received in the Workshop	209
10.1	DEIA-Enhanced CoP Framework	228

Tables

2.1	Hegemonic versus Non-Hegemonic VE	42
3.1	Structure of the *GearUp!* VE	65
3.2	Countries and Institutions Participating in the First Round of *GearUp!* VE	66
4.1	COIL Project Assignments	83
4.2	Emergent Themes in Discrimination Narratives	85

5.1	Heritage Language and Art Curricular Outline, Grades 6–8 (SY 2022–2023)	99
6.1	The "What" of Multiliteracies: Designs of Meaning	125
7.1	Learners' Perception of Difficulty	157
7.2	Learners' Perception of the SDS Interface	157
7.3	User Experience: Ease of Speaking with an Avatar	158
7.4	User Experience: Comfort Level	159
7.5	Language Development	160

Acknowledgments

We would like to thank all those who have been involved in the process of bringing this volume to fruition. We are most grateful to CALICO for showing keen interest in our topic and giving us the opportunity to edit this volume. The series editor, Stephanie Link, has been most supportive of the book idea from the onset and has worked alongside us tirelessly in all stages of the project. We would also like to thank the editorial personnel at Equinox and the University of Toronto Press for guiding us through the entire publication process.

There are many individuals we are thankful to for contributing to the volume's content. These include not only the authors themselves but also participants, students, as well as other collaborators who have been involved in their research and pedagogical projects. Many of the dedicated contributors to this volume have also judiciously reviewed chapters. Below are the names of reviewers who provided this additional service:

Ángela M. Alonso Morais	University of León, Spain
Rahmi H. Aoyama	Northern Illinois University
Lulu Ekiert	Holyoke Public Schools
Luca Giupponi	Michigan State University
Deniz Gokcora	Borough of Manhattan Community College/CUNY
Reza Neiriz	Iowa State University
Raymond Oenbring	University of the Bahamas
Maw Maw Tun	Northern Illinois University
Koen Van Gorp	Michigan State University
Kamilia Rahmouni	Virginia Commonwealth University
An Nguyen Sakach	Arizona State University

Sabine Siekmann University of Alaska Fairbanks
Joan Parker Webster University of Alaska Fairbanks

Finally we thank our families and friends for their interest, comradery, and support as we worked on this volume.

Təşəkkürlər! Danke! ¡Gracias! 谢谢！にふぇーでーびる！

Abbreviations

AATA	American Association of Teachers of Arabic
ACTFL	formerly known as American Council on the Teaching of Foreign Languages
AI	artificial intelligence
ANLC	Alask Native Language Center
API	application programming interface
AR	augmented reality
ASR	automatic speech recognition
ATC	Arabic Teacher Council
ASU	Arizona State University
BMCC	Borough of Manhattan Community College
CALL	computer-assisted language learning
CARLA	Center for Advanced Research on Language Acquisition
CDL	critical digital literacy
CeLTA	Center for Language Teaching Advancement
CERCLL	Center for Educational Resources in Culture, Language and Literacy
COIL	Collaborative Online International Learning
CoP	communities of practice
COTI	Consortium for the Teaching of Indonesian
COTSEAL	Council of Teachers of Southeast Asian Languages
CVE	critical virtual exchange
DC-ATC	District of Columbia Arabic Teachers' Council
DEIA	diversity, equity, inclusion, and accessibility
DI	differentiated instruction
ECTS	European Credit Transfer and Accumulation System
ERT	emergency remote teaching

ESL	English as a second language
EU	European Union
EUROCALL	European Association for Computer Assisted Language Learning
GCE	global citizenship education
GSACS	Global Scholars Achieving Career Success
HEI	higher education institution
HL	heritage language
IaH	internationalization at home
ICT	information and communication technologies
IoC	internationalization of the curriculum
JUST	Jordan University of Science and Technology
LARC	Language Assessment Research Conference
LCTL	less commonly taught language
LMS	learning management system
MENA	Middle East and North Africa
MLA	Modern Language Association
MSA	Modern Standard Arabic
MSU	Michigan State University
NAFOSTED	National Foundation for Science & Technology Development (Vietnam)
NCOLCTL	National Council of Less Commonly Taught Languages
NGO	non-governmental organization
NIU	Northern Illinois University
NLRC	National Less Commonly Taught Languages Resource Center
OER	open educational resource
OLT	online language teaching
OPI	Oral Proficiency Interview
PD	professional development
PIC-RAT (model)	PIC: passive, interactive, creative; RAT: replace, amplify, transform
PSA	public service announcement
QFI	Qatar Foundation International
SAE	Standard American English
SDG	Sustainable Development Goal (United Nations)
SDS	spoken dialogue system
SEA	Southeast Asian

SEALC	Southeast Asian Language Council
SVG	Scalable Vector Graphics (format)
SY	school year
TESOL	Teaching English to Speakers of Other Languages
TIP	technology integration plan
TTS	text to speech
UAF	University of Alaska Fairbanks
VALIANT	Virtual Innovation and Support Networks for Teachers
VE	virtual exchange
ZPD	zone of proximal development

1 Introduction to Critical CALL across Institutions and Borders

Emma R. Britton, Angelika Kraemer, Theresa Austin, Hengyi Liu, and Xinyue Zuo

1 Introduction

This volume recognizes computer-assisted language learning (CALL) as a field supporting language educators' own sensemaking and criticality about the role of technology in instruction. While the term "critical" carries many understandings and meanings across the disciplines, this volume draws from understandings in the field of critical applied linguistics. From this vantage point, criticality involves questioning "the assumptions that lie at the basis of our praxis" as language educators, considering beliefs and practices that "have become naturalized and are not called into question" (Helm et al., 2015, p. xiii; see also Chapter 2 by Hauck, this volume). In other words, criticality prompts us as practitioners to question what we may have taken for granted about digital technology's numerous advantages for language learners and teachers, drawing attention to ways that technology is increasingly commodifiable in the realm of language learning (Hellmich, 2019) and may "exacerbate problems of discrimination, marginalization, and inequity" (Gleason & Suvorov, 2019, p. i).

Critical CALL practitioners therefore directly engage their practice with issues of power, dominance, justice, and inequity, recognizing the project of language teaching and learning as one that is connected to broader social, cultural, and political systems (Helm et al., 2015). Critical CALL practitioners discern which modes of technology-enhanced instruction can disrupt social injustices, as well as which modes can sustain them. They ask thought-provoking questions that contributors to this volume bring to light, such as "How can technology be leveraged to support diversity, equity, inclusion, and accessibility (DEIA) in my language education context?" or "How does technology contribute to social inequities in my language education context?" Such questions subsequently inform their work with language learners. In this sense, critical CALL is intended not just for teachers or program administrators but also for learners, who can subsequently develop criticality through instruction and also by questioning and reflecting on assumptions of their belief systems and considering societal issues of equity, marginalization, and power in their local and global worlds (see Chapter 2 by Hauck, this volume).

Moving forward, we presume that teachers and learners with access to computer-based technologies are more and more likely to rely on these tools to support language learning, which only increases the need for a critical mindset. Alongside increased use of technology, human-machine interactions will continue to become progressively sophisticated and commodifiable. In this evolving sociotechnical landscape – increasingly characterized by fast-paced algorithmic culture, bots, and machine learning (Godwin-Jones, 2021) – the CALL field cannot be assumed to be a neutral or an apolitical domain (Hellmich, 2019). In the future, fast-paced innovation in computer applications will increase language learners' access to learning resources. However, the quality of these tools cannot be guaranteed, and their use cannot guarantee successful intercultural communication with other target language users since such relations are "intersubjectively constructed in each specific context of interaction" (Canagarajah, 2007, p. 925). Localized languages used by specific populations may not be adequately addressed in computer applications, further marginalizing these users and the status of their language (Koenecke et al., 2020). This issue is compounded by the loss of embodied human communication, which relies on interpreting and producing cues such as gaze, body movement, gestures, and prosodic elements (Sax, 2022). Intercultural negotiation skills will therefore remain essential to CALL, and the need to recast critical CALL as a humanitarian project that "goes beyond technicist references to skills and competences" (Fassetta et al., 2020, p. 119) seems greater now than ever before.

With this in mind, the goal of this volume is to feature interinstitutional and transnational partnerships that bring critical CALL objectives to the forefront of multilingual education. This volume features and advocates for CALL innovations leveraging social collaboration to support humanistically oriented goals in multilingual learning. We understand such goals as focused on developing participants' ethics and global citizenry, cultivating "an appreciation of diversity and otherness" and fostering "empathy, care, love, unity and solidarity in human relations" (Porto et al., 2023, p. 281). We understand that humanistically oriented objectives are aligned with critical CALL, which centres social issues of power, equity, discrimination, and dominance within social worlds that are ever increasingly impacted by technology. We define "interinstitutional partnerships" as those that involve knowledge and resource sharing across more than one institution and "transnational partnerships" as those that include stakeholders located across national borders.

The contributions to this volume offer possibilities for partnership in three key thematic ways: learner-oriented exchanges, teaching and learning of less commonly taught languages, and language teachers' professionalization and collaboration. First, critical CALL emerges in learner-oriented exchanges where students in under-resourced settings gain opportunities to interact online with other speakers of the target language outside their institution, extending their learning networks to their greater communities or even to spaces that are geographically distant. Such transnational exchanges and community-oriented partnerships are featured in Part One of the volume. Second, given the dominant focus on English language teaching in learner-oriented exchanges and in CALL research more broadly (Ward, 2018; Zak, 2021), critical CALL emerges through the teaching and learning of less commonly taught languages (LCTLs). The National Council of Less Commonly Taught Languages (NCOLCTL) defines LCTLs as "all languages other than English and the commonly taught European languages of German, French and Spanish" (NCOLCTL, n.d.). CALL collaborations supporting the teaching and learning of LCTLs are featured in Part Two. Third, critical CALL is realized not only through online exchanges that support language learners but also through those that support language teachers' equity, professionalization, collaboration, and development of multilingual dispositions (Yazan et al., 2021). Part Three features cases of virtual professional development communities occurring across institutions and national borders.

2 The Impetus for This Volume

The need for critical CALL practitioners across educational contexts has become even more important since the *Advances in CALL Research and Practice* book series – to which this volume belongs – was launched in 2016. Since that time, the CALL field has seen rapid pedagogical transformations and developments, as advances in information and communication technology based on mobile and computer-assisted instructional applications have all the more frequently been called into use in language education contexts (Saylan et al., 2023). The COVID-19 pandemic particularly demanded that language teachers and learners – across all educational levels and geographic contexts – participate in some form of online teaching during disruptive times (Goertler & Gleason, 2024; Jin et al., 2022). This shift to digital interaction, often replacing face-to-face communication, underscored the integral role of technology in educational continuity.

While studies conducted prior to 2020 suggested that online language learners "fare[d] at least as well as their face-to-face counterparts" (Moser et al., 2021, p. 1), such abrupt and extensive migrations to emergency remote teaching often exacerbated social inequities and impacted the CALL field profoundly (Goertler & Gleason, 2024; Thomas & Yamazaki, 2021). Mass and unanticipated migrations to online learning heightened the collective trauma of social isolation and brought to bear many new challenges in relation to DEIA – especially for language learners and teachers from disenfranchised populations (Wiley-Camacho et al., 2022), including those from underserved backgrounds residing in scarcely resourced countries or areas. The inequities that were exacerbated and brought to light by these mass migrations continue to be challenges at the present time, reminding us that equitable access to CALL technologies cannot be presumed. For instance, learners in remote areas or areas of political conflict continue to encounter recurrent power outages and limited internet connectivity (see Chapter 2 by Hauck, this volume; Shahnama et al., 2021), while others in condensed households continue to experience learning struggles related to home life (e.g., the lack of a workspace conducive to learning). Those in countries under authoritarian regimes continue to face censorships to learning content (Fassetta et al., 2020; Wiley-Camacho et al., 2022; Yang & Roberts, 2023).

Disproportionately privileged mass migrations to online learning have also brought to light immeasurable challenges for language teachers across the globe, showing that teachers need continuous support in implementing CALL innovations. Some reports have attempted to document the challenges exacerbated by the pandemic. One report targeting teachers' perceptions of online teaching during the pandemic in a Chinese context (Yang, 2020) identified difficulties that the 15,438 surveyed teachers encountered in online teaching across multiple educational settings. Among the difficulties, unstable internet connections, teachers beginning to use available relevant technology for the first time, and limited interaction with learners were recurring challenges as teachers were forced to switch instruction from in person to online abruptly in coordination with a national strategy to cope and limit the spread of the pandemic. While this volume is not focused on describing CALL innovations intended for emergency remote teaching, which the previous series volume did (Goertler & Gleason, 2024), many CALL partnerships featured here have been implemented during time frames overlapping with the pandemic, making clear to us not only that technologies have contributed to social inequities in these recent years but also that creative CALL innovations have emerged in support of DEIA.

We see the present moment as opening an important opportunity for reimagining CALL as a transformative vehicle (Freire, 2005) for community building, equity, inclusion, empowerment, and emancipation for language learners and their teachers. Within this volume, we recognize these transformations as happening through three types of interinstitutional collaborative CALL models, which correspond to the book's three parts. In the following Sections 2, 3, and 4, we offer conceptualizations of these models, drawing attention to some of their affordances, as well as citing relevant examples from the volume's contributors. In Section 5, we identify the chapters that are included in each of the three parts and summarize the content of each chapter.

3 CALL In/Through Transnational and Community-Oriented Learner Exchange

Particularly in the CALL field, the term "exchange" is most commonly associated with interaction occurring exclusively through digitally mediated channels, yet contributors to this volume have prompted us to broaden our conceptualization beyond virtual exchange (which we define in the next paragraph). In this volume, interinstitutional exchange can involve a range of "collaborative strategies" adopted between two or more institutions that share interest in "increasing the quality of education, even as they cope with limited or diminishing resources" (Charitos et al., 2017, p. 2). In this regard, Ekiert and Austin's Chapter 5 shows that interinstitutional exchange can involve not only technology-mediated channels but also local community involvement, when purposed to support language learners. The chapter describes a three-way exchange between a university, a school, and the local community, illustrating the various ways that technologies become embedded in artefacts and artistic creations, as well as in hybrid interactions occurring offline and in person.

Over the last 20 years, virtual exchange (VE) has been developing as a subfield of CALL (Benini & Thomas, 2021). This development is evidenced in part by a dedicated journal devoted to the topic, *Journal of Virtual Exchange*, which had its first issue published in 2018 (O'Dowd, 2018). According to Helm (2015), VE is a "systematic process of communicating and working with people from different locations through online or virtual means for the development of language and/or intercultural competence" (p. 187). It is facilitated by two or more faculty who are geographically separated and enables language learners to engage in academic conversations, collaborative projects or assignments, as well as joint synchronous classes or lectures (Zak, 2021). VE can occur either synchronously or asynchronously, with faculty employing a range of technologies to support interactions. Videoconferencing and chat tools can support synchronous interactions, whereas text platforms like email, forums, or other online tools can support asynchronous interactions. However, to reach – rather than exclude – learners in under-resourced communities in the world, Hauck (Chapter 2, this volume) advocates for the use of low-bandwidth technologies; these include text-based tools such as chat or discussion forums. To further promote inclusion during exchange, Ekiert and Austin (Chapter 5, this volume) demonstrate repurposing widely accessible and existing technologies to develop student inquiry, art-making, and development for wellness that extends the classroom into various multilingual communities.

As noted by O'Dowd (2018), alongside the increased interest in the area, there has been an increasing number of terminologies circulating that are used to describe and characterize VE. While the origins of VE arguably lie in the field of language education (see Chapter 2 by Hauck, this volume), VE is also a pedagogical approach that has been used in subject-specific areas that fall outside the realm of language teaching. It is beyond our scope to introduce and define all these terms; for this purpose, readers can consult O'Dowd (2018) or Zak (2021) for literature-informed characterizations.

Here, we distinguish two overarching linguistic models of VE significant in the CALL field. The first model involves bilingual exchange among learners and the second employs a lingua franca approach, where one shared language is used for communication (Gutiérrez & O'Dowd, 2021).

In the first model, commonly referred to as e-tandem or teletandem, students at both partner sites have some knowledge of both languages that will be used in the exchange. While there are no extensive examples of e-tandem featured in this volume, it is important to emphasize the value of the model here, as e-tandem engages learners in reciprocal language exchange, using both languages during interactions for purposes of intercultural learning alongside language development (Gutiérrez & O'Dowd, 2021). In reciprocal exchanges, both partners benefit from the exchange, and both provide support to help their partner learn. Peers can act as informal linguistic tutors, providing feedback on each other's language usage, thus facilitating skill development through authentic communication and support (Gutiérrez & O'Dowd, 2021; O'Rourke, 2007). Guo and Xu's (2023) study of a nine-week VE involving 22 students learning Chinese as an additional language from one British university is one example of the e-tandem model. In this instance, the Chinese language learners were paired with speaking partners from a Chinese university who were studying to be Chinese language teachers. In their study of this e-tandem exchange, Guo and Xu (2023) explored how translanguaging – which involves interlocutors in moving dynamically and fluidly between the conventionally named languages in their repertoires – naturally emerged during online conversations between the partners. In this volume, Hauck in Chapter 2 conceptualizes translanguaging (which has especially been documented as occurring in e-tandem) as an integral part of critically oriented VE, as it promotes positive and inclusive views of multilingualism.

In the lingua franca approach, the second overarching VE model, learners across the partner sites share knowledge of one common language, which becomes the lingua franca for communication, but do not share the same first language (Lenkaitis & Loranc, 2021). For example, Gokcora and Oenbring's Collaborative Online International Learning (COIL) project (featured in Chapter 4, this volume) used English as the lingua franca for exchange, as the project involved US-based English-as-a-second-language students (who spoke a number of different first languages) and Jordan-based students majoring in paramedics, for whom Arabic was a first language. Similarly, as described by Alonso Morais in Chapter 3, this volume, the *GearUp!* VE model, which prepares students for study abroad experiences, was intentionally designed to accommodate students from a wide range of cultural backgrounds and therefore used English as a lingua franca of the exchange.

Both models of VE – e-tandem and lingua franca – can enhance DEIA for learners, and we draw attention to DEIA benefits here. In general, VE communities have been shown to increase access to authentic language-learning opportunities and foster intercultural collaborative learning. It is particularly beneficial for individuals residing in rural areas or regions with limited or scarce educational resources (e.g., media, electricity, formal education). Additionally, it extends to those for whom education abroad experiences are infeasible (Machwate et al., 2021) due to financial constraints, familial responsibilities, or restricted mobility due to immigration status (Zak, 2021). Technologies can therefore provide drastic shifts to education, opening spaces for learning within larger connected networks, where traditional approaches to teaching and learning are no longer appropriate (Kannan & Munday, 2018), and helping language learners take the initiative and develop as autonomous learners (Schwienhorst, 2009).

Participation in VE also serves to empower multilingual learners by facilitating meaningful intercultural encounters and promoting open and purposeful communication, especially during times of turmoil and suffering (Moore & Simon, 2015). For instance, Porto et al. (2023) describe a four-week VE project involving English language learners at the Universidad Nacional de La Plata in Argentina and undergraduate students participating in a course on intercultural communication at the University of Maryland, Baltimore County. The project, which took place during the COVID-19 crisis in June 2020, involved students in exploring artistic expressions in their home communities illustrating the discomfort of the pandemic and also in co-creating expressive multimodal artefacts. Findings showed the process of creating these multimodal artworks across nations to be transformative, disturbing learners' affective responses to the pandemic in productive ways. Moreover, participation in transnational online communities contributes to the development of learners' identities as multilingual individuals. For example, Song (2021) analysed how an informal online community composed of Korean women in diasporic settings forged identities through the use of English as an additional language. Her analysis of their discourses evidenced resistance to, as well as recirculation of, dominant ideologies about language learning and the participating women's Koreanness.

4 CALL In/Through Less Commonly Taught Languages

LCTLs carry smaller numbers of speakers worldwide (compared to the more commonly taught languages), making CALL innovations crucial for broadening otherwise limited access to learning opportunities and resources (see Heidrich Uebel et al., 2024). As mentioned previously, some scholars consider an LCTL to be any language other than the most commonly taught languages of English, German, French, or Spanish (NCOLCTL, n.d.). However, the Modern Language Association (MLA), which keeps track of US higher education enrolments for all languages other than English, offers a narrower definition, understanding LCTLs as all languages other than the "top fifteen" enrolments (Lusin et al., 2023, p. 15). These 15 languages included Spanish, French, American Sign Language, Japanese, German, Chinese/Mandarin, Italian, Arabic, Latin, Korean, Russian, Ancient Greek, Biblical Hebrew, Portuguese, and Modern Hebrew when reports were last tabulated for the fall 2021 semester. While there are many languages taught in Western contexts that meet the LCTL classification outside these 15, Farsi, Vietnamese, and Hindi are just a few examples with which readers may already have familiarity, given that each of these languages has many millions of speakers. Indigenous languages (which often have smaller numbers of speakers) also classify as LCTLs. Indigenous languages are those spoken by "indigenous communities, peoples and nations" who have a "historical continuity with pre-invasion and pre-colonial societies that developed on their territories" (Martínez, 1986, as cited in Lane & Makihara, 2016, p. 300). This volume features Yup'ik, Alutiiq, and Ahtna, three of the Indigenous languages of Alaska (see Chapter 6 by Siekmann et al.), as well as Indonesian and Burmese (see Chapter 7 by Aoyama et al.), both of which are LCTLs spoken primarily in Southeast Asia.

While many languages known as LCTLs have millions of speakers residing in their localized contexts, learners rarely encounter these languages in formal educational spaces outside of their localities. Promoting learners' access to LCTLs is therefore synonymous with enhancing DEIA within educational institutions. From a critical standpoint, more commonly taught languages such as English are known as colonial languages. The global spread of dominant languages throughout centuries of colonialism has threatened the survival of Indigenous and local languages (Meighan, 2022). Meighan (2022), for instance, notes that "two-third of the world's 7,000–7,500 languages are Indigenous languages; one-third are experiencing loss" (p. 2). Therefore, when offering Indigenous or other LCTL languages, institutions are creating a more inclusive environment that recognizes and affirms the multilingual and diverse identities of heritage speakers and promotes access to worldviews and ways of knowing that emerge through these languages (see Chapter 8 by Heidrich Uebel et al., this volume). It is important to note that learners' motivations for learning LCTLs resonate with DEIA concerns and are often different from motivations to learning more commonly taught languages (Ward, 2018). Learners often enrol in more commonly taught languages for career reasons or for compulsory reasons (Murphy et al., 2022). By contrast, learners often enrol in LCTLs for "cultural, heritage, and language preservation reasons" (Ward, 2018, p. 116). Indigenous languages face particular threats in sustaining strong numbers of speakers who will continue to carry their cultural, spiritual, and economic survival across generations, making their institutional availability a key factor for decolonizing language education (Meighan, 2022).

In the US educational context, LCTL programs are often unavailable in K–12 settings due to the limited number of LCTL speakers residing in these communities and the predominant monolingual English ideology that is often perpetuated in schools. While relatively rare, some K–12 schools have taken a role in supporting Indigenous language maintenance and revitalization efforts in communities where a substantial number of heritage learners reside. For instance, McCarty et al. (2021) note that Hawaii medium schooling represents the most comprehensive system of Indigenous language immersion in the United States, with 27 Kaiapuni schools existing at the time their article was written. In Chapter 6, this volume, Siekmann et al. note that there are established programs delivering instruction in the medium of the local Alaska Indigenous languages, including Yup'ik immersion or Yup'ik/English dual language programs. While these examples are promising, many learners do not have the opportunity to enrol in studying a LCTL until they attend university.

Yet, even in higher education contexts, LCTLs comprise less than a quarter of US higher education enrolments (Lusin et al., 2023), and as a result, LCTL instructors face challenges that are distinct from those teaching the more commonly taught languages. These include low enrolment rates, limited availability of quality instructional materials (Heidrich Uebel et al., 2024), and limited opportunities for learners to interact with experienced speakers outside of the language classroom (see Chapter 7 by Aoyama et al., this volume). LCTL programs tend to be significantly smaller than programs in more commonly taught languages, and there is often just one instructor teaching the associated language for various learner levels, which means that institutions often do not have the capability to consistently offer language sequences from year to year. In some institutions, instructors may not be able to offer advanced courses at all, given that any language program will experience attrition in the number of enrolled students as the levels increase (Heidrich Uebel et al., 2024).

Interinstitutional collaboration via course-sharing (or resource-sharing) models has been established as a common CALL-based strategy to overcome some of the challenges that are unique to LCTLs. Course sharing can take different forms but often involves two or more institutions in a "bilateral language exchange," where each institution has a LCTL it can offer to the other without the exchange of funds (Heidrich Uebel et al., 2024). Angelika Kraemer, co-editor of this volume, co-directs one instantiation of an LCTL course-sharing effort in her current role at Cornell University in the United States. The Shared Course Initiative is an interinstitutional agreement between Columbia, Cornell, and Yale universities to share instruction in more than 20 LCTLs using high-definition videoconferencing technology. These three institutions have established a memorandum of understanding, which permits students to enrol in any LCTL shared by the other institutions without paying tuition to the sending institution. To give an example, a Cornell student who is interested in enrolling in Elementary Modern Tibetan (offered through Columbia) can enrol in the course as a Cornell student. The student can attend all courses in person (alongside any other enrolled Cornell students) at Cornell's Language Resource Center. However, their Tibetan faculty is physically based at Columbia's Language Resource Center, where a group of Columbia students also attend the course. In some cases, shared LCTL courses have students attending across all three institutions, with each connecting at their three respective language centre locations and connecting via videoconferencing technologies built into the classrooms. The recently published volume, *Sharing Less Commonly Taught Languages in Higher Education*, edited by Emily Heidrich Uebel, Angelika Kraemer, and Luca Giupponi, provides other examples of sharing structures and established consortia. In that volume, Heidrich Uebel et al. (2024) further explain how LCTLs have been leveraging CALL technologies through course-sharing efforts as a core element of promoting DEIA in institutional planning. Furthermore, Aoyama et al. (Chapter 7, this volume) describe one innovative interinstitutional resource-sharing effort facilitated by LCTL instructors at Northern Illinois and Iowa State universities in the United States to develop an AI-based spoken dialogue system in Indonesian and Burmese.

5 CALL In/Through Teacher Professional Development

As multiple contributors to this volume note, language teachers often experience isolation, especially prevalent among LCTL instructors, who may be the only individual teaching their language at their institution. Technology-enabled interinstitutional professional development (PD) is therefore an important strategy supporting teachers in developing distributed communities of practice – communities that collaborate in learning and reflecting on practice to arrive at new personal as well as collective understandings (see Chapter 8 by Heidrich Uebel et al., this volume). For this purpose, telecollaboration has increasingly been used not just for language learner exchanges but also for professional exchanges among teachers (Medina Riveros et al., 2022; Üzüm et al., 2020).

For language teachers – whether they are in practice or in training – virtual and interinstitutional partnerships have been shown to increase access to quality PD opportunities (Giupponi et al., 2021) and to promote development of CALL-based competencies via collaboration in professional communities (Karatay & Hegelheimer, 2021). As noted by Chen (2022), quality PD opportunities can support teachers in meeting their already existing responsibilities for curriculum development, technology-enhanced instruction, and assessment of student learning outcomes; PD also facilitates teachers' process of reflecting on their instructional practices. Current literature aiming at CALL in or through teacher PD has often examined the following aspects: understanding CALL-based tools and resources, assessment and evaluation, reflection after action practices, and professional learning communities. In order to implement CALL-based tools and resources in their own classrooms, teachers undoubtedly benefit from having online exchanges where they interact with others using similar technological tools. Furthermore, PD opportunities involving transnational collaboration across national borders have also been shown to cultivate interculturality that teachers need to be effective with learners (Üzüm et al., 2020). It includes developing translingual communication strategies to navigate across diverse linguistic backgrounds (Yazan et al., 2021).

A critical CALL lens prompts consideration of how technology-enabled PD can disrupt or sustain social injustices faced by language teachers. One powerful example of transnational teacher exchange, offered by Fassetta et al. (2020), illustrates the potential of PD to disrupt social justice and employment concerns faced by language teachers in Palestine as they further developed understandings of CALL-based tools and resources. Particularly for Palestinians, who face unemployment challenges exacerbated by immobility and blockades, "the internet represents ... a far from ideal yet very important way to engage with the rest of the world" (Fassetta et al., 2020, p. 118). The Israeli government removed Arabic as one of its official languages in 2018, an action that has limited Arabic teachers' prospects to teach the language locally. Reporting on the PD's successes and challenges, Fassetta et al. (2020) note that the program's use of online collaborative tools supported employment prospects for language teachers seeking to overcome their geopolitical constraints while "living an enduring situation of crisis" (Fassetta et al., 2020, p. 120). With renewed global interest in learning Arabic for religious or cultural reasons, the authors posit that online teaching opportunities may become increasingly viable for Gazans with improvements to internet stability. While this possibility is promising, contributors to this volume illustrate disparities that can emerge between language teachers participating in transnational PD opportunities. For instance, Sakach and Phan (Chapter 9, this volume) bring critical attention to issues such as unreliable internet connectivity, lack of a private workspace, and generational gaps in digital literacy, which limited the involvement of some teachers participating in one transnational PD for Southeast Asian languages. Their chapter shows the need to carefully design these opportunities to promote inclusion of all participating language teachers.

Contributors in Part Three also illustrate the range of information and communication technologies and infrastructures that have been employed to promote accessibility of geographically dispersed language teachers participating in online PD. These can include learning management systems, videoconferencing platforms, text messaging or social media apps, and other cloud-driven collaborative tools (such as Google Workspace). The interinstitutional PD opportunities featured in this section have been offered by different types of institutions, including universities and professional organizations, and were made available to teachers located across national borders. The PD opportunities described have taken different forms and modalities, including short-term summer courses for language teachers offered online (see Chapter 8 by Heidrich Uebel et al., this volume), as well as topic-driven workshops with synchronous and asynchronous collaborative components (see Chapter 9 by Sakach and Phan, and Chapter 10 by Rahmouni, this volume).

6 An Overview of the Volume

Following this Introduction, this volume is comprised of three parts. Part One, "CALL In/Through Transnational and Community-Oriented Learner Exchange," consists of four chapters. Three of these chapters explore virtual exchanges designed for language learners in transnational and university settings. The last chapter in this section is the only chapter taking place in a K–12 setting; it illustrates how technology-mediated exchanges can emerge in three ways: between grade levels in school, with a university, and with local community partners. Part Two, "CALL In/Through Less Commonly Taught Languages," consists of two chapters, which illustrate how technology strengthens learners' access, opportunity, and engagement with Indigenous languages spoken in Alaska as well as with Indonesian and Burmese. Part Three, "CALL In/Through Teacher Professional Development," contains three chapters. Each of these illustrates how virtual exchange communities have supported language instructors for Southeast Asian languages, Arabic, as well as other LCTLs.

In "Critical Virtual Exchange: At the Interface of Critical CALL, Critical Digital Literacy, and Critical Global Citizenship Education," Hauck argues for the importance of critical virtual exchange (CVE) projects as part of internationalization at home efforts in higher education. Given that the majority of university students are not "internationally mobile," the author offers that VE can support immobile students in developing intercultural capacities associated with studying abroad, such as openness, empathy, and proficiency in other languages; these capacities are especially important for learners who are marginalized or under-represented in higher education. The chapter argues that traditional VE models that have been popular in higher education are not inherently inclusive. CVE is therefore put forward as an approach that responds to the global digital divide, intentionally seeking the involvement of learners from backgrounds that have often been excluded from traditional exchanges, and centres social justice content in dialogues across partner sites. The chapter offers two examples of CVE projects that highlight the interrelationship between critical digital literacy, critical CALL, and critical global citizenship education to address issues of social justice and inclusion.

In "Advancing Inclusion through Pre-Mobility Virtual Exchange," Alonso Morais conceptualizes VE as a pre-mobility model for university students who are interested in studying abroad. While pre-mobility programs prepare sojourners for travels to a new country, the chapter explains in detail how such models can, at the same time, foster inclusion for learners who experience disadvantages that prevent their mobility as well as for students from under-represented backgrounds. It describes in further detail one such program called *GearUp!*, an eight-week program sponsored by the University of León in Spain, where students collaborate using English as the lingua franca for their exchange. The program, which has been promoted in 18 different countries across Europe and Latin America, aims to prepare students for study abroad but also provides an alternative intercultural experience for those for whom study abroad is infeasible. The chapter describes the program's first two rounds of implementation, which occurred in 2022 and 2023.

In their chapter "COILing Discrimination Narratives across Continents: A Virtual Exchange Project between a Community College in New York City and a Four-Year College in Jordan," Gokcora and Oenbring feature a three-way Collaborative Online International Learning (COIL) project involving 81 students across two countries. The project connected 33 community college students from New York City in the United States with 48 paramedic students in Jordan. During the exchange, students collaborated in binational groups, and each crafted narratives based on interviews they conducted with one individual in their community about their experiences of discrimination. Collectively, these narratives highlighted a range of discrimination types in relation to race, age, employment, immigration status, gender, and faith. Students then analysed these discrimination narratives for similarities and differences across the two international contexts, making connections about the experiences of immigrants in the United States and Jordan. The chapter illustrates how critical CALL can be reimagined to help students make authentic connections with peers across the globe while exploring how issues of injustice emerge in their local communities.

In "Using Technology and Art in a Middle School Exploratory Heritage Language Program: Diversity Matters," Ekiert and Austin document an ongoing three-way partnership between a school, a university, and the greater local community that makes use of multiple technologies to support the linguistic repertoires of learners in an exploratory middle school heritage program, which involves participants from different heritage language backgrounds. Their chapter describes ways that technology and art were continuously integrated together in a new curriculum for purposes of developing students' linguistic repertoires through critical language awareness and wellness concurrently. The authors highlight a community night and art show as one culminating curricular project that allowed students to take on leadership roles, use technology in authentic ways (such as for publicity and the design of the art show program), and connect with the broader community, as the students explained their projects to visitors. Ekiert and Austin note that challenging moments occurred with the integrated use of technology, as students experienced disruptions to technological applications that were used for their projects. In future iterations, the authors reflect that the addition of evaluative activities, such as composing feedback to app designers, could further empower learners through language.

Part Two begins with the chapter "Indigenizing Language Pedagogies with Technology: Entangling Human and Non-Human Affordances for Indigenous Language and Culture Maintenance, Revitalization, and Reclamation," by Siekmann, Parker Webster, and Thorne. This chapter presents four practitioner-teacher action research projects occurring in the context of Indigenous language and cultural maintenance and revitalization efforts. Using the Western pedagogical framework of multiliteracies, Vygotskian sociocultural theory, and Indigenous ways of being-knowing-doing, the authors analyse how the teachers' projects use technology alongside Indigenous ways of being-knowing-doing to disrupt monoglossic and monolingual ideologies. Specific instances of technology integration are highlighted in the teachers' projects, including creation of instructional videos by Elders and students, digital storytelling, and a place-based mobile augmented reality game. The chapter concludes by explaining how the projects' technology use makes visible relatedness and entanglement among people, language, culture, teaching, and learning, forming the foundation for revitalization through sustainable Indigenous language and culture processes.

"Developing an Interactive AI-Based Spoken Dialogue System for Improving Oral Proficiency in Indonesian and Burmese" is written by Aoyama, Tun, and Neiriz. This chapter represents an interinstitutional endeavour to develop three AI-based prototypes supporting learners' oral proficiency in two LCTLs: Indonesian and Burmese. The prototypes, known as spoken dialogue systems (SDSs), facilitate learners' oral interactions with AI avatars in the associated target languages. Noting the limited number of instructional resources available for LCTLs and the challenges that learners face in finding experienced speakers to interact with outside of class, the authors describe their collaborative process of developing the SDS prototypes as well as learners' perspectives on their use. To understand students' perspectives on SDS, they conducted a pilot study involving 29 students studying Indonesian and Burmese at Northern Illinois University in the United States. Learners engaged with the SDS avatars through three interactive tasks and then completed a survey designed to assess their perceptions about perceived difficulty level, SDS interface, user experience, and language development during their engagements with the SDS avatar. A subsample of students additionally participated in interviews about their experiences. Findings indicate that students enjoyed using SDS for practice and that SDS could be an alternative practice tool used outside of the classroom.

Part Three begins with "Technology-Enabled Interinstitutional Professional Development for Less Commonly Taught Languages" by Heidrich Uebel, Giupponi, Van Gorp, and Garza, which features technology-mediated language teacher PD opportunities that have been offered through Michigan State University's Center for Language Teaching Advancement in the United States. The chapter explores the synergies existing between the institutional availability of LCTLs and institutional DEIA strategies, and highlights ways that interinstitutional and technologically mediated course-sharing efforts can help create an equitable and inclusive learning experience for all LCTL participants. It explains the distinctive PD needs of LCTL educators, especially within course-sharing models, and offers successful examples of establishing a community of practice among language instructors across institutions through shared online PD. The chapter illustrates the transformative potentials of technology-enabled interinstitutional PD, drawing on examples from two advanced online PD courses.

Sakach and Phan's chapter, "Interinstitutional and Transnational Language Teacher Professional Development: Teachers' Critical Reflections and Future Directions," explores a collaborative PD model for language teachers that was initiated by the Southeast Asian Language Council. The model they describe utilized information and communication technologies, incorporating both interinstitutional and transnational components, and involved teachers from the United States, Southeast Asia, and Europe. PD participants were involved in long-term projects focused on reading assessment design and reading materials development, which included both initial workshop components as well as post-workshop collaborative components. In the follow-up study presented in this volume, the authors examine the telecommunication and digital collaboration tools used both during and beyond the workshops, identifying their advantages and drawbacks. Teachers used multiple telecommunication tools such as videoconferencing, text messaging, and shared cloud storage to communicate across the globe. Examining participants' reflections on their collaborative PD experiences, the authors found that the model cultivated global partnerships and support for teachers across different LCTLs. However, findings show that ongoing refinement and adaptation of telecommunication-based PD models is necessary to promote further inclusivity and address emerging challenges such as time zone differences, limited internet connectivity, and disparities in comfort levels using digital tools.

In "Advancing Arabic Language Education: Empowering Teachers and Promoting Critical CALL through the Arabic Teachers' Council," Rahmouni discusses some of the challenges confronting Arabic language educators related to diglossia, teaching approaches, and the often-encountered limited foundational training and resource constraints. The chapter describes the circumstances of linguistic variation existing among many spoken varieties of Arabic, as well as six distinctive pedagogical approaches that each address this diglossic situation in different ways. Noting the limited networking opportunities existing for Arabic language educators, the chapter offers a communities of practice framework that is responsive to issues of DEIA, outlining ways to empower teachers through technology-enhanced collaboration and resource sharing. To exemplify this framework, the chapter describes the work of the Arabic Teachers' Council, which has been offering a number of PD workshops, primarily in online modalities, since 2020 to Arabic teachers in both K–12 and higher education settings.

Taken together, the volume's 10 chapters illustrate the variety of ways that partnerships are forged across institutions and borders to advance CALL innovations that are critical and humanistically oriented in nature. They take critical considerations into account, articulating social problems that are related to the local context or language(s) featured and explaining ways that the featured CALL innovation can promote more equitable conditions for under-represented and underserved language teachers and learners. We hope therefore that readers – who include language teachers, language program administrators, and CALL scholars – gain insights into the ways that criticality can be advanced in their own contexts, as well as inspiration to cultivate interinstitutional and transnational collaborations in their CALL projects, whether these are designed holistically to support language learners, the teaching of LCTLs, or language teachers.

About the Authors

Emma R. Britton is the volume's lead editor. She currently works as a Postdoctoral Fellow for the Study of Deeper Learning with the American Educational Research Association. Her research and praxis centres on applications of critical linguistic, post-humanist, sociocultural, and multimodal theories in a variety of digitally mediated second and world language settings. Her publications have appeared in journals such as *Journal of Language, Identity, and Education*; *Language Awareness*; *Foreign Language Annals*; *TESOL Quarterly*; and *Journal of Second Language Writing*. She has been learning Azerbaijani via virtual exchange throughout and beyond the COVID-19 pandemic.

Angelika Kraemer is the director of the Language Resource Center at Cornell University. Her research interests include language centre management, technology-enhanced language learning, and assessment. She has published in various journals and edited volumes such as *CALICO Journal*, *CALICO Monograph Series*, *Foreign Language Annals*, *Languages*, and *Die Unterrichtspraxis/Teaching German*. She is co-editor of *Language Center Handbook* (2021, 2025, IALLT) and *Sharing Less Commonly Taught Languages in Higher Education: Collaboration and Innovation* (2024, Routledge).

Theresa Austin is a critical sociolinguist in education and a professor of language, literacy, and culture at UMass Amherst. She is a member of the European collaborative network of scholars, Language in the Human-Machine Era (LITHME). She has collaborated on developing digital CALL applications, assessments, and transnational teacher professional development opportunities. She has published widely in various applied-linguistic journals and served as a co-editor for *Critical Inquiry in Language Studies* and *Languages and Linguistics*.

Hengyi Liu recently completed PhD studies in language, literacy, and culture at UMass Amherst. Hengyi brings to the CALL field more than a decade of language teaching experience with multilingual learners in elementary, middle, and high schools across China and the United States. Hengyi's research spans the areas of classroom discourse and multiliteracies in after-school settings in the US context. He is particularly interested in drawing on sociocultural theories of learning to understand the use of semiotics in multiliteracies.

Xinyue Zuo recently earned a PhD from the Department of Teacher Education and Curriculum Studies at UMass Amherst. Her research interests lie in instructional design and technology, interpreting in educational settings, second language acquisition, and bilingualism. Her publications have appeared in *ECNU Review of Education*, *Journal of International Students*, and *Başkent University Journal of Education*, and her research work has been presented at local and international conferences including AERA, CATESOL, and CIE.

References

Benini, S., & Thomas, M. (2021). Project-based language learning, virtual exchange and 3D virtual environments: A critical review of the research. In M. Thomas & K. Yamazaki (Eds.), *Project-based language learning and CALL* (pp. 21–56). Equinox Publishing.

Canagarajah, S. (2007). Lingua franca English, multilingual communities, and language acquisition. *Modern Language Journal*, *91*(s1), 923–939. https://doi.org/10.1111/j.1540-4781.2007.00678.x

Charitos, S., Kaiser, C., & Van Deusen-Scholl, N. (2017). From interinstitutional competition to interinstitutional collaboration. *EuropeNow Journal*, *8*, 1–7. https://www.europenowjournal.org/2017/06/05/from-interinstitutional-competition-to-interinstitutional-collaboration/

Chen, M. (2022). Digital affordances and teacher agency in the context of teaching Chinese as a second language during COVID-19. *System*, *105*, 102710. https://doi.org/10.1016/j.system.2021.102710

Fassetta, G., Al-Masri, N., Attia, M., & Phipps, A. (2020). Gaza teaches Arabic online: Opportunities, challenges and ways forward. In G. Fassetta, N. Al-Masri, M. Attia, & A. Phipps (Eds.), *Multilingual online academic collaborations as resistance: Crossing impassable borders* (pp. 117–130). Multilingual Matters. https://doi.org/10.21832/9781788929608

Freire, P. (2005). *Pedagogy of the oppressed*. Continuum International Publishing Group.

Giupponi, L., Heidrich Uebel, E., & Van Gorp, K. (2021). Strategies for language centers to support online language instruction. In E. Lavolette & A. Kraemer (Eds.), *Language center handbook 2021* (pp. 61–90). International Association for Language Learning Technology.

Gleason, J., & Suvorov, R. (2019). Promoting social justice with CALL. *CALICO Journal*, *36*(1), i–vii. https://doi.org/10.1558/cj.37162

Godwin-Jones, R. (2021). Evolving technologies for language learning. *Language Learning & Technology*, *25*(3), 6–26. https://doi.org/10125/73443

Goertler, S., & Gleason, J. (Eds.). (2024). *Technology-mediated crisis response in language studies*. Equinox Publishing.

Guo, Z., & Xu, X. (2023). Understanding intercultural virtual exchange through a translanguaging lens in Chinese as a foreign language. *Journal of China Computer-Assisted Language Learning*, *3*(1), 132–167. https://doi.org/10.1515/jccall-2022-0018

Gutiérrez, B.F., & O'Dowd, R. (2021). Virtual exchange: Connecting learners in online intercultural collaborative learning. In T. Beaven & F. Rosell-Aguilar (Eds.), *Innovative language pedagogy report* (pp. 17–22). Research-publishing.net. https://doi.org/10.14705/rpnet.2021.50.1230

Heidrich Uebel, E., Kraemer, A., & Giupponi, L. (Eds.). (2024). *Sharing less commonly taught languages in higher education: Collaboration and innovation*. Routledge. https://doi.org/10.4324/9781003349631

Hellmich, E.A. (2019). A critical look at the bigger picture: Macro-level discourses of language and technology in the United States. *CALICO Journal*, *36*(1), 39–58. https://doi.org/10.1558/cj.35022

Helm, F. (2015). The practices and challenges of telecollaboration in higher education in Europe. *Language Learning & Technology*, *19*(2), 197–217. https://doi.org/10125/44424

Helm, F., Bradley, L., Guarda, M., & Thouësny, S. (Eds.). (2015). *Critical CALL: Proceedings of the 2015 EUROCALL Conference, Padova, Italy*. Research-publishing.net. https://files.eric.ed.gov/fulltext/ED564162.pdf

Jin, L., Deifell, E., & Angus, K. (2022). Emergency remote language teaching and learning in disruptive times. *CALICO Journal*, *39*(1), i–x. https://doi.org/10.1558/cj.20858

Kannan, J., & Munday, P. (2018). New trends in second language learning and teaching through the lens of ICT, networked learning, and artificial intelligence. *Círculo de Lingüística Aplicada a la Comunicación*, *76*, 13–30. https://doi.org/10.5209/CLAC.62495

Karatay, Y., & Hegelheimer, V. (2021). CALL teacher training – considerations for low-resource environments: Overview of CALL teacher training. *CALICO Journal*, *38*(3), 271–295. https://doi.org/10.1558/cj.20159

Koenecke, A., Nam, A., Lake, E., Nudell, J., Quartey, M., Mengesha, Z., Toups, C., Rickford, J.R., Jurafsky, D., & Goel, S. (2020). Racial disparities in automated speech recognition. *PNAS*, *117*(14), 7684–7689. https://doi.org/10.1073/pnas.1915768117

Lane, P., & Makihara, M. (2016). Indigenous peoples and their languages. In O. García, N. Flores, & M. Spotti (Eds.), *The Oxford handbook of language and society* (pp. 299–320). Oxford University Press. https://doi.org/10.1093/oxfordhb/9780190212896.013.7

Lenkaitis, C.A., & Loranc, B. (2021). Facilitating global citizenship development in lingua franca virtual exchanges. *Language Teaching Research*, *25*(5), 711–728. https://doi.org/10.1177/1362168819877371

Lusin, N., Peterson, T., Sulewski, C., & Zafer, R. (2023). *Enrollments in languages other than English in US institutions of higher education, fall 2021*.

Modern Language Association. https://www.mla.org/content/download/191324/file/Enrollments-in-Languages-Other-Than-English-in-US-Institutions-of-Higher-Education-Fall-2021.pdf

Machwate, S., Bendaoud, R., Henze, J., Berrada, K., & Burgos, D. (2021). Virtual exchange to develop cultural, language, and digital competencies. *Sustainability*, *13*(11), 5926. https://doi.org/10.3390/su13115926

McCarty, T.L., Noguera, J., Lee, T.S., & Nicholas, S.E. (2021). "A viable path for education": Indigenous-language immersion and sustainable self-determination. *Journal of Language, Identity and Education*, *20*(5), 340–354. https://doi.org/10.1080/15348458.2021.1957681

Medina Riveros, R.A., Botelho, M.J., Austin, T., & Pérez, D.A.P. (2022). Teachers inquiring into translanguaging and multimodal pedagogies: Emerging creative and critical entanglements during transnational professional development. In R.A. Mora, Z. Tian, & R. Harman (Eds.), *Translanguaging and multimodality as flow, agency, and a new sense of advocacy in and from the global south* (pp. 53–77). Routledge. https://doi.org/10.4324/9781003435235-4

Meighan, P.J. (2022). Indigenous language revitalization using *TEK-nology*: How can traditional ecological knowledge (TEK) and technology support intergenerational language transmission? *Journal of Multilingual and Multicultural Development*, *43*, 1–19. https://doi.org/10.1080/01434632.2022.2084548

Moore, A.S., & Simon, S. (Eds.). (2015). *Globally networked teaching in the humanities: Theories and practices*. Routledge. https://doi.org/10.4324/9781315754925

Moser, K.M., Wei, T., & Brenner, D. (2021). Remote teaching during COVID-19: Implications from a national survey of language educators. *System*, *97*, 102431. https://doi.org/10.1016/j.system.2020.102431

Murphy, D., Sarac, M., & Sedivy, S. (2022). Why U.S. undergraduate students are (not) studying languages other than English. *Second Language Research & Practice*, *3*(1), 1–33. https://doi.org/10125/69866

NCOLCTL (National Council of Less Commonly Taught Languages). (n.d.). *Frequently asked questions: What is a less commonly taught language or LCTL?* Retrieved March 11, 2025, from https://ncolctl.org/about/frequently-asked-questions/#toggle-id-2

O'Dowd, R. (2018). From telecollaboration to virtual exchange: State-of-the-art and the role of UNICollaboration in moving forward. *Journal of Virtual Exchange*, *1*, 1–23. https://doi.org/10.14705/rpnet.2018.jve.1

O'Rourke, B. (2007). Models of telecollaboration (1): eTandem. In R. O'Dowd (Ed.), *Online intercultural exchange: An introduction for foreign language teachers* (pp. 42–61). Multilingual Matters. https://doi.org/10.21832/9781847690104-005

Porto, M., Golubeva, I., & Byram, M. (2023). Channelling discomfort through the arts: A Covid-19 case study through an intercultural telecollaboration project. *Language Teaching Research, 27*(2), 276–298. https://doi.org/10.1177/13621688211058245

Sax, D. (2022). *The future is analog: How to create a more human world*. PublicAffairs.

Saylan, E., Kokoç, M., & Tatlı, Z. (2023). A systematic review of empirical studies on computer-assisted language learning. *Waikato Journal of Education, 28*(1), 89–107. https://doi.org/10.15663/wje.v28i1.1091

Schwienhorst, K. (2009). Learning a second language in three dimensions: Potential benefits and the evidence so far. *Themes in Science and Technology Education, 2*(1–2), 153–163.

Shahnama, M., Yazdanmehr, E., & Elahi Shirvan, M. (2021). Challenges of online language teaching during the COVID-19 pandemic: A process tracing approach. *Teaching English as a Second Language* (formerly *Journal of Teaching Language Skills*), *40*(3), 159–195. https://www.learntechlib.org/p/148625/

Song, R. (2021). *Caught between spaces: Korean adult EFL/ESL female speakers' negotiating social identities in online English study groups* [Doctoral dissertation]. UMass Amherst. https://doi.org/10.7275/22362798.0

Thomas, M., & Yamazaki, K. (2021). Introduction: Projects, pandemics and the re-positioning of digital language learning. In M. Thomas & K. Yamazaki (Eds.), *Project-based language learning and CALL* (pp. 1–20). Equinox Publishing.

Üzüm, B., Akayoglu, S., & Yazan, B. (2020). Using telecollaboration to promote intercultural competence in teacher training classrooms in Turkey and the USA. *ReCALL, 32*(2), 162–177. https://doi.org/10.1017/S0958344019000235

Ward, M. (2018). Qualitative research in less commonly taught and endangered language CALL. *Language Learning & Technology, 22*(2), 116–132. https://doi.org/10125/44639

Wiley-Camacho, G., Hillaire, G., Buttimer, C.J., & Colwell, R. (2022). Remote language revitalisation efforts during COVID-19. *Technology, Pedagogy and Education, 31*(3), 1–15. https://doi.org/10.1080/1475939x.2022.2077819

Yang, E., & Roberts, M.E. (2023). The authoritarian data problem. *Journal of Democracy, 34*(4), 141–150. https://doi.org/10.1353/jod.2023.a907695

Yang, X. (2020). Teachers' perceptions of large-scale online teaching as an epidemic prevention and control strategy in China. *ECNU Review of Education*, *3*(4), 739–744. https://doi.org/10.1177/2096531120922244

Yazan, B., Üzüm, B., Akayoglu, S., & Mary, L. (2021). Telecollaboration as translingual contact zone: Teacher candidates' translingual negotiation strategies. In O. Barnawi & A. Ahmed (Eds.), *TESOL teacher education in a transnational world: Turning challenges into innovative prospects* (pp. 139–157). Routledge. https://doi.org/10.4324/9781003008668-9

Zak, A. (2021). An integrative review of literature: Virtual exchange models, learning outcomes, and programmatic insights. *Journal of Virtual Exchange*, *4*, 62–79. https://doi.org/10.21827/jve.4.37582

PART ONE
CALL IN/THROUGH TRANSNATIONAL AND COMMUNITY-ORIENTED LEARNER EXCHANGE

2 Critical Virtual Exchange: At the Interface of Critical CALL, Critical Digital Literacy, and Critical Global Citizenship Education

Mirjam Hauck

1 Introduction

Language learning and teaching – as Satar et al. (2023) remind us – increasingly means using multimodal, multicultural, and multilingual skills in digitally mediated environments. Undoubtedly, there are many benefits to such multifaceted and instant communication across time zones and geographical distance. Yet, it can also lead, both locally and globally, to polarization between individuals, communities, and nations (Dooly & Darvin, 2022) and – consequently – raise equity and inclusion issues in language education. "While digital affordances have enabled diverse groups of people to interact with one another," Dooly and Darvin (2022) pointed out, "they have also amplified existing inequalities and forms of Othering" (p. 354). Similarly, Helm (2019) observed that the great potential of online technologies to increase intercultural communication and constructive engagement with divergent worldviews has been put into perspective by the way they are being used, or rather abused, to polarize communities, entrench hate, and radicalize youth. "The result," the author concluded, "is individuals' self-segregation in online 'echo chambers' where their opinions are reinforced, and they have little exposure to diverse views" (p. 140). Thus teachers – including language teachers – in societies that are becoming increasingly diverse face the challenge of how to prepare students as citizens who can engage with complex issues in ways that reflect equity and justice. Hence, the task at hand for educators in general and language educators in particular is to prepare learners – including teachers as learners (teacher trainees) – for both agentive and inclusive engagement in digitally mediated communication contexts. An additional challenge arises for higher education institutions (HEIs) as a whole, as they are being held responsible for preparing young people for the twenty-first-century labour market in a globally interconnected world and for helping them develop their international and intercultural skills such as openness, collaboration, critical thinking, and language proficiency.

Virtual exchange (VE), an educational practice that combines the deep impact of intercultural dialogue with the broad reach of digital technology (EVOLVE Project Team, 2020), has emerged as one way to successfully approach most of these challenges. For over two decades, VE has enjoyed increasing popularity in university education, especially in initial (language) teacher education programs (O'Dowd, 2018). Collaborating online with colleagues and students from different cultural backgrounds and educational systems has allowed trainees to experience and reflect on issues related to technology and pedagogy in authentic linguistic and intercultural settings. Unsurprisingly, a considerable amount of VE research has been carried out in university language education and pre-service language teacher education contexts (for an overview, see Hauck et al., 2020).

VE has also been proposed as an ideal means to foster critical intercultural and global awareness (Reljanovic Glimäng, 2022), that is, for global citizenship education (GCE) as framed by Andreotti (2006, 2014). This author argued for a critical approach to GCE with notions of power, voice, and difference at its core and informed by their conceptualization of critical literacy as "a level of reading the word and the world that involves the development of skills of critical engagement and reflexivity" (p. 7), which, in turn, draws on Freire and Macedo's (1987) seminal work on "reading the word and the world," a phrase anchored in the educational aim of empowering learners to gain agency and a critical consciousness through dialogic inquiry around real-world issues. Critical GCE, according to Andreotti (2006), enables learners to engage in "the analysis and critique of the relationships among perspectives, language, power, social groups and social practices" (p. 49).

Yet, critical perspectives, in the sense of Choi's (2016) "critical resistance," remain underexplored in VE, including in exchanges that evolve around the learning and teaching of languages and cultures. Choi (2016) promotes "more creative, innovative, non-linear, and non-hierarchical forms of participation potentially leading to a deeper level of digital engagements"

(p. 581) while "challenging the status quo and promoting social justice" (p. 584). There is considerable potential, though, for exchanges to explicitly align with educational social justice agendas (Hauck, 2019, 2020, 2023) and to address global topics in transnational settings (O'Dowd, 2020). VEs focused on GCE topics – as O'Dowd (2020) suggests – can offer particularly rich contexts for intercultural interaction while also engaging participants in promoting change for social improvement.

This mostly conceptual contribution to the nascent field of critical virtual exchange (CVE) – VE through the social justice and inclusion lens – puts the spotlight on the interface between critical computer-assisted language learning (CALL), critical digital literacy, critical global citizenship education, and CVE. After a brief introduction to VE in Section 2, CVE is presented and discussed in Section 3. The concepts of critical digital literacy, critical CALL, and critical global citizenship education and their relevance for CVE will be expounded by drawing on scholars like Helm (2015, 2019), Darvin (2017), Andreotti (2006, 2014), and Stein and Andreotti (2021), whose work is grounded in critical pedagogy and postcolonial theory. Section 4 is dedicated to the presentation of two concrete examples that speak to the CVE agenda before Section 5 brings this chapter to a conclusion.

2 Virtual Exchange

There is a great variety of types of VE[1] that are used as an educational intervention across the education sector. A recent European Union (EU) Erasmus+ funded project – Engaging Languages in Intercultural Virtual Exchange (E-LIVE),[2] with participants from primary, secondary, vocational, higher, and further education institutions – captures the richness of the field. In E-LIVE, partners from several European countries worked on developing innovative, digital teaching methods to improve the quality of modern language teaching through meaningful and authentic VE-based

---

1. For an overview of the different models and approaches to VE currently being used in HEI contexts and a short historical review of the major developments and trends in VE to date, see O'Dowd (2018).
2. More details about the project can be found on the E-LIVE website at https://sites.google.com/view/eliveproject

interaction. Their aim was to scale up the impact of pedagogical innovation to include the broad educational field of language teaching. One of their main strategies to augment such impact in schools was to engage trainee teachers and provide them with the necessary know-how and experience needed to integrate these pedagogical innovations later in their teaching careers.

VE initiatives outside of HEIs that focus on social justice and inclusion challenges are scarce though. A recent exception is Hinshaw et al.'s (2022) study, which explicitly considered "the opportunities and barriers facing the implementation of virtual exchange in K-12 education, and the perceptions of access to these opportunities for underrepresented students in the context of the federal US education system" (p. 1). Another exception is a recent study funded by the US-based Stevens Initiative, *The ABC of Young Learners and Virtual Exchange (VE): Access, Benefits, and Content* (Alami et al., 2023), which focused on geographical regions where young learners traditionally do not have access to global learning opportunities, as well as on young learners with VE experience, to establish the benefits they draw from their participation. It was a follow-up study to Alami et al. (2022), which investigated reasons for marginalization and under-representation in global VE initiatives in tertiary education, highlighting region-specific challenges.

The origins of VE lie in the fields of applied linguistics and language education, where it was initially referred to as telecollaboration (Belz, 2003). Thus, it is a form of CALL and has been hailed as an experiential learning opportunity that offers participants (semi) authentic interactions with peers, mediated by technology (Helm & Hauck, 2022). Yet, VE has shown learning gains for students across all disciplines, and both VE practice and research have benefited from cross- and multidisciplinary approaches (O'Dowd, 2018).

Today VE is understood as a practice, supported by research, that consists of sustained, technology-enabled, people-to-people education programs or activities in which constructive communication and interaction takes place between individuals or groups who are geographically separated and/or from different cultural backgrounds, with the support of educators or facilitators. It combines the deep impact of intercultural dialogue and exchange with the broad reach of digital technology (EVOLVE Project Team, 2020, p. 20).

It has been acknowledged as a strong catalyst in advancing the internationalization of HE curricula, known as "internationalization at home" (IaH; Beelen & Jones, 2015; O'Dowd & Beelen, 2021).

VE has developed over 30 years from experience in educational exchange and study abroad and can prepare for, deepen, or extend physical exchanges, or as shown by COVID-19, can also approximate physical mobility. Having an alternative to physical exchanges is particularly relevant as outward student mobility is still limited, with, for example, only 7.8 per cent of UK undergraduate students opting for a study abroad experience in 2019 (UUKI, 2022) and less than 6 per cent of American college students studying abroad in 2023 (US Department of State's Bureau of Educational and Cultural Affairs, 2023). Hence, VE is also a means to achieve a more equitable and inclusive education, removing much of the cost of studying internationally, which disproportionately impacts socially disadvantaged students who may experience financial constraints.

In this chapter, the focus is on exchanges that are jointly designed and implemented by two or more university educators from the same or different disciplinary fields and who want to integrate an international and intercultural dimension into their pre-existing courses. These VEs last on average six to eight weeks and are known to prepare students for the globalized digital workplace as they focus on transversal skills like problem solving, teamwork and leadership, languages and communication, critical and innovative thinking, and media and information literacy (Crawford, 2021). The exchanges have also been recognized as the ideal set-up for learners' digital skills development (Hauck, 2019), as VE is – by definition – mediated by technology. Usually a learning management system (e.g., Moodle or Canvas) functions as the hub for an exchange, and various online tools and applications are embedded or linked from the hub, depending on VE activity design and student learning goals.

COVID-19 has brought challenges regarding inclusion and exclusion to the fore. Such challenges have been caused – in many cases – by lack of access to and familiarity with online tools and applications, thereby preventing educators and students from around the globe to take part in online (language) learning and teaching, and thus also VE. This situation, in combination with the work of scholars who draw on critical pedagogy and call attention to critical global issues, sustainability, and aspects of (in)equity in and through VE (Helm et al., 2023; Helm & Hauck, 2022; Klimanova & Hellmich, 2021), has given rise to a new line of VE research and practice termed "critical virtual exchange" (CVE; Hauck, 2020; Klimanova & Hellmich, 2021), which – in the case of language (teacher) education – is informed by and informs critical CALL (Helm, 2015). Moreover, I have begun to frame CVE as a conduit for critical GCE as understood by Andreotti (2006, 2014) and have argued that CVE constitutes an ideal space for transnational critical inquiry in (language) education (Hauck, 2019). The defining elements of CVE are outlined in the next section.

3 Critical Virtual Exchange

While IaH wants to reach all students, many VE practices are still electives available to a limited group of students only, and it has been established that upscaling VE to include all students requires considerable effort (EVOLVE Project Team, 2020). Thus VE-based IaH is not yet inherently inclusive. On the contrary, it is as prone to Western hegemonies and power imbalances among the participants as any other form of online or hybrid education influenced by access to and experience with technology, the linguistic competence of educators and students in relation to the dominance of the English language in VE and IaH, institutional constraints (e.g., lack of support, acknowledgment, and resources), gender, race, age, and also sociopolitical and geopolitical challenges (Helm, 2019). Not all young people, for example, have equal access to a reliable internet connection or sufficient hardware to participate in VE (Alami et al., 2022). This digital divide can reproduce or perpetuate existing exclusion or even create new (digital) inequalities (Satar & Hauck, 2021).

Moreover, as Selwyn and Facer (2013) have pointed out already over a decade ago, the political and social dimensions of technology use in education tend to be underestimated, as are the power dynamics created by bespoke educational practices, that is, the prioritization of certain knowledges – usually those from the Global North – which reinforce social and epistemic inequalities and injustices. "In a context of radical economic, political, and educational inequality," they put forward, "technology is usually arranged around certain values, power is centralized, hierarchies are embedded, allocation is uneven, and there are structural constraints between social classes" (p. 10). As a result, the use of digital technology in educational settings is "often not a wholly inclusive, dialogic, or equitable process in which all actors have equal power in participating" (p. 14) and where all actors can determine what or how educational technology is used. The authors deconstructed the overarching "means-end" and "deterministic" thinking (Selwyn & Facer, 2013, p. ix) that has dominated the integration of educational technology in education in many parts of the world and established the need to question the seemingly value-neutral claims made in the name of digital technologies and to identify the inequalities of access, power, and skills that influence and mediate their use and perpetuate the aforementioned injustices. This need to question also applies to VE. Therefore, O'Dowd and Beelen (2021) concluded, "we need to find out more ... [about] how processes of inclusion and exclusion play out in virtual settings" (n.p.).

Kastler and Lewis (2021) have made a first attempt at conceptualizing VE across the curriculum through a diversity, equity, inclusion, and accessibility (DEIA) lens: Equitable partnerships in VE programs must welcome participants from all demographics including minority-serving institutions and institutions in non-English speaking countries. At the same time, institutional leadership needs to prioritize the creation of resources, training, and support for exchange implementers, that is, the teachers. They, in turn, need to prioritize the inclusion of activities that intentionally explore social issues and justice topics as a part of the student exchange dialogue. Importantly, exchanges need to be designed to serve all participating communities, rather than the community of the leading partner, by finding common issues to tackle or by customizing exchange projects for local realities. The most urgent issues, however, are inequalities in terms of access to software and hardware and/or internet connectivity. Figure 2.1 illustrates the Global North/Global South divide in this respect. Thus, while technology has the capacity to empower and liberate, it also has the capacity to exclude and marginalize (Darvin, 2016). Therefore, careful consideration needs to be given to technology choices in VE. It is noteworthy that language-related DEIA challenges remain unaddressed in Kastler and Lewis's (2021) considerations.

Building and expanding on Kastler and Lewis's (2021) work, I have introduced the concept of CVE (Hauck, 2020, 2023), which sees VE as a vehicle for action, public engagement, and sociopolitical change. CVE

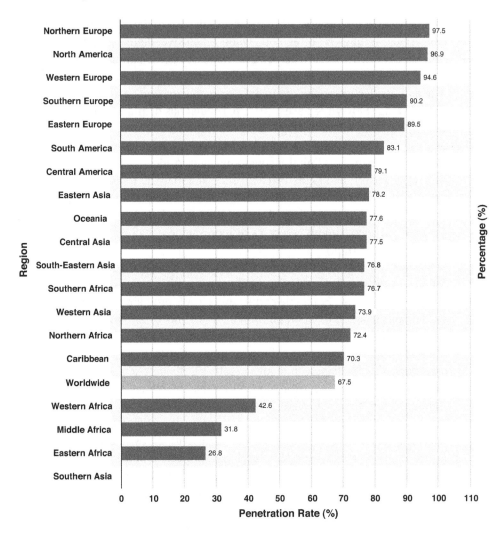

Figure 2.1 Internet World Penetration Rates

Source: Petrosyan (2024). We Are Social; DataReportal; Meltwater; GWI © Statista 2024. Additional information from Worldwide; DataReportal; GWI; October 2024.

explicitly sets out to address social justice and inclusion at institutional and individual levels. It aims to ensure more equitable and inclusive student exchange experiences and is characterized by the following elements (see Figure 2.2):

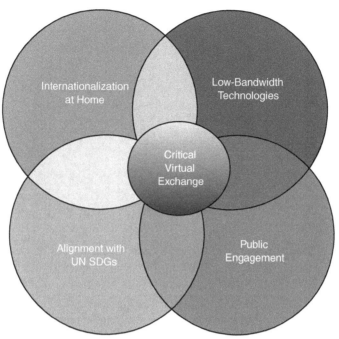

Figure 2.2 Critical Virtual Exchange
Source: Hauck (2023), Figure 1.

- use of low-bandwidth technologies
- systematic inclusion of students often under-represented in IaH (e.g., those from low socio-economic backgrounds)
- exchange topics informed by local and global, that is, "glocal" (Robertson, 1995) challenges and aligned with the UN Sustainable Development Goals (SDGs) (United Nations, 2015)
- integration of local student outreach work with businesses, non-governmental organizations (NGOs), and charities to promote transversal skills development, enhance graduate employability, and further support SDGs achievement

In addition, I have started to propose the systematic integration of translanguaging approaches as a defining element of CVE, particularly but not exclusively in exchanges where the learning and teaching of languages and cultures is the focal point (see Figure 2.3). Translanguaging means the

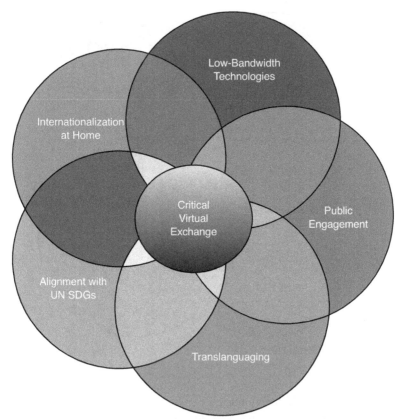

Figure 2.3 Critical Virtual Exchange – Expanded Framework
Source: The author.

fluid use of multiple linguistic and semiotic resources as a single repertoire (Clavijo Olarte et al., 2023). It encourages learners to use their full linguistic and semiotic repertoire to help them realize their multimodal communication potential. Multimodal communicative competence is the ability to make meaning and express ideas across a wide range of modes including words (spoken or written), images (still and moving), sound, 3D models, and any combinations of these (Kress, 2003). Promoting translanguaging in CVE means fostering positive attitudes towards multilingualism and multimodal communication.

Multimodality and social semiotics are also at the core of the conceptualization of *critical* digital literacy (CDL) by Bilki et al. (2022). The authors see CDL reflected in learners' awareness of the impact of meaning-making potential – affordances and limitations – of digital media and the way in which they exercise agency while gaining intercultural understandings and establishing (symbolic) power relationships in VE. Their approach is inspired by Darvin's (2017) definition of CDL as "the examination of how meanings are represented in ways that maintain and reproduce relations of power" (p. 5) and Hauck's (2019) argument that engaging in VE can help learners become critically digitally literate, that is, aware of how operating in digital spaces impacts ways of thinking and doing, and thus meaning-making (see also Satar et al., 2023).

This understanding of CDL is another element that distinguishes CVE from conventional VE and its acknowledged benefits in terms of promoting traditional digital literacy and techno-pedagogical skills development (Hauck et al., 2020). Further explanations of the nature of CDL, its affinity with critical CALL, and their interrelationship with CVE are provided in Section 3.1.

3.1 Critical Digital Literacy, Critical CALL, and CVE

CVE is both informed by CDL and can also provide new insights for CDL, which "examines how the operation of power within digital contexts shapes knowledge, identities, social relations, and formations in ways that privilege some and marginalize others" (Darvin, 2017, p. 2). Darvin suggested that digital literacy from a critical perspective helps us understand how technologies are used in situated and encultured ways – akin to Thorne's (2003, 2016) "cultures-of-use" in CALL – and how the material dimensions of online spaces can be indicative of dominant ideologies, economies, and institutions (Darvin, 2017). Thorne's (2003, 2016) cultures-of-use refer to the way learners select and employ digital devices and apps for personal and social purposes, and the implications for using technology for more formal language learning and teaching purposes.

In relation to VE, Helm (2019) has pointed out that the online environments which form the backdrop for exchanges are not ideologically neutral, nor are they inherently equitable. Moreover, the author highlighted that, the use of English as a lingua franca in the majority of VEs to this day inevitably limits the types of communities and knowledges that one can engage with, as does the use of online technologies, considering that neither English language competence nor internet connectivity are ubiquitous. Helm and Hauck (2022) illustrated how VE environments steer learners to normative behaviours and meanings, how learners position each other, how they perform identities, and how information is legitimated and distributed. The e-tandem-based model of VE, for example, is generally considered as bilingual, but in its prescriptive instantiations, it operates on a monolingual one-language-at-a-time ideology, with a temporal separation of named languages and a deficit view (and even proscription) of translanguaging practices.

By contrast, CVE explicitly encourages translanguaging approaches (see Figure 2.3) and wants participants to draw on their entire "semiotic budget" (Hauck & Satar, 2018, p. 155), that is, all modes available to them online to make meaning, communicate, and interact with each other, including language. Using multimodal conversation analysis, Guo and Xu (2023) illustrated instantiations of translanguaging in VE interactions and showed how British learners of Chinese and their peers from a Chinese university leveraged a range of linguistic, semiotic, and multimodal resources to communicate with their partners. A recent study by Satar et al. (2024) illustrated how translanguaging practices are, in fact, also present in e-tandem. Using a social semiotics perspective (Bezemer & Kress, 2016), the authors' analysis of recorded video conferencing sessions from a Brazilian-American exchange showed how participants drew on all the resources in their "complete language repertoire" (García & Wei, 2014, p. 22) through translingual and transmodal practices. This allowed the participants to make meanings beyond what they could express within their target language proficiency, thus providing an opportunity to extend their semiotic repertoires. Satar et al.'s (2024) findings suggest that the separation of languages principle in e-tandem is unhelpful, if not inappropriate, as it neither works in practice nor seems to reflect current perspectives in language learning and teaching. The authors proposed a reframing of the principle as the "translanguaging principle" (Satar et al., 2024, n.p.), based on an understanding of translanguaging as co-learning, where each participant takes on fluid roles of expert/learner and capitalizes on opportunities to extend each other's semiotic repertoires within multilingual and multimodal interaction (see also Section 4.1).

CDL, then, also echoes Helm's (2015) understanding of critical CALL, that is, the systematic "engagement with issues of power and inequality and an understanding of how our classrooms and conversations are related to broader social, cultural and political challenges" (p. xiii). Critical CALL takes as a premise that the world is "inequitably multilingual and technologized" (Gleason & Suvorov, 2019, p. ii). For CALL practitioners, it means acknowledging that technology tools and services are not neutral and considering their use in the light of factors such as gender, race, and social class (Anwaruddin, 2019; Hellmich, 2019).

Both CDL and critical CALL presuppose a sense of agency on behalf of the learners, more specifically critical consciousness and critical agency as framed by Freire (1970) and Giroux (1981): the ability to read the world critically and the ability to act in the world to change it, which starts with an understanding of one's power in relation to another's power. In CVE, such agency is key to avoiding uneven global power relations and power representations that are being reproduced in VE-based IaH including, of course, exchanges that centre on language and culture learning.

Moreover, CDL, as Darvin (2017) explained, "equips learners with the tools to examine the linguistic and non-linguistic features of digital media, to identify their embedded biases and assumptions, in order to access the truth" (p. 2). It also leverages digital technologies for social justice–oriented action and change (Jiang & Gu, 2022; Mirra & Garcia, 2020), for example, by providing access to a wider and more diverse range of participants. To achieve this leverage, however, Brown (2017) demanded that digital literacy provision needs to be anchored in real-life settings in a more principled way and that it needs to take account of the sociopolitical context. He sees this requirement as core to defining and understanding digital literacies and the much wider concept of "critical citizenry" (Brown, 2017, n.p.) in the digital era.

CVE happens in real-life settings and has reflexive use of technology as one of its defining elements. It provides an ideal setting for such contextualization and for exercising critical agency and citizenry through, for example, collaborative UN SDG-aligned student project work (see Section 4 for examples).

Next, thoughts on the interconnection between GCE and CVE are provided.

3.2 Critical Global Citizenship Education and CVE

UNESCO's (2014) broad definition of GCE is centred on the aim to "empower learners to engage and assume active roles, both locally and globally, to face and resolve global challenges and ultimately to become

Table 2.1 Hegemonic versus Non-Hegemonic VE

Hegemonic	Non-Hegemonic
• specific body of knowledge/competences to be mastered • global competences for employability • surfs diversity and evokes positive feelings • manages diversity, tolerates difference so collaborative tasks can be completed • forgets or ignores history and focuses on so-called common values • Global North seeks solutions to challenges in the Global South • enhances liberal elite cosmopolitanism of the individual	• based on reciprocity and *mutualismo*[a] • creates opportunities for unlearning, learning, and relearning • makes participants' locus of enunciation relevant and reflects on situatedness of knowledges • "chang[es] the terms of the conversation and not only its content" (Mignolo, 2007, p. 133) in order to re-localize the global • listening at the core • participants are challenged and changed by their interactions

Note. [a] *mutualismo*: mutual dependence and protection (Trott, 2017).
Source: Hauck and Helm (2020).

proactive contributors to a more just, peaceful, tolerant, inclusive, secure and sustainable world" (p. 15). Scholars like Stein and Andreotti (2021) question such common understandings of GCE that foreground self-improvement and the development of leadership skills to save the world rather than address the economic and cultural roots of the inequalities in the way power and wealth/labour are distributed in a global complex and uncertain system. They challenge hegemonic discourses, the masking of global complexity, and the perpetuation in education of colonial ideologies, and they encourage us "to think otherwise" (Andreotti, 2006, p. 7).

In a similar vein, Hauck and Helm (2020) distinguish between hegemonic and non-hegemonic forms of VE (see Table 2.1), while acknowledging that elements of both can be found in many exchanges.

Drawing on Hauck (2020), Reljanovic Glimäng (2022) added an additional conceptual layer to this distinction, namely the notion of safe (hegemonic) versus brave (non-hegemonic) spaces in VE, where learners can engage in thinking otherwise rather than being lured into the "illusion of commonality" (Ware & Kramsch, 2005, p. 200). Like Hauck and Helm's (2020) understanding of hegemonic and non-hegemonic configurations of VE as a continuum, Reljanovic Glimäng (2022) sees safe and brave spaces in VE as a continuum. While moving from safe, hegemonic to brave, non-hegemonic VE, maybe even within the same exchange, learners will exercise varying degrees of critical agency (Freire, 1970; see Section 3.1) and show varying levels of epistemological humility, that is, the realization that one's beliefs and views may be limited and situated (Ess, 2007, as cited in Hauck, 2020).

Non-hegemonic, brave VE, then, is CVE that is an instantiation of critical GCE in Andreotti's (2006, 2014) sense, involving "analysis and critique of the relationships among perspectives, language, power, social groups and social practices by the learners" (Andreotti, 2006, p. 51). It also reflects the defining characteristics of critical CALL, that is, a concern for social equity (see Section 3.1.).

For Andreotti (2006), however, exercising criticality goes beyond assessing that something is either right or wrong, biased or unbiased, or true or false. She sees it rather as an endeavour to unearth the origins of assumptions and implications. In contrast to Darvin's (2017) understanding of "critical" in CDL, for Andreotti (2006) critical literacy is not about the learners "unveiling" the "truth" but about giving learners the opportunity and encouraging them

> to reflect on their context and their own and others' epistemological and ontological assumptions: how we came to think/be/feel/act the way we do and the implications of our systems of belief in local/global terms in relation to power, social relationships and the distribution of labour and resources. (p. 7)

The following section features two concrete examples of exchanges that speak to the CVE agenda, with each case meeting at least two or three of the defining criteria of CVE, including multimodal approaches to student project work and outcomes as propounded in the expanded CVE framework (see Figure 2.3).

4 CVE Examples

4.1 Reading the City and Making Your City Sustainable

In this exchange, university students in Buenos Aires (Argentina), Poznan (Poland), and Malmö (Sweden) were involved in critically exploring their different urban environments through the lens of UN SDG 11: Make cities inclusive, safe, resilient, and sustainable (United Nations, 2015). There were two iterations of this exchange, one in 2020 and one in 2021.

Both iterations were seven-week-long trinational, interdisciplinary collaborations between undergraduate student groups from three disciplines: multimodal communication (Argentina, $n = 21$), tourism (Poland, $n = 21$), and teacher education (Sweden, $n = 12$). The educators had met during the VE training offered as part of the EU Erasmus+ funded EVOLVE project. The students were randomly organized into 10 international teams, with one to three representatives from each institution, and used English as a lingua franca in their synchronous and asynchronous interactions. However, as Reljanovic Glimäng (2022) pointed out, the focus was on content and communication, rather than on language acquisition, and "the participants were encouraged to use multimodal and multilingual resources to convey meaning in online interactions" (p. 67).

The projects followed a three-stage task sequence (O'Dowd & Waire, 2009): (a) connecting in international teams, (b) critically exploring topics, and (c) co-creating multimodal artifacts.

4.1.1 Reading the City: Popular, Personal, and Critical Perspectives on Urban Culture

In the first iteration, the main aim was for the students to develop critical, creative, and digital skills by collaboratively analysing and designing representations of their cities. After familiarizing themselves with different online tools in preparation for the main project phase (Task 1), students moved on to explore the potentials of multimodal meaning-making by sharing and critically analysing popular and official tourist websites depicting their respective cities (Task 2). The focus was on the content of these websites and the stories and values that they promote. By contrast, students then selected and shared examples of how their cities figure in aesthetic texts such as literature, poetry, or music to identify critical or controversial issues. These could concern challenges such as segregation, poverty, crime, prejudice, and so forth (Task 3). Finally, students worked in cross-cultural teams and designed their own multimodal city-texts based on a critical theme chosen by each group (Task 4).

4.1.2 Making Your City Sustainable

For the second iteration of this CVE, the educator team decided to put more emphasis on critical agency and citizenry. In this iteration, the student teams researched sustainability issues in urban settings, starting from the questions: How is SDG 11 addressed in your city? Where are the opportunities/challenges? They co-created sustainability campaigns relevant in all three cities. The collaborative process involved going into town and exploring problems and existing initiatives, and talking to local experts and/or grassroots activists engaged in topics ranging from recycling and pollution to strategies for saving the bees in the city and making cities safer spaces for women. Thus, this CVE not only addressed sustainability in terms of environmental challenges but also tackled social sustainability by addressing social justice issues.

The aim was to foster students' critical reflection and critical global citizenship skills by

- investigating and comparing sustainability issues within and across cities
- recognizing how sustainability goals must be understood considering local socio-economic, political, and historical realities
- negotiating ideas in international teams and using translanguaging, digital tools, and multimodal resources to share meaning across varying proficiency levels in English
- co-creating multimodal digital campaigns as a way of sharing and implementing new knowledge and taking action

A representative student quote from the e-portfolios the participants kept during their exchanges reads as follows: "This kind of project can really open up other ways of thinking. You can see the bigger picture and that you are actually a global citizen."

However, drawing on her notion of brave, non-hegemonic spaces in VE where learners can engage in thinking otherwise, Reljanovic Glimäng (2022) observed that brave spaces, manifesting through development of critical intercultural and global awareness, mostly emerged during the students' individual reflections after the campaigns had been co-created. She concluded that the task sequence the students engaged in needed to be modified and proposed a shift in focus that foregrounds critical intercultural reflexivity over the action-oriented pedagogical task. "What comes after co-creation," she proposed, "should become the salient dialogic part according to a non-hegemonic approach to VE, and a critical approach to GCE" (pp. 78–79).

Still, both iterations of this CVE provided the learners with an opportunity to exercise agency, engage with issues of power and inequality, and develop an understanding of how our (online) classrooms and conversations are related to broader social, cultural, and political challenges, which are the tenets of critical CALL.

In the second CVE example, participants took a first stab at social entrepreneurship.

4.2 Youth Entrepreneurship for Society (YES)

The YES project took place within an English for specific purposes setting, which – like the first example – also took account of the students' wider sociopolitical contexts, thus reflecting the interface between CVE, critical CALL, and CDL, leveraging digital technologies for sociopolitical action, public engagement, and change (see Section 3.1). Business communication and management students from Cyprus University of Technology ($n = 27$) and the University of Valencia in Spain ($n = 15$) engaged in the co-construction and sharing of authentic and meaningful artefacts. The aim was to connect the respective classrooms with the outside world through the involvement of local organizations and to promote students' transversal skills development – intercultural, linguistic, and digital skills and teamwork – as well as to develop a social entrepreneurial mindset. Since this project was a second language CVE, participants interacted in English at B2 level according to the Common European Framework of Reference for Languages. They collaborated in international groups of four and interacted both synchronously and asynchronously using English as a lingua franca over the course of one semester (fifteen weeks).

Via the HEI engagement offices at both institutions, the students were put in contact and worked with local associations and NGOs in Spain and Cyprus (11 Spanish and 11 Cypriot), identifying the main challenges faced by those organizations. In their cross-cultural groups, the students discussed and proposed solutions to social challenges in their respective local communities and designed their own initiatives including elevator pitches and digital campaigns, which they subsequently presented in an online social entrepreneurship fair (Sevilla-Pavón, 2019).

The result is a model for new local employer/HEI collaborations to support employability skills development through CVE. To this effect, the two educators concluded it was "necessary to go beyond the syllabus and the classroom's physical four walls in order to foster solidarity, equality and respect in the broader social context" (Sevilla-Pavón & Nicolaou, 2022, p. 1662). The CVE experience equipped their learners with "the tools to tackle problems of discrimination, marginalisation and inequality … both in the classroom and in society" (p. 1663). They saw the students become "active change champions" (p. 1650) who had become aware of the importance of advocacy and social entrepreneurship to achieve social change.

The preliminary conclusions that can be drawn from these practical applications of the concepts underpinning CVE are summarized in the final section of this chapter.

5 Conclusions and Outlook

The examples presented in Sections 4.1 and 4.2 testify to the potential of CVE as a brave space for "thinking otherwise" (Andreotti, 2006, p. 7), which means CVE is a space for developing critical agency and citizenry, and a space where students gain an understanding of how our classrooms and conversations are related to broader social, cultural, and political challenges as encapsulated in critical CALL (Helm, 2015). They also illustrate how criticality and DEIA challenges in CALL can be realized through interinstitutional and transnational partnerships, which can also involve businesses and organizations.

CVE allows teachers and learners to move beyond standard content such as insights into "food, fashion, folklore and festivals," which still characterize many VE projects (Hauck, 2020, n.p.), and to engage in meaningful interactions on glocal challenges, that is, those that combine local and global dimensions (Robertson, 1995). It also responds to Helm's (2016) call to pay attention to "phatic exchanges between learners" (p. 151), where complexity often gets downplayed, if not avoided, and where superficial views of otherness and the world tend to prevail.

Moreover, the examples suggest that CVE can serve as an inclusive, sustainable, and scalable strategy for IaH in general and *critical* IaH in particular. As an embedded IaH strategy, CVE has the potential to instigate transformative change at individual, institutional, and policy levels and can – as has been shown – lead to new forms of collaborations between employers and organizations and HEIs. These, in turn, can enhance graduate employability, particularly for students from low socio-economic backgrounds who are under-represented in an already small percentage of learners who study abroad. CVE can allow them to experience new ways of acquiring international and intercultural skills including languages. In addition, CVE participation helps learners move beyond uncritical consumption of technology and offers them an opportunity to develop CDL skills and engage in critical CALL.

However, not only can CVE effect real change, both locally and globally, through student CVE projects focusing, for example, on the UN SDGs, but it also has potential to enrich VE and IaH research by creating new legacies in IaH based on an understanding of research as "living knowledge" (Facer & Enright, 2016, n.p.), which concerns bringing together community knowledge with academic expertise. In the case of CVE, it means connecting praxis knowledge – lived experiences of students, educators, and administrators involved in CVE – with the body of global critical knowledge in international and intercultural education and transversal skills building (problem solving, teamwork and leadership, languages and communication, critical and innovative thinking, and media and information literacy).

Adhering to the multidisciplinary, multimodal, and inclusive approaches exemplified above will enable CVE practitioners to counteract technology-induced polarization and forms of othering (Dooly & Darvin, 2022), to make a significant contribution to systemic change in IaH in HE, and to – hopefully – set a new agenda for *critical* IaH through CVE.

Acknowledgments

I would like to express my gratitude to the colleagues who have shared their CVE examples with me: Malin Reljanovic Glimäng, Ana Sevilla-Pavón, and Anna Nicolaou. I would also like to thank the editors for their very helpful feedback and their creative suggestions for amendments to this chapter.

About the Author

Mirjam Hauck is associate head for internationalization, equality, diversity, and inclusion in the School of Languages and Applied Linguistics at the Open University/UK and a senior fellow of the UK's Higher Education Academy. She has published widely on the use of technologies for the learning and teaching of languages and cultures. She is the president of the European Association for Computer Assisted Language Learning (EUROCALL) and associate editor of the *CALL Journal*.

References

Alami, N., Albuquerque, J., Ashton, L., Elwood, J., Ewoodzie, K., Hauck, M., Karam, J., Klimanova, L., Nasr, R., & Satar, M. (2022). Marginalization and underrepresentation in virtual exchange: Reasons and remedies. *Journal of International Students*, *12*(S3), 57–76. https://doi.org/10.32674/jis.v12iS3.4665

Alami, N.H., A-Saab, S.A., Ashton, L.S., Elwood, J., Ewoodzie, K., Hauck, M., Klimanova, L., & Satar, M. (2023). *The ABC of young learners and virtual exchange (VE): Access, benefits, and content.* Stevens Initiative. https://www.stevensinitiative.org/wp-content/uploads/2023/05/Stevens-Initiative-Sponsored-Research-Final-Report-The-ABCs-of-Young-People-and-Virtual-Exchange-Access-Benefits-and-Content.pdf

Andreotti, V. (2006). Soft versus critical global citizenship education. *Policy & Practice: A Development Education Review*, *3*, 40–51. https://www.developmenteducationreview.com/issue/issue-3/soft-versus-critical-global-citizenship-education

Andreotti, V. (2014) Critical literacy: Theories and practices in development education. *Policy & Practice: A Development Education Review*, *19*, 12–32. https://www.developmenteducationreview.com/issue/issue-19/critical-literacy-theories-and-practices-development-education

Anwaruddin, S.M. (2019). Teaching language, promoting social justice: A dialogic approach to using social media. *CALICO Journal*, *36*(1), 1–18. https://doi.org/10.1558/cj.35208

Beelen, J., & Jones, E. (2015). Redefining internationalization at home. In A. Curaj, L. Matei, R. Pricopie, J. Salmi, & P. Scott (Eds.), *The European higher education area* (pp. 59–72). Springer. https://doi.org/10.1007/978-3-319-20877-0_5

Belz, J.A. (2003). Linguistic perspectives on the development of intercultural competence in telecollaboration. *Language Learning & Technology*, *7*(2), 68–117. https://doi.org/10125/25201

Bezemer, J., & Kress, G. (2016). *Multimodality, learning and communication: A social semiotic frame*. Routledge.

Bilki, Z., Satar, M., & Sak, M. (2022). Critical digital literacy in virtual exchange for ELT teacher education: An interpretivist methodology. *ReCALL, 35*(1), 58–73. https://doi.org/10.1017/S095834402200009X

Brown, M. (2017, May 29). *Exploring the underbelly of digital literacies*. oeb Insights. https://oeb-insights.com/exploring-the-underbelly-of-digital-literacies

Choi, M. (2016). A concept analysis of digital citizenship for democratic citizenship education in the internet age. *Theory & Research in Social Education, 44*(4), 565–607. https://doi.org/10.1080/00933104.2016.1210549

Clavijo Olarte, A., Medina, R.A., Calderon-Aponte, D., Rodríguez, A., Prieto, K., & Náder, M.C. (2023). Raising awareness of the city as a text: Multimodal, multicultural, and multilingual resources for education. In A. Salmon & A. Clavijo-Olarte (Eds.), *Handbook of research on socio-cultural and linguistic perspectives on language and literacy development* (pp. 239–264). IGI Global. https://doi.org/10.4018/978-1-6684-5022-2.ch013

Crawford, I. (2021). Employer perspectives on virtual international working: Essential skills for the globalised, digital workplace. In S. Swartz, B. Barbosa, I. Crawford, & S. Luck (Eds.). *Developments in virtual learning environments and global workplace* (pp. 178–204). IGI Global. https://doi.org/10.4018/978-1-7998-7331-0.ch010

Darvin, R. (2016). Language and identity in the digital age. In S. Preece (Ed.), *Routledge handbook of language and identity* (pp. 523–540). Routledge. https://doi.org/10.4324/9781315669816-39

Darvin, R. (2017). Language, ideology, and critical digital literacy. In S. Thorne & S. May (Eds.), *Language, education and technology* (3rd ed., pp. 17–30). Springer. https://doi.org/10.1007/978-3-319-02237-6_35

Dooly, M., & Darvin, R. (2022). Intercultural communicative competence in the digital age: Critical digital literacy and inquiry-based pedagogy. *Language and Intercultural Communication, 22*(3), 354–366. https://doi.org/10.1080/14708477.2022.2063304

EVOLVE Project Team. (2020). *The impact of virtual exchange on student learning in higher education: EVOLVE project report*. https://research.rug.nl/en/publications/the-impact-of-virtual-exchange-on-student-learning-in-higher-educ

Facer, K., & Enright, B. (2016). *Creating living knowledge: The Connected Communities Programme, community-university relationships and the participatory turn in the production of knowledge*. University of Bristol. https://hdl.handle.net/1983/9560334f-7114-4a30-b669-1cbb56c3a149

Freire, P. (1970). *Pedagogy of the oppressed*. Penguin.

Freire, P., & Macedo, D. (1987). *Literacy: Reading the word and the world*. Routledge. https://doi.org/10.4324/9780203986103

García, O., & Wei, L. (2014). *Translanguaging: Language, bilingualism and education*. Palgrave Macmillan. https://doi.org/10.1057/9781137385765

Giroux, H. (1981). *Ideology, culture and the process of schooling*. Temple University Press.

Gleason, J., & Suvorov, R. (2019). Promoting social justice with CALL. *CALICO Journal*, *36*(1), i–vii. https://doi.org/10.1558/cj.37162

Guo, Z., & Xu, X. (2023). Understanding intercultural virtual exchange through a translanguaging lens in Chinese as a foreign language. *Journal of China Computer-Assisted Language Learning*, *3*(1), 132–167. https://doi.org/10.1515/jccall-2022-0018

Hauck, M. (2019). Virtual exchange for (critical) digital literacies skills development. *European Journal of Language Policy*, *11*(2), 187–210. https://doi.org/10.3828/ejlp.2019.12

Hauck, M. (2020, September 15). Towards global fairness in the digital space through VE [Conference session]. 3rd International Virtual Exchange Conference (IVEC), Newcastle, UK. https://iveconference.org/2020-conference/

Hauck, M. (2023). From virtual exchange to critical virtual exchange and critical internationalization at home. In Diversity Abroad (Ed.), *The global impact exchange: Virtual exchange as a tool to advance equity and inclusion* (pp. 9–12). Stevens Initiative. https://diversityabroad.org/public/DIVaPublic/GIE-Archives/GIE-2023/GIE-Sp2023/GIE-Sp23-Article-1.aspx

Hauck, M., & Helm, F. (2020). Critical internationalisation through critical virtual exchange [Video]. Critical Internationalization Studies Network. https://youtu.be/S1EZL4DLjew

Hauck, M., Müller-Hartmann, A., Rienties, B., & Rogaten, J. (2020). Approaches to researching digital-pedagogical competence development in VE-based teacher education. *Journal of Virtual Exchange*, *3*, 5–35. https://doi.org/10.21827/jve.3.36082

Hauck, M., & Satar, M. (2018). Learning and teaching languages in technology-mediated contexts: The relevance of social presence, co-presence, participatory literacy, and multimodal competence. In R. Kern & C. Develotte (Eds.), *Screens and scenes: Multimodal communication in online intercultural encounters* (pp. 133–157). Routledge. https://doi.org/10.4324/9781315447124-7

Hellmich, E.A. (2019). A critical look at the bigger picture: Macro-level discourses of language and technology in the United States. *CALICO Journal*, *36*(1), 39–58. https://doi.org/10.1558/cj.35022

Helm, F. (2015). The practices and challenges of telecollaboration in higher education in Europe. *Language Learning & Technology*, *19*(2), 197–217. https://doi.org/10125/44424

Helm, F. (2016). Facilitated dialogue in online intercultural exchange. In R. O'Dowd & T. Lewis (Eds.), *Online intercultural exchange: Policy, pedagogy, practice* (pp. 150–172). Routledge. https://doi.org/10.4324/9781315678931

Helm, F. (2019). EMI, internationalisation, and the digital. *International Journal of Bilingual Education and Bilingualism*, *23*(3), 314–325. https://doi.org/10.1080/13670050.2019.1643823

Helm, F., Baroni, A., & Acconcia, G. (2023). Global citizenship online in higher education. *Educational Research for Policy and Practice*, *23*, 1–18. https://doi.org/10.1007/s10671-023-09351-6

Helm, F., & Hauck, M. (2022). Language, identity and positioning in virtual exchange. In L. Klimanova (Ed.), *Identity, multilingualism and CALL* (pp. 24–28). Equinox. https://doi.org/10.1558/equinox.43408

Hinshaw, N., Gonzalez, S., & Engel, L. (2022). Internationalization of K–12 schooling through virtual exchange: Opportunities in a fractured context. *Journal of International Students*, *12*(S3), 1–16. https://doi.org/10.32674/jis.v12iS3.4624

Jiang, L., & Gu, M.M. (2022). Toward a professional development model for critical digital literacies in TESOL. *TESOL Quarterly*, *56*(3), 1029–1040. https://doi.org/10.1002/tesq.3138

Kastler, K., & Lewis, H. (2021). Approaching VE through an equity lens. In Diversity Abroad (Ed.), *The global impact exchange: Exploring opportunities for global engagement within local communities* (pp. 17–19). Stevens Initiative.

Klimanova, L., & Hellmich, E.A. (2021). Crossing transcultural liminalities with critical virtual exchange: A study of shifting border discourses. *Critical Inquiry in Language Studies*, *18*(3), 273–304. https://doi.org/10.1080/15427587.2020.1867552

Kress, G. (2003). *Literacy in the new media age*. Routledge. https://doi.org/10.4324/9780203299234

Mignolo, W.D. (2007). INTRODUCTION: Coloniality of power and de-colonial thinking. *Cultural Studies*, *21*(2–3), 155–167. https://doi.org/10.1080/09502380601162498

Mirra, N., & Garcia, A. (2020). "I hesitate but I do have hope": Youth speculative civic literacies for troubled times. *Harvard Educational Review*, *90*(2), 295–321. https://doi.org/10.17763/1943-5045-90.2.295

O'Dowd, R. (2018). From telecollaboration to virtual exchange: State-of-the-art and the role of UNICollaboration in moving forward. *Journal of Virtual Exchange, 1*, 1–23. https://doi.org/10.14705/rpnet.2018.jve.1

O'Dowd, R. (2020). A transnational model of virtual exchange for global citizenship education. *Language Teaching, 53*(4), 477–490. https://doi.org/10.1017/S0261444819000077

O'Dowd, R., & Beelen, J. (2021, September 7). *Virtual exchange and Internationalisation at Home: Navigating the terminology*. European Association for International Education. https://www.eaie.org/blog/virtual-exchange-iah-terminology.html

O'Dowd, R., & Waire, P. (2009). Critical issues in telecollaborative task design. *Computer Assisted Language Learning, 22*(2), 173–188. https://doi.org/10.1080/09588220902778369

Petrosyan, A. (2024). Internet penetration rate worldwide 2024, by region. *Statista*, 5 November 2024. Released October 2024. https://www.statista.com/statistics/269329/penetration-rate-of-the-internet-by-region/

Reljanovic Glimäng, M. (2022). Safe/brave spaces in virtual exchange on sustainability. *Journal of Virtual Exchange, 5*, 61–81. https://doi.org/10.21827/jve.5.38369

Robertson, T. (1995). Glocalization: Time-space and homogeneity-heterogeneity. In M. Featherstone, S.M. Lash, & R. Robertson (Eds.), *Global modernities* (pp. 25–44). Sage. https://doi.org/10.4135/9781446250563.n2

Satar, M., Aranha, S., Spatti Cavalari, S.M., & Almijiwl, W. (2024). Low proficiency level learners' translingual and transmodal practices in teletandem: Challenging the separation of languages principle. *System, 120*, 103187. https://doi.org/10.1016/j.system.2023.103187

Satar, M., & Hauck, M. (2021). Exploring digital equity in online learning communities. In A.M. Sousa Aguiar de Medeiros & D. Kelly (Eds.), *Language debates: Digital media* (pp. 270–290). John Murray Learning.

Satar, M., Hauck, M., & Bilki, Z. (2023). Multimodal representation in virtual exchange: A social semiotic approach to critical digital literacy. *Language Learning & Technology, 27*(2), 72–96. https://hdl.handle.net/10125/73504

Selwyn, N., & Facer, K. (2013). Introduction: The need for a politics of education and technology. In N. Selwyn & K. Facer (Eds.), *The politics of education and technology* (pp. 1–17). Palgrave Macmillan. https://doi.org/10.1057/9781137031983_1

Sevilla-Pavón, A. (2019). L1 versus L2 online intercultural exchanges for the development of 21st century competences: The students' perspective. *British*

Journal of Educational Technology, *50*(2), 779–805. https://doi.org/10.1111/bjet.12602

Sevilla-Pavón, A., & Nicolaou, A. (2022). Artefact co-construction in virtual exchange: "Youth Entrepreneurship for Society." *Computer Assisted Language Learning Journal*, *35*(7), 1642–1667. https://doi.org/10.1080/09588221.2020.1825096

Stein, S., & Andreotti, V. (2021). Global citizenship otherwise. In E. Bosio (Ed.), *Conversations on global citizenship education: Perspectives on research, teaching, and learning* (pp. 13–36). Routledge.

Thorne, S.L. (2003). Artifacts and cultures-of-use in intercultural communication. *Language Learning & Technology*, *7*(2), 38–67. https://doi.org/10125/25200

Thorne, S.L. (2016). Cultures-of-use and morphologies of communicative action. *Language Learning & Technology*, *20*(2), 185–191. https://doi.org/10125/44473

Trott, E. (2017). *Bodies of water: Politics, ethics, and relationships along New Mexico's Acequias* [Doctoral dissertation]. University of New Mexico. https://digitalrepository.unm.edu/anth_etds/138

UNESCO. (2014). *Global citizenship education: Preparing learners for the challenges of the 21st century*. UNESCO. https://unesdoc.unesco.org/ark:/48223/pf0000227729

United Nations. (2015). *Transforming our world: The 2030 agenda for sustainable development*. United Nations. https://sdgs.un.org/2030agenda

US Department of State's Bureau of Educational and Cultural Affairs. (2023). *Using data to open doors*. https://opendoorsdata.org/

UUKI (Universities UK International). (2022). *Internationalisation at home: Developing global citizens without travel*. UUKI Publications. https://www.universitiesuk.ac.uk/universities-uk-international/insights-and-publications/uuki-publications/internationalisation-home-developing

Ware, P., & Kramsch, C. (2005). Toward an intercultural stance: Teaching German and English through telecollaboration. *The Modern Language Journal*, *89*(2), 190–205. https://doi.org/10.1111/j.1540-4781.2005.00274.x

3 Advancing Inclusion through Pre-Mobility Virtual Exchange

Ángela M. Alonso Morais

1 Introduction

Spending a term or a year abroad offers substantial advantages for language learning, as it provides a more authentic experience than textbooks can offer (Kinginger, 2016; Richardson, 2016), and immersion in a new culture can bring "cultural sensitivity and proficiency in the host language" (Jackson, 2020, p. 445). This international experience remains, however, exclusive and elitist, as it is only available to a reduced number of students who can afford it (Byram & Dervin, 2008; Richardson, 2016). Furthermore, recent studies have questioned the assumption that a study abroad experience will automatically lead to the enhancement of students' language proficiency levels or intercultural competence (Coleman, 2013; Jackson, 2020; Kinginger, 2011, 2016). Intercultural competence (Byram, 1997) refers to the ability to interact successfully in intercultural contexts and encompasses knowledge of the self and others; skills of interpretation, relation, discovery, and interaction; as well as attitudes of curiosity and openness.

According to Vande Berg et al. (2012), students acquire effective intercultural learning during their time abroad only through deliberate and strategic intervention by educators. This intervention may acquire diverse shapes, including pre-departure, during, or post-departure workshops or seminars in face-to-face or online environments (Jackson, 2020). Pre-departure pedagogical interventions can also be referred to as "pre-mobility" interventions. Pre-mobility can be defined as a preparatory phase prior to planned mobility, which is deliberately implemented by institutions or educators themselves to equip future sojourners with the necessary language, intercultural, and soft skills to maintain successful and appropriate intercultural interactions when studying abroad.

Higher education institutions (HEIs) are responsible for ensuring the efficacy and success of the learning outcomes, and international education plays a crucial role in this regard – exposing students to diverse cultures, educational systems, as well as fostering skills such as critical thinking or adaptability. One of the most popular international education initiatives are study abroad programs. Study abroad can be defined as "a subtype of education abroad that results in progress toward an academic degree at a student's home institution" but excludes "the pursuit of a full academic degree at a foreign institution" (Forum on Education Abroad, 2011, n.p.).

Mobility rates for study abroad have risen substantially recently (European Commission, 2022b), but they are still only available for a reduced number of students who can afford the considerable expenses incurred in the international experience (Byram & Dervin, 2008; de Wit & Jones, 2018; Richardson, 2016). Financial constraints can initially include insufficient mobility grant funding provided by universities, followed by the high cost of accommodation, travel expenses, city transport, and other exceptional expenses that are subsequently incurred. The budget required for studying abroad is exorbitant, and in the European context, students often cite inadequate funding from the Erasmus grant, which is awarded to full-time university students meeting Erasmus+ program criteria, as the primary reason for declining the opportunity (European Parliament & Directorate-General for Internal Policies, 2010). Among the challenges that hinder students' access to education overseas, we also often find the participants' personal motivations and expectations, individual traits, and program variations or the lack of information about these learning opportunities (Jackson, 2020).

Even though higher education is evolving in terms of diversity, equity, inclusion, and accessibility (DEIA), there still must be a push to provide wider access to intercultural learning and advance social justice in policy and in practice. As Tienda (2013) highlights, "integration is not an automatic by-product of campus diversity; therefore ... institutional leaders must pursue deliberate strategies that promote inclusion" (p. 467). HEIs worldwide have elaborated numerous internationalization plans to apply on campus and within the curriculum to develop students' intercultural skills (de Wit & Jones, 2018) and to broaden the scope of intercultural opportunities accessible to students (Jackson, 2020).

Internationalization at home (IaH) rose to prominence recently and is, by nature, more inclusive than other forms of internationalization as it also offers activities to non-mobile students. IaH is concerned with the incorporation of interculturality "into the formal and informal curriculum for all students in domestic learning environments" (Beelen & Jones, 2015, p. 69). It is often combined with the internationalization of the curriculum (IoC), which integrates the intercultural dimension into the curriculum, learning outcomes, tasks, or assessment of students (Leask, 2015). These initiatives have produced a shift in focus from "mobility for some" to "international learning opportunities for all" (O'Dowd, 2023a, p. 43) and offer a more equitable approach to the development of global skills (Richardson, 2016).

To enhance accessibility to intercultural learning, we can actively promote the inclusion of international strategies and diversity of cultures in the classroom, thereby helping to increase the number of students benefiting from international education. Online approaches such as virtual exchange (VE) or blended intensive programs have flourished with the advent of the COVID-19 pandemic and newly developed technologies (Farnell et al. 2021). These initiatives have the potential to offer intercultural experiences to a wider range of students, including those who cannot participate in study abroad programs due to financial, family, or personal reasons (O'Dowd, 2023b). These approaches to intercultural learning are innovative opportunities to advance DEIA in higher education through strategic international partnerships, which this volume promotes.

VE connects learners from diverse cultural contexts to partake in language and intercultural exchange and collaboration as part of course work and with the support of educators (O'Dowd, 2018). VE is on the rise, particularly in language learning contexts, and despite the obstacles it overcame to finally settle in the educational system, it now seems to be a much-loved device to promote IaH (O'Dowd, 2023a). Nevertheless, thinking that institutional DEIA goals will be achieved by simply offering the more sustainable and accessible VE experiences may risk being considered naive because, as de Wit and Jones (2018) point out, offering a wider range of international education opportunities is not enough. Internationalization must be available to all students, and HEIs must recognize its relevance in students' future.

With this idea in mind, this chapter reviews the affordances of pre-mobility VE, which refers to the employment of VE initiatives as a preparatory phase to mobility for the advancement of equity and inclusion in intercultural education. It provides an overview of an innovative model organized by the University of León (Spain). The *GearUp!* VE model is proposed in the following sections as a sustainable tool to prepare undergraduate students to study abroad and to maximize their learning outcomes regarding intercultural, linguistic, and transversal skills. *GearUp!* participants collaborate in teams for eight weeks to complete six tasks that revolve around the theme of studying abroad. This VE, designed and coordinated by the author of this chapter, has been implemented twice in partnership with different institutions across the world. Its structure will be outlined in Section 3 of this chapter, which concludes with some pedagogical implications for educators and international staff at universities who are committed to helping a wider range of students boost their intercultural competence and language proficiency.

2 The Role of Pre-Mobility Virtual Exchange in Promoting Inclusion

Over the past decade, there has been a noticeable shift towards promoting diversity in higher education (Tienda, 2013). However, these initiatives often lack a global outlook, and DEIA efforts need to be extended and incorporated into the institutional internationalization strategies as well (Özturgut, 2017). Inclusion and accessibility initiatives have sometimes been treated as part of a "social justice agenda" that results in a commercialization of diversity (Özturgut, 2017, p. 84). The need for inclusion has typically been treated as just one more item on a checklist, used as part of a marketing strategy, but that is far from the initial mission of HEIs of maximizing the pedagogical benefits for students (Tienda, 2013). Organizations responsible for international programs have been urged to adopt a more inclusive and accessible approach to offer intercultural learning to a wider range of students (European Commission, 2022b).

VE has been proposed and implemented several times with the goal of broadening access to international education (Batardière et al., 2019; O'Dowd, 2023a). Although VE does not have magical powers, it is thought to have the potential to bring about inclusion in a number of ways (O'Dowd, 2023b). VE initiatives, and pre-mobility VE in particular, serve as a sustainable tool to support the inclusion of those students in disadvantaged situations (due to financial, geographical, personal, family, or safety reasons, among others), students with no motivation to participate in study abroad, students whose language level would hinder their mobility, or students who belong to under-represented cultures or marginalized backgrounds.

2.1 Accessibility and Environmental Sustainability

The main argument in favour of the employment of VE is its accessibility. Universities and teachers themselves can set up international VE programs and easily offer them to diverse cohorts of students, including those who would otherwise never have an international mobility experience during their studies. As O'Dowd (2023b) reviewed, VE can suit those students who cannot afford the cost of physical mobility programs, students and teachers who find themselves isolated (O'Dowd & Vinagre, 2024) or in unsafe geographical regions, or language learners who are initiating their first intercultural interactions in their target language.

Even though VE is not to be seen as an alternative to physical mobility for disadvantaged students, it is clear that access to these hands-on intercultural experiences is much easier. Students who cannot afford to travel abroad, who have family constraints, or those who are differently abled can take pleasure in this activity too. Physical or intellectual impairments can hinder accessibility to study abroad programs, along with health issues, educational barriers, or discrimination (European Commission, 2022b). Constraints such as integration in the host community, the lack of learning materials adapted to special needs, the physical environment, or access to grant funding make it impossible for such students to participate in mobility or fully benefit from it. By eliminating these barriers, VE can foster authentic intercultural interaction among students from diverse and marginalized backgrounds, as it is an intercultural experience that can be made available to large cohorts of students with access to technology. This advantage should not encourage institutions and organizations to replace physical mobility, reduce its funding (European Students' Union & the Erasmus Student Network, 2022), or feel complacent with their low mobility rates. On the contrary, virtual and physical mobility should be combined to enhance students' international education (O'Dowd, 2023a). VE models such as the one proposed in this chapter have the potential to reach and involve cohorts of students "who would otherwise be unwilling or unable to travel due to physical, social, or financial reasons" (Sabzalieva et al., 2022, p. 15), which was the case for some of the participants in *GearUp!* who worked part time, had already-established families, or were in their final academic year.

Virtual approaches also provide a more environmentally sustainable path towards international education than traditional study abroad programs (Sabzalieva et al., 2022). The Stevens Initiative (2023) works to connect young people across continents and cultures, and advocates for the use of VE to broaden access to this sort of international experience. The initiative remarks that the use of VE eliminates the high cost of traditional mobility, the difficulty in acquiring a visa for certain participants, and the time spent away from family, work, or the educational context. For these reasons, VE can be considered a more easily accessible tool to international education than traditional study abroad programs.

However, VE presents the problem of equitable access to the internet, as not all students can rely on stable connections or a Wi-Fi network to connect to. This situation poses the risk of widening the gap between those students who can afford international education and those who cannot. One of the participants of the *GearUp!* VE highlighted this problem: "In the same way that being online allows you the benefit of being able to do it from anywhere, it has against you the fact that you need a stable Wi-Fi connection" (R2_STUD1). Though VE should not be considered a substitute for mobility, it remains a resource that is more readily available compared to study abroad programs because, if planned efficiently and with the necessary funding, it can reach larger groups of students and be sustainable over time.

2.2 Increased Motivation and Reduced Anxiety

The employment of VE also has the potential to enhance the inclusivity of international education by fostering greater participation of students in physical mobility programs. The Erasmus+ KA3 project EVOLVE, which analysed the impact of VE on students learning across all HEI disciplines, found that 60 per cent of VE participants were interested in physical mobility (EVOLVE Project Team, 2020).

A recent study confirmed that participation in VE can lead to an increased motivation to study abroad (Lee et al., 2022). The authors explain that being in contact and engaging with other cultures through VE enhances students' intercultural experience and sense of harmony, which, in turn, may lead to a higher interest in and demand for mobility programs, an outcome they call the "exposure effect" (p. 4). Their study also suggests that the intercultural learning that occurs as a result of VE could mitigate the anxiety associated with studying abroad and the possible challenges students may find in the host environment. The study authors claim that VE can offer support for students to feel more confident, prepared, and eager to go abroad, paving the way for physical mobility. This VE approach can be beneficial for those students who choose not to take part in international mobility due to the stress or anxiety it may cause. In this way, VE creates a safe space for them to practice and increase their motivation to study abroad.

The *Blended Mobility Implementation Guide* (European Commission, 2022a), which aims to inspire and encourage institutions that are considering incorporating blended mobility activities, also supports the idea that blended learning may lead students to participate in long-term mobility. Erdei and Káplár-Kodácsy (2020) also suggest that VE can serve as a tool for students to establish friendships and create an international network that can prepare them for a longer mobility. Many of the students who participated in *GearUp!* pointed out that this sort of academic work gave them the opportunity to discover new cultures and that they became attracted to intercultural contexts and thus felt more eager to participate in physical mobility in the near future. When asked about whether the VE had changed their opinion about studying abroad, one *GearUp!* participant from the second round of implementation stated, "It definitely has. I'm not intimidated as much about meeting new people, and I'd gladly go to Germany or Portugal, because I would already have friends there" (R2_STUD21). This example evidences the potential of VE to increase motivation and reduce anxiety towards studying abroad.

2.3 Accommodating Learners with Differences in Language Proficiency

VE initiatives in the context of language learning also have the potential to cater to a higher number of students than other more traditional classroom activities (Kinginger, 2016). VE programs can accommodate those students who are skilled in oral production but also those who may feel uncomfortable speaking another language, as they offer students a first real encounter with language use both online and within the classroom context. This wider range of accommodation is particularly the case when VEs combine synchronous and asynchronous components (O'Dowd, 2023a). Asynchronous tasks provide them with time to reflect on their language use or to ask questions of their local peers and teachers, making their first interactions more relaxed and fine-tuned. The Evaluating and Upscaling Telecollaborative Teacher Education (EVALUATE) project, which examined the impact of VE on the early stages of teacher education across Europe, also reported a similar outcome regarding the reassurance and opportunity for rehearsal that an online environment, especially asynchronous, may offer (Baroni et al., 2019). VE scaffolds students' intercultural and language learning and allows them to get ready for future in-person interactions in a safe environment. The Stevens Initiative (2023) mentions that over 80 per cent of their participants "feel they can be their true selves, are valued by fellow peers, are included in all aspects of programming, and belong in their virtual exchange" (p. 13).

2.4 Under-Represented Cultures

Moreover, VE gives commonly under-represented cultures the opportunity to be seen and valued more easily than with traditional study abroad programs. The online learning environment has expanded the horizons for international collaboration, and it is now feasible to explore destinations once considered impractical for physical mobility (Torres & Statti, 2022). International VE gives diverse student cohorts a chance to discover countries and cultures that would otherwise not catch their attention or be thought of as possible destinations because, when students choose a destination, practicality tends to be their top priority instead of choosing regions that are too far away or that exceed their budget.

The Stevens Initiative serves as a representative example of this inclusive trait of VE, as it has been organizing successful VEs between the United States and the regions of the Middle East and North Africa (MENA) since 2015. Students in the MENA region experience the challenges of high unemployment rates, water scarcity, multiple conflicts, and inequality, which lead many students to work and focus on survival rather than study. These VEs offer MENA region students the opportunity to explore other cultures and languages, and engage in safe, neutral, and entertaining online interaction. The *Virtual Exchange Impact and Learning Report* (Stevens Initiative, 2023) also highlights the effectiveness of VE in broadening access to intercultural learning and engaging communities that are often neglected in global educational initiatives.

2.5 Pre-Departure VE Preparation and Appreciation of Diversity

Though there are cohorts of students that VE cannot reach, a pre-departure phase employing VE can be beneficial for students facing certain disadvantages, such as learning needs, discrimination, or health issues. Pre-mobility VE can begin the conversation of preparation for these students and help them reflect on their future needs. This phase may provide students with a space for reflection and preparation for their experience regarding DEIA in their future host environment (Adams et al., 2023). Students may take this phase in their mobilities to reflect on how to prepare for their experience on site regarding their specific needs and uniqueness. It may include reflection on their skills and capabilities, their ethnicity, sexual orientation, health, background, and on how all these aspects of identity may play into their host community. On the one hand, participants can potentially reflect on how they may be perceived and, on the other, learn to build a more inclusive and tolerant environment by being aware of diversity. According to the *2022 Global Education Experience Student Survey* (Kasravi, 2023), more than 50 per cent of respondents were negatively impacted due to their feeling stereotyped or isolated while abroad. This finding points to the need for further pre-departure preparation. This is a clear asset of VE initiatives, which, when implemented as pre-departure interventions, can have a positive impact on the on-site experiences of students.

Appreciation of diversity is also a skill that students often develop when participating in VE. Learning how to appreciate other cultures present in the exchange was something many *GearUp!* participants mentioned. One student from the first round of implementation showed the potential of VE to foster appreciation for diversity: "I realized that life in my country is different than in other countries in the world, and [it] taught me to appreciate every difference I may find" (R1_STUD12). Students also enhance their empathy and tolerance, competences which go hand in hand with the embrace of inclusion and diversity, as they develop the skill set necessary to build a truly diverse and inclusive society. One student commented, "I did develop some more empathy for my teammates and think this is a skill I will also make use of outside of the exchange" (R2_STUD98).

3 A Pre-Mobility Model: *GearUp!*

GearUp! is a model of VE designed to prepare undergraduate students for a study abroad experience regarding intercultural, linguistic, and transversal skills. It was inspired by the initiative *Ready, Mobility, Go!* (Batardière et al., 2019), which also proposed a pre-mobility VE as a tool to prepare students from Spain, Belgium, and Ireland, among others, to go on exchanges. *GearUp!* aims to prepare students for a study abroad experience but also offers an easily accessible opportunity for those students (a) who cannot afford its expenses, (b) whose personal situation does not allow them to participate in mobility programs, or (c) who are in their last year of studies and their opportunities to study abroad have passed.

Six tasks (see Table 3.1) related to the theme of study abroad guide students throughout their eight-week online interactions. Every week, students are asked to attend an online supervision session that involves guidance on the tasks, support and feedback on the work done weekly, and talks by experts on the themes of the exchange. Students must also attend a preparatory workshop and read the student handbook (created particularly for this VE) before their interactions start. They are teamed up in multicultural groups and collaborate using English as the lingua franca of the exchange. *GearUp!* was deliberately designed with no specific target cultures in mind in order to accommodate as many students and cultural backgrounds as possible. As a consequence, a wide range of participants can collaborate in teams and carry out the tasks successfully, as these are not culture specific. When their interactions finish, students must reflect on them by completing an e-portfolio that is used as part of the assessment.

3.1 First Round of Implementation

In its first round of implementation in 2022, the initiative primarily targeted students who intended to study abroad as part of their degree, but it was made available to any undergraduate student interested in expanding their

Table 3.1 Structure of the *GearUp!* VE

Week 1	Workshop on online intercultural communication; student handbook for the *GearUp!* VE
Week 2	Task 1: Getting to know each other
Week 3	Task 2: University life across countries
Week 4	Task 3: Overcoming stereotypes
Week 5	Task 4: Elements of culture
Week 6	Task 5: Cultural misunderstandings
Week 7	Task 6: Challenges of studying abroad (accommodation, health services, and public transport)
Week 8	Reflective e-portfolio

views or meeting other students in different countries. It was promoted in 18 different countries in Europe and South America (see Table 3.2) among universities that had previously partnered with the University of León in Spain. Students from any year and discipline could apply and have the chance to interact with other university students across the globe. Forty-two students successfully completed all stages of the VE.

To enrol in the program, students had to complete a Google Form that was sent to them via the international offices of each institution or, as some students reported, found via the social media pages created specifically for the exchange. Only undergraduate students were allowed to apply. The selection process was complex, as a large number of applications came from Mexico and the matching of students for the ensuing group interactions had to be fully multicultural. The demand for VE initiatives in Mexico seemed to be substantially higher than that in other countries. Due to this unequal distribution of students from various countries and to ensure the success of the virtual teams and the tasks, a decision was made to prioritize applications based on their submission order.

Students were teamed up in groups of three to five participants from different cultural backgrounds to allow for a richer comparison of cultures. Some participants were international students in their own institutions pursuing a full degree, which helped represent an even wider range of cultures. This cohort brought even more perspectives and experiences into the exchange and benefited those students who had never had any form of intercultural interaction.

Table 3.2 Countries and Institutions Participating in the First Round of *GearUp!* VE

Country	Institution
Austria	Montanuniversität Leoben
Chile	Universidad Finis Terrae
Finland	Seinäjoki University of Applied Sciences
France	Université Côte D'Azur, Campus La Salle, Saint-Etienne
Germany	Hawk Hildesheim – Hawk Göttingen
Hungary	University of Győr
Italy	Università Degli Studi di Macerata, Università Degli Studi Gabriele D'Annunzio
Lithuania	Vilnius University
Mexico	Benemérita Universidad Autónoma de Puebla
Montenegro	Mediterranean University Podgorica
Netherlands	Windesheim University of Applied Sciences
Peru	Universidad San Martin de Porres
Poland	University of Warsaw, Silesian University of Technology
Portugal	Universidade de Aveiro
Romania	University of Babes-Bolyai
Spain	University of León, University of Valladolid
Sweden	Kristianstad University
Turkey	Anadolu University, Ankara University

3.2 Second Round of Implementation

In its second round of implementation in 2023, *GearUp!* was offered to five student cohorts from the University of León (Spain), Université de Bordeaux (France), FH Campus Wien (Austria), Middle East Technical University (Turkey), and Baku Higher Oil School (Azerbaijan). Five innovative and committed teachers partnered to integrate the exchange into their corresponding modules. They recognized students' hard work by granting a percentage of the module's final grade or extra European Credit Transfer and Accumulation System (ECTS) credits, which are used by universities all over Europe to represent the amount of workload a student completes. This major shift in the recruitment of students and structure of the VE was due to the tremendous workload that the first round involved for the VE coordinator, who is also the author of this chapter.

Not only did this new class-to-class VE structure allow students to receive guidance online as in the first round, but it also allowed them to count on local support from the partner teachers on a weekly basis. This teacher partnership, the strong relationship established among all five educators, and the frequent local support proved beneficial to maintain student motivation and foster a cohesive community during this implementation of the VE.

Ninety-five participants successfully completed all stages of the 2023 implementation. These were undergraduate students from various disciplines such as English or Spanish studies, teacher education, engineering, or sustainable packaging. The majority of students were in their second academic year and had the possibility to go on exchange as part of their undergraduate studies.

Students were teamed up in groups of six to eight participants from the different partner institutions with the aim of creating multiple multicultural groups. This round of implementation allowed collaboration between the eastern and western parts of Europe, which encouraged students from the five countries involved to appreciate cultural diversity and get in contact with cultures they would have otherwise never thought of selecting as study abroad destinations. A student explained:

> Thanks to this program I would like to visit Turkey and why not, maybe doing the Erasmus exchange. All the cultural and organizational aspects have called my attention. That is why we talked about it more, and she sent me a beautiful video about her university. (R2_STUD64)

This initiative is ideally designed to prepare undergraduate students to study abroad (as traditional mobility programs such as Erasmus+ do, aiming to develop students' intercultural communicative skills or enhance their language skills). Yet, traditional mobility programs do not always succeed in this regard. Many students cannot afford the experience financially (Byram & Dervin, 2008); some do not feel prepared; and others who embark on the journey often return reporting negative attitudes towards the host culture (Byram & Fleming, 1998). Besides this issue, the more recent pandemic situation increased the number of obstacles that students face in their journey to become interculturally aware. With travel restrictions occurring during the COVID-19 pandemic, mobility rates fell in recent years (European Commission, 2022b), and HEIs were forced to make greater use of new technological approaches that allowed students to interact with other students from universities in diverse geographically distant locations (Farnell et al., 2021).

Nevertheless, IaH strategies such as *GearUp!* have proven to be educational approaches to advance inclusion in the internationalization of higher education. Pre-mobility VE offers everyone a chance to partake in certain intercultural experiences that they might otherwise miss due to financial or family constraints. When asked about their plans to study abroad in the future, one of the *GearUp!* participants from the second round of implementation explained, "I am a little older, and I already have my life settled in León … Unfortunately I'm not going to work or study abroad, but it has helped me meet people from other countries that I wouldn't have met otherwise" (R2_STUD1).

Another participant said, "Probably the only thing I'm afraid of in moving abroad is society's rejection of me" (R2_STUD16). The *GearUp!* exchange also helped this student feel understood and comfortable when speaking another language, probably paving the way for her to further develop her language skills, confidence, and interest in other cultures, thus correlating with other VE outcomes from projects outlined above. The same student highlighted VE's potential to foster understanding and empathy by commenting that "people who share a situation … are more humble and kind. Therefore, when it comes to communication, we are more polite, we try not to make other people feel bad, and we create situations so that they can improve in what we can help" (R2_STUD16). With this student's insight into her VE experience, we can reassert its potential to bring about empathy and tolerance for diversity. Through pre-mobility VE, students have the opportunity to enhance their awareness of the advantages of diversity, develop a genuine appreciation for it, and foster a heightened enthusiasm for international experiences.

VE initiatives should not be considered, however, as a mere alternative to or substitute for traditional study abroad programs (O'Dowd, 2023a), nor should they be perceived as exacerbating the disadvantages faced by the most underprivileged students who end up enrolling in this more affordable experience. Instead, these initiatives should be recognized as an independent opportunity that promotes the inclusion of all students in global education. This view acknowledges the necessity for organizations and institutions to persist in their efforts to secure funding and continue to improve international education opportunities.

4 Pedagogical Implications and Conclusion

It is common to see HEIs implementing new strategies to advance DEIA, but this excitement among institutions often fades away when the initiatives cannot be sustained over time. Institutions must continue to evolve their knowledge and skills to achieve more inclusive, equitable, diverse, and accessible intercultural learning for all students (Adams et al., 2023), and educators' role in this regard is crucial. This section of the chapter offers advice, recommendations, and a final conclusion on what teachers, institutions, and staff at international offices can do to offer inclusive international education through carefully structured VE initiatives. Some aspects to consider in order to make VE a more inclusive and easily accessible approach to intercultural learning are the following:

1. **VE task design**. Developing tasks that allow for synchronous and asynchronous dialogue and scaffolding students' learning process offers students with diverse learning needs and styles the opportunity to participate in intercultural dialogue. This approach can help address the imbalances in language levels of participants and increase confidence and comfort when communicating in another language (Baroni et al., 2019; O'Dowd, 2023a). Designing tasks with a wide range of objectives and in a variety of media can allow different learning needs and styles to be met, which is vital to advance inclusion. *GearUp!* combined synchronous interaction in the form of workshops, talks, and videoconferences to carry out tasks, with asynchronous dialogue using instant messaging apps. The tasks in *GearUp!* combined reading, writing, listening to videos, information exchange, collaboration on the creation of a product, group discussions, and comparison of images. This structure resulted in diverse forms of cultural comparison and language practice in an authentic environment.
2. **Choice of partners**. When designing a VE for your institution or module, reflecting on the expected learning outcomes is crucial before choosing future partners, as the language level, discipline, year, or country can determine the feasibility of a partnership. VE can reach disadvantaged students and help them engage in equitable intercultural dialogue if we

adapt our initiatives to students' context and needs. Partnerships with teachers from commonly under-represented cultures and/or less commonly taught languages can create a diverse space to explore interculturality and language learning (O'Dowd, 2023b; Stevens Initiative, 2023).

3. **Pedagogical mentoring.** Guiding participants through the whole VE cycle is crucial (Gutiérrez et al., 2022), especially to enhance their intercultural competence, language learning, and motivation. The frequent supervision sessions that *GearUp!* offered for all participants, both online and locally, proved to be very beneficial to sustain motivation levels and to create a safe space to discuss ideas while creating a sense of community. In these sessions, it is vital to address cultural differences, stereotypes, and concerns to guide conversations outside their comfort zones (Dooly, 2011) and to support changes in students' awareness about diversity and inclusion. Pedagogical interventions must also include critical reflection on their language skills and on the tools to further their development and heighten their self-efficacy levels.

4. **Recognition of students' work.** When possible, all students should be granted equal recognition to ensure fairness and prevent any form of inequality (O'Dowd, 2018). Recognition can take the form of ECTS credits or badges for VEs that are implemented as a stand-alone activity or a percentage of the grade for VEs that are embedded in university modules, for example. All participants should receive equivalent levels of recognition, as it may affect how they view the exchange, their partners, or cause issues among student teams. With this point in mind, institutional support and flexibility must be achieved to successfully implement an inclusive approach (Stallivieri, 2020).

In conclusion, the consistent evolution in internationalization strategies in higher education and the exclusive character of current study abroad programs have led institutions and teachers themselves to adopt more inclusive and easily accessible approaches to intercultural learning, like VE. This activity offers students in remote locations or those with limited financial resources the opportunity to engage in guided intercultural conversations, thus having meaningful communication that can serve as pre-departure preparation. When tasks and partners are carefully selected, VE is likely to bring inclusion and diversity into the classroom. Institutions, teachers, and staff at international offices should invest in and strive to create accessible, ethical, and inclusive VE opportunities for all students because, when carefully designed, VE has the potential to cater to diverse groups of students (Krabill, 2023). Pre-mobility VE, in particular, also has the potential to foster the inclusion of a wider range of students into study abroad programs and enrich their education by supporting their language development, transversal skills, and intercultural competence in order to benefit fully from the experience overseas.

About the Author

Ángela M. Alonso Morais is a postdoctoral researcher in the Department of Modern Languages at the University of León, Spain, where she also works as an EFL/ESP teacher. She has collaborated on the Erasmus+ European policy experiment Virtual Innovation and Support Networks for Teachers (VALIANT; 2021–2024) and has been coordinating the *GearUp!* virtual exchange program (https://gearupvirtualexchange.wordpress.com/). Her major research interests lie in the area of pre-mobility virtual exchange, second language education, and intercultural learning.

References

Adams, A., Hertel, A., & Frost, C. (2023). *Bridging the gap between diversity, equity, and inclusion and global learning*. Diversity Abroad. https://diversityabroad.org/public/DIVaPublic/Articles/Article-Items/DEI_Gap_GlobalEd.aspx

Baroni, A., Dooly, M., Garcés García, P., Guth, S., Hauck, M., Helm, F., Lewis, T., Mueller-Hartmann, A., O'Dowd, R., Rienties, B., & Rogaten, J. (2019). *Evaluating the impact of virtual exchange on initial teacher education: A European policy experiment*. Research-publishing.net. https://doi.org/10.14705/rpnet.2019.29.9782490057337

Batardière, M.-T., Giralt, M., Jeanneau, C., Le-Baron-Earle, F., & O'Regan, V. (2019). Promoting intercultural awareness among European university students via pre-mobility virtual exchanges. *Journal of Virtual Exchange*, 2, 1–6. https://doi.org/10.14705/rpnet.2019.jve.4

Beelen, J., & Jones, E. (2015). Redefining internationalization at home. In A. Curaj, L. Matei, R. Pricopie, J. Salmi, & P. Scott (Eds.), *The European higher education area* (pp. 59–72). Springer. https://doi.org/10.1007/978-3-319-20877-0_5

Byram, M. (1997). *Teaching and assessing intercultural communicative competence*. Multilingual Matters. https://doi.org/10.21832/9781800410251

Byram, M., & Dervin, F. (Eds.). (2008). *Student, staff and academic mobility in higher education.* Cambridge Scholars Publishing.

Byram, M., & Fleming, M. (1998). *Language learning in intercultural perspective: Approaches through drama and ethnography.* Cambridge University Press.

Coleman, J.A. (2013). Researching whole people and whole lives. In C. Kinginger (Ed.), *Social and cultural aspects of language learning in study abroad* (pp. 17–44). John Benjamins. https://doi.org/10.1075/lllt.37.02col

de Wit, H., & Jones, E. (2018). Inclusive internationalization: Improving access and equity. *International Higher Education, 94,* 16–18. https://doi.org/10.6017/ihe.2018.0.10561

Dooly, M.A. (2011). Crossing the intercultural borders into 3rd space culture(s): Implications for teacher education in the twenty-first century. *Language and Intercultural Communication, 11*(4), 319–337. https://doi.org/10.1080/14708477.2011.599390

Erdei, L.A., & Káplár-Kodácsy, K. (2020). *International student mobility at a glance: Promising potential and limiting barriers of non-traditional mobility.* ELTE Eötvös Loránd University Department of Erasmus+ and International Programmes. https://www.hlitl-project-eu.uvsq.fr/literature-review

European Commission, Directorate-General for Education, Youth, Sport and Culture. (2022a). *Blended mobility implementation guide for Erasmus+ higher education mobility KA131.* Publications Office of the European Union. https://data.europa.eu/doi/10.2766/467485

European Commission, Directorate-General for Education, Youth, Sport and Culture, (2022b). *Erasmus+ annual report 2021.* Publications Office of the European Union. https://data.europa.eu/doi/10.2766/635340

European Parliament & Directorate-General for Internal Policies. (2010). *Improving the participation in the ERASMUS programme.* https://publications.europa.eu/resource/cellar/f6b3644b-2b19-497c-819e-542163b5c047.0003.02/DOC_1

European Students' Union & the Erasmus Student Network. (2022). *Bringing the student perspective to the debate on mobility, virtual exchange and blended learning.* https://www.esn.org/sites/default/files/news/esn_esu_policy_paper_-_mobility_and_virtual_blended_activities.pdf

EVOLVE Project Team. (2020). *The impact of virtual exchange on student learning in higher education: EVOLVE project report.* https://research.rug.nl/en/publications/the-impact-of-virtual-exchange-on-student-learning-in-higher-educ

Farnell, T., Skledar Matijević, A., & Šćukanec Schmidt, N. (2021). *The impact of COVID-19 on higher education. A review of emerging evidence:*

Analytical report. Publications Office of the European Union. https://doi.org/10.2766/069216

Forum on Education Abroad. (2011). *Education abroad glossary.* https://www.forumea.org/glossary.html

Gutiérrez, B.F., Glimäng, M.R., Sauro, S., & O'Dowd, R. (2022). Preparing students for successful online intercultural communication and collaboration in virtual exchange. *Journal of International Students, 12*(S3), 149–167. https://doi.org/10.32674/jis.v12iS3.4630

Jackson, J. (2020). The language and intercultural dimension of education abroad. In J. Jackson (Ed.), *The Routledge handbook of language and intercultural communication* (pp. 444–472). Routledge. https://doi.org/10.4324/9781003036210-34

Kasravi, J. (2023). *2022 Global education experience student survey.* Diversity Abroad. https://diversityabroad.org/public/DIVaPublic/Resources-Services/Research-Reports/2022_Student_Survey/22_Student_Survey.aspx

Kinginger, C. (2011). Enhancing language learning in study abroad. *Annual Review of Applied Linguistics, 31,* 58–73. https://doi.org/10.1017/S0267190511000031

Kinginger, C. (2016). Telecollaboration and student mobility for language learning. In S. Jager, M. Kurek, & B. O'Rourke (Eds.), *New directions in telecollaborative research and practice: Selected papers from the second conference on telecollaboration in higher education* (pp. 19–29). Research-publishing.net. https://doi.org/10.14705/rpnet.2016.telecollab2016.487

Krabill, R. (2023). Disentangling virtual exchange and study abroad discourses in equity and inclusion. In Diversity Abroad (Ed.), *The global impact exchange: Virtual exchange as a tool to advance equity and inclusion* (pp. 64–65). Stevens Initiative. https://diversityabroad.org/public/DIVaPublic/GIE-Archives/GIE-2023/GIE-Sp2023/GIE-Sp23-Article-17.aspx

Leask, B. (2015). *Internationalizing the curriculum.* Routledge. https://doi.org/10.4324/9781315716954

Lee, J., Leibowitz, J., & Rezek, J. (2022). The impact of international virtual exchange on participation in education abroad. *Journal of Studies in International Education, 26*(2), 202–221. https://doi.org/10.1177/10283153211052777

O'Dowd, R. (2018). From telecollaboration to virtual exchange: State-of-the-art and the role of UNICollaboration in moving forward. *Journal of Virtual Exchange, 1,* 1–23. https://doi.org/10.14705/rpnet.2018.jve.1

O'Dowd, R. (2023a). *Internationalising higher education and the role of virtual exchange*. Routledge. https://doi.org/10.4324/9781315393704

O'Dowd, R. (2023b). Issues of equity and inclusion in virtual exchange. *Language Teaching*, 1–13. https://doi.org/10.1017/S026144482300040X

O'Dowd, R., & Vinagre, M. (2024). *Virtual innovation and support networks for teachers: Exploring the impact of virtual exchange in teacher education*. Peter Lang. https://doi.org/10.3726/b21769

Özturgut, O. (2017). Internationalization for diversity, equity, and inclusion. *Journal of Higher Education Theory and Practice*, *17*(6), 83–91. https://articlegateway.com/index.php/JHETP/article/view/1529

Richardson, S. (2016). *Cosmopolitan learning for a global era*. Longman. https://doi.org/10.4324/9781315871004

Sabzalieva, E., Mutize, T., & Yerovi, C. (2022). *Moving minds: Opportunities and challenges for virtual student mobility in a post-pandemic world*. UNESCO. https://unesdoc.unesco.org/ark:/48223/pf0000380988

Stallivieri, L. (2020, May 23). *International virtual education needs greater support*. University World News. https://www.universityworldnews.com/post.php?story=20200518150642841

Stevens Initiative. (2023). *2023 virtual exchange impact and learning report*. The Aspen Institute. https://www.stevensinitiative.org/resource/2023-virtual-exchange-impact-and-learning-report

Tienda, M. (2013). Diversity ≠ inclusion: Promoting integration in higher education. *Educational Researcher*, *42*(9), 467–475. https://doi.org/10.3102/0013189X13516164

Torres, K., & Statti, A. (2022). Learning across borders through immersive virtual technologies. *International Research and Review*, *12*(1), 18–32. https://files.eric.ed.gov/fulltext/EJ1380645.pdf

Vande Berg, M., Paige, R.M., & Lou, K.H. (2012). *Student learning abroad: What our students are learning, what they're not, and what we can do about it*. Stylus Publishing, LLC.

4 COILing Discrimination Narratives across Continents: A Virtual Exchange Project between a Community College in New York City and a Four-Year College in Jordan

Deniz Gokcora and Raymond Oenbring

1 Introduction

While in the first few decades of its existence the field of computer-assisted language learning (CALL) traditionally focused on drill and practice approaches, more recently CALL practitioners have focused on communicative approaches, such as Collaborative Online International Learning (COIL), also known as virtual exchange. In a COIL project, students work in transnational groups to engage on a project to learn from each other about the selected topic, develop cross-cultural communication skills, global citizen skills, and refine research skills (O'Dowd, 2018). While sharing narratives between multinational groups is a central element of virtual exchange, the research on using cross-group narrative analysis as part of a COIL project is very limited. Accordingly, in this study, we describe the potential of using narratives of discrimination and injustice collected by students as part of a virtual exchange, focusing on a case study of a three-way COIL collaboration among three courses at two institutions. The specific courses that participated in the study were the following: one remedial reading and writing course and one human services course in social sciences at the Borough of Manhattan Community College (BMCC) of the City University of New York; and one paramedics course at Jordan University of Science and Technology (JUST) in Irbid, Jordan. In particular, we focus on compare and contrast as an accessible strategy for language learners to use when evaluating discrimination narratives across diverse sites. As a whole, the study highlights ways that CALL can be reframed using contemporary digital technologies to lead to collaborative learning and to encourage students to build connections between their experiences and larger social issues.

2 Literature Review

In the past few decades, a significant body of research on COIL projects has developed, focusing on bilingual and bicultural exchanges (Çiftçi & Savaş, 2018; Lewis & O'Dowd, 2016). Notably, as COIL practices have evolved over the past 20 years, there has been a growing interest in using English or any common language as the lingua franca in these collaborations (O'Dowd, 2021a, 2021b). Helm (2016), for example, framed these lingua franca collaborative projects as platforms to practise critical approaches, addressing social and political challenges in an increasingly polarized world/society marked by conflict, injustice, and social inequalities. More recently, Poe's (2022) study described the potentials of international virtual exchange programs to broaden identities and foster global citizenship among under-represented students in higher education in the United States.

Furthermore, Teaching English to Speakers of Other Languages (TESOL) scholars have increasingly argued that English as a second language (ESL) classes should be a place for students to craft narratives focusing on their own identity formation, including their experiences with discrimination (e.g., Gokcora & Oenbring, 2023). These narratives assist students to develop their communication skills and to critically respond to their sociopolitical environments. Sharmin (2021), for example, argues that, when ESL students craft multimodal discrimination narratives as part of their coursework, it helps "learners enter the external community ... and negotiate racism and linguicism" (p. vi).

Notably, however, most of the existing studies examining narratives of discrimination in the ESL classroom have primarily revolved around teacher-researchers' analysis of discrimination narratives produced by students (or analysis of their own narratives of discrimination as teachers) rather than treating the exchange and analysis of narratives produced by students within the class as a pedagogical technique. For example, Ates et al. (2015) argued for the value of including instructor discrimination narratives in TESOL teacher-training courses. Further, James (2018) used narrative inquiry to conduct a close examination into the experiences of a single ESL nursing student, finding family, language, and persistence as the emerging themes. For example, living with a family can bring some additional stress; however, the support from the family can alleviate that stress. Similarly, ESL students can experience discrimination and culturally insensitive behaviour as a result of their issues speaking English. In another study, Shapiro (2014) assessed narratives produced by Black former refugee students in the United States, critically analysing the effects of deficit discourse on their lived experiences. As all of these studies suggest, the research on using the exchange and analysis of discrimination narratives as a pedagogical technique has yet to be brought into the discourse on virtual exchange. That is what we attempt here.

In a COIL project, students from two or more nations collaborate using digital technologies as part of classwork to build communication skills, exchange information, and learn from each other. Researchers such as Ramírez-Marín et al. (2020) contended that participating in virtual exchange projects encourages students to establish "positive attitudes, respect, openness, curiosity, self-awareness, sociolinguistic awareness, perspective-taking, empathy, relationship building, and interconnectedness" (p. 115), which are essential for a successful collaboration in any field of work. In a recent study, Porto et al. (2023) argued that language and intercultural communication education in universities should include "discomforting themes" so that students will be aware of these topics of human suffering and respond to them in innovative and positive ways. Following these lines, we contend that virtual exchanges offer students a unique opportunity to build connections with diverse groups, as well as to develop a deeper understanding of their identities and situatedness through comparison and contrast with other groups of students. Further, following Porto et al. (2023), we believe in the value of virtual exchange as an approach to develop humanistic values in students. Accordingly, we argue for the pedagogical value of having students craft, present, and analyse discrimination narratives as part of CALL virtual exchange collaborations.

3 "Reducing Inequalities" COIL Project

The current COIL project was a product of an overarching Global Scholars Achieving Career Success (GSACS) grant. GSACS is based on a larger grant received from the Stevens Initiative, which was sponsored by the US Department of State with funding provided by the US government and administered by the Aspen Institute. GSACS is a multinational collaboration between five colleges of the City University of New York (specifically LaGuardia Community College, Borough of Manhattan Community College, Hostos Community College, Guttman Community College, and Queens College) and four universities in the Middle East and North Africa (MENA) region, specifically Morocco (Abdelmalek Essaadi University), Egypt (American University in Cairo), Jordan (Jordan University of Science and Technology), and Palestine (Palestine Ahliya University). For the overarching GSACS grant, the principal investigators recruited faculty members from the five CUNY colleges and matched them with professors in the MENA region. Faculty fellows from all partner schools agreed to lead COIL project activities involving at least one CUNY institution and at least one MENA institution.

This specific project under the GSACS banner between students at JUST and BMCC focused on the United Nations Sustainable Development Goal (UN SDG) #10, which involves exploring ways to reduce inequality among and within nations. The courses involved in the study were cross-disciplinary; therefore, we understood that reducing inequalities as a suitable general theme would connect an ESL writing course (ESL 96), a human services course (HUM 101), and a critical care course (PARA 486). Students' main goal for the project was to explore the shared inquiry question, How and why do people discriminate against each other in the United States and Jordan? We believe studies such as ours, which encourage globally and locally marginalized students to understand the ways discrimination manifests itself in diverse environments (as well as suggesting ways to reduce discrimination), are especially important, given the current unrest in the Middle East and increasing nativist populism in many Western nations, including the United States.

4 Instructors' Positionality

As previously mentioned, this project involved three instructors, the first two ESL and social science instructors at a US urban community college and the third a paramedics instructor at a university in Jordan. All three instructors collaborating in the COIL project have previous international experience and were genuinely interested in social justice issues. The ESL instructor, the lead author of the current chapter, is originally from Turkey but has been living in the United States for 35 years and has selected social justice as a general theme in her courses. The BMCC social science professor is originally from India and has been teaching at BMCC for several years, integrating social justice issues in their courses. The JUST paramedics professor has advanced degrees from institutions in the United States; therefore, he is familiar with the social context related to social injustices there. All instructors had engaged in a different COIL project before, but this project was the first time they had worked in a three-way virtual exchange. Further, the lead author wanted to deepen her experience in a new way, since this project revisited UN SDG #10 (reducing inequalities), by introducing various forms of discrimination through an additional collaborator in human services.[1]

5 Students' Perspectives

The COIL project took place in spring 2023, and all students ($n = 81$) participated in the project, 48 from JUST and 33 from BMCC (11 in the ESL class and 22 in the human services class). Apart from providing unique learning opportunities for the students, the exchange was designed as a three-way, three-class exchange because the number of students in the JUST paramedics class outnumbered the number of students in each of the BMCC classes.

As previously mentioned, BMCC is a metropolitan community college in New York City. The institution is culturally and linguistically diverse; there are 155 different languages spoken among 20,000 students enrolled in the college. The students in the BMCC ESL class were largely first-year, first-generation, post-secondary students, including recent immigrants to the United States, international students, and students who were born and raised in the United States but have other first/home languages. Immigrant students in the ESL class stemmed from a variety of nations,

---

1. The BMCC social science professor and the JUST paramedics professor did not participate in the composition of this chapter. The chapter is the work of the lead author (the ESL instructor) and a collaborator with whom they have published previously regarding virtual exchange and global social justice issues who did not directly participate in the virtual exchange presented here. He is an American expatriate teaching at a university in the anglophone Caribbean. These two authors are the authorial "we" of the chapter.

including Pakistan, Japan, Venezuela, Ecuador, the Ivory Coast, Senegal, and Ukraine. Students enrolled in BMCC human services class were similarly diverse. As is common for immigrant students in this context, most BMCC students receive some form of financial aid and work full-time or part-time jobs while being students.

Conversely, the JUST students, native speakers of Arabic, were fourth-year paramedics majors and were either ethnic Jordanians or had roots in Palestine, since Jordan is one of the countries with the most Palestinian immigrants. Out of the 48 paramedics students, 22 had a Palestinian background with Jordanian citizenship. While the BMCC students were all first-year students and thus were at the start of their post-secondary journey, all the JUST students were experienced matriculated students, and thus they were much more experienced in their college-related tasks. (Notably, Irbid, the city where JUST is located, is in Jordan but is within 50 kilometres [31 miles] of both the West Bank and Syria.) JUST students of Palestinian descent had similar socio-economic backgrounds to those whose families stemmed from Jordan. Further, on average, JUST students had had much less contact with diverse international individuals than had the BMCC students and had travelled less than the US-based students. Without having much international contact, many JUST students were determined to participate and complete requirements to obtain advanced degrees in their field.

6 The COIL Project

When planning the COIL project, the instructors established four student learning outcomes for the five-week virtual exchange module. By the end of the five-week COIL project, students would

- have deepened their knowledge of language, cultures, traditions, and communication habits in the partner country
- be able to shift perspectives and behaviours into an alternative cultural worldview while exploring United Nations Sustainable Development Goals
- use technology to present ideas and communicate across cultures
- communicate and collaborate effectively on tasks with international peers

In the project, all students were grouped into one of five binational groups and completed a total of three group assignments. In the project, students from each of the classes worked together on a group project. Specific volunteer students were asked to present their topics at the GSACS student conference and converse with their COIL partners to compare how the UN SDG was experienced in Jordan and the United States.

At the beginning of the semester, the instructors arranged Zoom meetings to introduce the virtual exchange project to students and for them to meet with each other. The instructors used Padlet as the learning management system to post materials and collect students' work. In order to keep the conversation going, one of the instructors at BMCC created a WhatsApp group so that students could ask quick questions and provide answers to each other.

In the next phase, students read texts and watched YouTube videos, all in English, on the subject of race and discrimination in the United States and Jordan, which had been selected by the instructors. For example, related to gender inequality, students read an online article on midwives and women's perspectives on family planning in Jordan, including human rights, gender equity, decision-making, and power dynamics. Another text for this particular assignment was a short reading about a "stop and frisk" incident of a Black professor, "I Fit the Description" by Steve Locke (2015). After reading Steve Locke's story and explaining their understandings about why the police racially profiled him, students were asked to explain the ways in which they could relate to this topic. If students chose to watch a video titled *Muslim NYPD Chaplain: Saluted in Uniform, Harassed as a Civilian* about unconscious bias, they were asked to explain (a) the reason why the Muslim officer was not respected as a civilian, (b) how they could relate to this topic, and (c) if people make decisions about them (students) due to unconscious bias. At this stage, students were asked to reflect upon their personal experiences with discrimination and post a response to the COIL Padlet using the provided texts and videos as springboards.

In the next stage, students interviewed a person who may be disadvantaged in some way, learned about their experiences, and acted as a professional who could offer them empathy and support. Using an interview guide with suggested questions, students interviewed someone in their community who has had experiences with overt or covert discrimination. Suggested questions included the following: Do you think certain groups (e.g., refugees, immigrants, women, elderly, etc.) are treated fairly in your community? Can you describe one situation where you were treated unfairly? How did this make you feel/impact your life? Students then wrote up the interviews into discrimination narratives. (Note that these narratives focused on the experiences of discrimination of the interviewees.)

After posting the discrimination narrative, the students were asked to read the narratives in their group and to write a short report about the similarities and differences between the social justice topics they found in the United States and those in Jordan. Next, ESL students at BMCC wrote a compare and contrast essay about the differences and similarities of injustices between Jordan and the United States, and posted a two-to-three paragraph piece to Padlet; students from the social services (HUM 101) class posted a narrative on difference and similarities they found in the narratives in their group to Padlet. Students from JUST were asked to create a PowerPoint presentation summarizing the findings (similarities and differences among inequalities between Jordan and the United States) from their group members.

Table 4.1 offers a summary of each step students completed in the project. The project started with an icebreaker activity, followed by reflection on selected videos about discrimination, so that students would be ready to conduct their interviews with individuals in their community.

7 Emergent Themes in Reflections

In their personal reflections on the springboard materials that students posted to Padlet, a number of themes emerged. First, immigrant students in the United States more readily commented on issues related to discrimination against women than students in Jordan. Second, older students in both the United States and Jordan were more likely to write about the topic of unconscious bias than first-year students. Third, immigrant students in the United States were able to contextualize discrimination based on skin colour, both in the United States and in their home countries, more often than students in Jordan. For example, in his reflection, one BMCC immigrant student from Peru explained the favouritism in his country towards students based on similar ethnic and social backgrounds. He indicated that

Table 4.1 COIL Project Assignments

Step No.	Description of Step
Task 1: Icebreaker	**Common tasks:** All students participated in the icebreaker activities.
Task 2: Reflection on videos and readings	**Common tasks:** All students watched the videos and made personal reflection posts on Padlet.
Task 3: Discrimination narratives	All students in three courses conducted an interview with someone in their community whom they identified as having been discriminated against. JUST students were asked to interview Syrian individuals aged 60+ (which was the focus of their class, PARA 486 Critical Care). An interview guide was provided to all students. **Common tasks:** All students submitted the narrative summarizing the survey results (two to three paragraphs) on Padlet and posted reflections on a binational partner's narrative, comparing and contrasting Jordanian and American narratives. They were asked to read a binational partner's reflection in the group and post a comparative reflection of one paragraph, explaining what they had learned from their partner. **Differentiated tasks:** BMCC HUM 101 students created a video, a poem, or a poster/meme about key ideas of discrimination they had read about Jordan. BMCC ESL students wrote a compare and contrast essay identifying two key findings of similarities or differences besides posting a narrative of their findings and a reflection on what they had learned from other students in their group. JUST students produced an oral presentation of their findings and posted their PowerPoint presentations to Padlet.

students who come from higher socio-economic backgrounds are favourably treated and given better grades than those who come from lower economic classes. He noted:

> In my country, Peru, race-bias still lies in education. First, most professors connect and interact more with students who share similarities with them,

either skin colour or background ... The professor will give more attention and importance to the student with whom he feels identified. Also, there is excessive prejudice in my country against socio-economic status. Educators often relate to white students with good economic solvency. Even though they don't know these learners, they tend to think that these students do not have to work hard in order to achieve their academic goals.

The above student is describing the intersectionality of skin colour and lower socio-economic background and identifies ways that race-related biases can emerge differently in Peruvian education contexts. In other words, he states that, although students with darker skin colour and lower socio-economic background might have better academic performance compared to the white students, they are perceived by some instructors as not as academically capable as the white and socio-economically advantaged students at school and in life. As we can see in the above quote, the Peruvian student was able to move beyond discussing racism as a personal experience and begin to respond critically to broader systemic injustices.

8 Emergent Themes in Discrimination Narratives

In their discrimination narratives produced based on their work with their interviewees, students at both BMCC and JUST highlighted a number of different types of discrimination, including discrimination based on religion (connected to individuals wearing certain types of religious clothing such as burkas and turbans), discrimination based on gender, discrimination based on skin colour, and discrimination based on body image and/or disability (e.g., a woman with alopecia, a form of hair loss). Table 4.2 presents a content analysis of emergent themes in the discrimination narratives.

As Table 4.2 indicates, the most common themes in the narratives collected by the BMCC were racial discrimination in job opportunities and gender-related discrimination. Remarkably, on the Jordanian side, 90 per cent of the 60+ Syrian interviewees' narratives mentioned discrimination based on age.

While many Syrian refugee informants recognized themselves to be victims of discrimination in Jordan based on their ethnicity, many Syrians mentioned their appreciation for the Jordanian government accepting them as immigrants in the narratives produced by JUST students. The following narrative produced by a JUST student is typical of others:

Table 4.2 Emergent Themes in Discrimination Narratives

BMCC (33 narratives)	JUST (48 narratives)
Racial discrimination in job opportunities (Persons of colour are not given equal opportunity in job applications) (11–33%)	Ageism (43–90%)
Gender-related discrimination (11–33%)	Immigrant status: lack of jobs (39–81%); lack of health services (40–83%)
Faith-based discrimination (4–12%)	Syrian women, even younger ones, were not encouraged to get jobs (32–67%)

[My interviewee] and his family experienced a few situations where they were treated unfairly … His children had trouble getting registered in school in their early years, which left them disappointed because it unexpectedly put a stop to their future and forced them to stay home and do nothing. As the number of Syrian refugees in Jordan rises year over year, numerous decisions and initiatives have been made and made public to interact with Syrians together with Jordanians … Children from Syria now have access to schools, and they have also received financial aid to make up for the lost previous academic years. As his farewell statement, [my interviewee] expresses his gratitude to everyone who has supported him and his family throughout the war and proclaims his appreciation for Jordan's warm welcome. He views Jordan as his home and considers himself fortunate to be here.

As this quote suggests, many Syrian interviewees expressed their gratitude to be in Jordan in comparison to being in the hostile and violent environment in Syria.

When comparing and contrasting the discrimination narratives, students at both BMCC and JUST recognized similarities among the interviewees in both the United States and Jordan, including lack of opportunities for employment, insufficient health care for immigrants or refugees, or giving immigrants and refugees some hard jobs and not providing them with the same compensation as the locals (financial abuse). One JUST student, for example, discussed the health care systems across two contexts, comparing the unequal treatment of refugees in Jordan with the treatment of undocumented workers in the United States, noting the following:

> [The refugee interviewed stated that] as a refugee, who was also being treated, in addition to being exposed to what all Jordanians suffer in government hospitals, the long duration of appointments and waiting, and due to her age and migration status, visiting the hospital was tiring her more. In other words, refugees must wait a long time, even when refugees really need to see a specialist urgently, to have the opportunity to see a doctor. Although the USA does not have as many refugees as Jordan, illegal immigrants suffer from the same treatment since they do not have any health insurance. Moreover, doctors in the USA are trying to give everyone with the full health service; however, illegal immigrants cannot receive due [to] their immigration status.

As is clear in the above quote, despite oftentimes painting in overly broad strokes (e.g., some undocumented individuals in the United States have some form of medical insurance), students were, nevertheless, able to make valuable connections between the experiences of migrants in diverse environments. Accordingly, this insight suggests the pedagogical value of having students compare and contrast discrimination narratives across diverse contexts.

Reading through the compare and contrast essays revealed that most BMCC ESL students were not aware of the Syrian refugee crisis in Jordan. Nonetheless, BMCC ESL students were also able to make meaningful connections between the experience of immigrants in the United States and that of Syrian refugees. One BMCC ESL student described a Mexican-American's experience when travelling to Mexico in the following manner:

> One of my friends [was] … born in United States, but she from Mexico. She was facing financial discrimination when she went on vacation in Mexico. She was view as a money provider, and she felt so bad for being use by her own people. So, her family in Mexico made her pay everything, after believing the stereotypes that people who came from United States are rich. But in Jordan it has some similarities with my story that talk about financial discrimination. The Syrian refugees face the same discrimination in Jordan. The discrimination was about the rising price of the rent in Jordan country for

the Syrians refugees. The Jordan countries was not taking care of the Syrians refugees by making their life difficult by increasing the rent price, and not providing enough job for them, and the necessities of living.

As noted, discrimination against Syrian refugees is a new reality for most new immigrant students (ESL students) at BMCC. Notably, one BMCC Japanese student stated that she has never thought of discrimination because, according to her, there is not a major problem about discrimination in Japan, noting in her compare and contrast piece that "I learned a lot of information and the attitude towards discrimination problems. So I explained it in my presentation; it is not like everyone needs to like each other because everyone has individual problems, so I just want everyone to understand each other and respect each other."

9 Conclusion

As suggested in this study, we contend that virtual exchange is a valuable tool for building awareness across international boundaries and diverse student groups, particularly for building connections to areas of the world such as the Levant with long and complex histories of interethnic strife and displacement. Moreover, we argue for the pedagogical value of comparing and contrasting discrimination narratives as part of COIL projects across diverse sites.

Although students at both campuses did not take any action or get involved in activities to address the inequalities directly as part of this project, they were, nevertheless, eager to share their ideas about a better world where change could be possible. The next step for future projects would be to address how virtual exchange participants could get involved in addressing inequalities in their communities. These activities could involve students in experiential learning experiences, using their skills or producing some creative work for the community. Nevertheless, through COIL engagement, students gain access to enriched intercultural experiences in a globalized world, and hopefully they are equipped with the necessary communication skills to embrace new challenges in their lives and careers. We believe that our COIL endeavours added value to the educational experiences of the students, and we as practitioners learned with our students and made the class much more engaging. Similar future virtual exchange projects would implement the seeds of a just and a more democratic world and prepare students to be conscientious and informed world citizens in their lives.

About the Authors

Deniz Gokcora is an associate professor in the Department of Academic Literacy and Linguistics at Borough of Manhattan Community College/ CUNY. She teaches ESL courses as well as linguistics. Her research focuses on faculty development, reading and frequent quizzes, and the use of technology in second language acquisition. She has published papers in *Journal of Computer Assisted Learning, Journal of Virtual Exchange, International Journal of Academic Development*, and others.

Raymond Oenbring is professor of English at the University of the Bahamas, where he serves as writing program coordinator. He is an editor of *Creole Composition: Academic Writing and Rhetoric in the Anglophone Caribbean*, winner of the Conference on College Composition and Communication (CCCC) Outstanding Book Award and the MLA's Mina P. Shaughnessy Prize.

References

Ates, B., Kim, S., & Grigsby, Y. (2015). Understanding English language learners: Incorporating our own cultural narratives in TESOL education. *Journal of Praxis in Multicultural Education*, *9*(1), 3. https://doi.org/10.9741/2161-2978.1074

Çiftçi, E.Y., & Savaş, P. (2018). The role of telecollaboration in language and intercultural learning: A synthesis of studies published between 2010 and 2015. *ReCALL*, *30*(3), 278–298. https://doi.org/10.1017/S0958344017000313

Gokcora, D., & Oenbring, R. (2023). Restructuring a developmental ESL course at an urban community college: Asking the right questions. *Michigan Reading Journal*, *56*(1), 12. https://scholarworks.gvsu.edu/mrj/vol56/iss1/12

Helm, F. (2016). Facilitated dialogue in online intercultural exchange. In R. O'Dowd & T. Lewis (Eds.), *Online intercultural exchange* (pp. 150–172). Routledge. https://doi.org/10.4324/9781315678931

James, N. (2018). Using narrative inquiry to explore the experience of one ethnically diverse ESL nursing student. *Teaching and Learning in Nursing*, *13*(1), 35–40. https://doi.org/10.1016/j.teln.2017.08.002

Lewis, T., & O'Dowd, R. (2016). Online intercultural exchange and foreign language learning: A systematic review. In R. O'Dowd & T. Lewis (Eds.), *Online intercultural exchange* (pp. 21–66). Routledge. https://doi.org/10.4324/9781315678931

Locke, S. (2015, December 4). I fit the description ... *Art and Everything After Blog*. https://www.stevelocke.com/blog/i-fit-the-description

O'Dowd, R. (2018). From telecollaboration to virtual exchange: State-of-the-art and the role of UNICollaboration in moving forward. *Journal of Virtual Exchange*, *1*, 1–23. https://doi.org/10.14705/rpnet.2018.jve.1

O'Dowd, R. (2021a). Virtual exchange: Moving forward into the next decade. *Computer Assisted Language Learning*, *34*(3), 209–224. https://doi.org/10.1080/09588221.2021.1902201

O'Dowd, R. (2021b). What do students learn in virtual exchange? A qualitative content analysis of learning outcomes across multiple exchanges. *International Journal of Educational Research*, *109*, 101804. https://doi.org/10.1016/j.ijer.2021.101804

Poe, J. (2022). Expanding identities and advancing global citizenship of underrepresented U.S. higher education students through international virtual exchange [Doctoral dissertation]. Georgia State University. https://doi.org/10.57709/30509455

Porto, M., Golubeva, I., & Byram, M. (2023). Channelling discomfort through the arts: A Covid-19 case study through an intercultural telecollaboration project. *Language Teaching Research*, *27*(2), 276–298. https://doi.org/10.1177/13621688211058245

Ramírez-Marín, F., Núñez-Figueroa, L. del C., & Blair, N. (2020). Collaborative Online International Learning: Language and cross-cultural experiences of university students. *Matices En Lenguas Extranjeras*, *14*(1), 118–162. https://doi.org/10.15446/male.v14n1.92144

Shapiro, S. (2014). "Words that you said got bigger": English language learners' lived experiences of deficit discourse. *Research in the Teaching of English*, *48*(4), 386–406. https://doi.org/10.58680/rte201425159

Sharmin, M. (2021). Multi-modal narrative practices in adult ESL: Fostering investment in language learning and negotiating racism, linguicism, & identity [Doctoral dissertation]. University of Memphis. https://digitalcommons.memphis.edu/etd/2768/

5 Using Technology and Art in a Middle School Exploratory Heritage Language Program: Diversity Matters

Lulu Ekiert and Theresa Austin

1 Introduction

In this curriculum report, we describe activities associated with developing a new program for middle school heritage language (HL) learners from different language backgrounds, which has been designed collaboratively between institutions. Our interinstitutional partnership represents an ongoing initiative to build a three-way school-community-university collaboration that makes use of various computer-assisted technologies, providing both tools and a medium for HL learners to leverage and develop their repertoires.

The interinstitutional collaboration was essential to build an understanding of a heritage language curriculum that represents an interdisciplinary approach integrating technology, critical language awareness, arts, and wellness. Our ongoing co-construction of the three-way collaboration is important to the stability of this type of programmatic undertaking as progress is slow, non-linear, and faces off with the hegemonic systems of oppression within public education and dominant societal language ideologies. The goals of the curriculum are to support diverse students in building critical language awareness and inspire them to further develop their language practices and abilities both in and out of the classroom. Accordingly, this type of exploratory program aims to increase use of HLs by members of the school, community, and university. When school, community, and university partners come together around the shared goal of developing HL learning through art and technology for youth, existing resources can become known and revitalized for wellness, which we understand as disrupting the effects of oppressive dominant practices. Through recognition and expansion of these resources, we can support equitable education and wellness within the participating communities.

We begin our report by introducing ourselves and how our collaboration has sustained a praxis from our learning and theorizing. Next, the setting and context for developing our curricular project is established, followed by our interinstitutional goals as they inform our curricular plan, technological affordances, and strategic decision-making to implement this project. We continue by describing the process of implementing this program to integrate arts into HL through technology. We conclude with the insights, lessons, and future possibilities for this ongoing collaboration. In the upcoming sections, we pose questions to guide the readers through the process of developing this type of school-community-university collaboration.

Through our ongoing programmatic collaboration, we strive to continue creating a mutually supportive context that can permit learners to use the arts supported by technologies to build connections to their HL communities and expand the understanding and use of these languages and cultures. In the long term, we expect this small effort may be able to positively impact acceptance of in-school use of diverse languages and impact usage in multiple communities. We look forward to making multilingual families and students feel seen, welcome, and valued.

2 Who Are We?

We are a middle school teacher and a university instructor who teamed up to develop a middle school HL program for students from diverse language backgrounds and with neurodiverse learning abilities.

The first author, Lulu, a multilingual middle school HL instructor, Polish/English/Spanish, has been building a program to heighten students' awareness of the value and use of an HL. The second multilingual author, Theresa, English/Spanish/Japanese, leverages her university position to consult on various ethnolinguistic projects to build long-term connections to many communities being served by the district. The third group of multilingual participants invited into planning are the students, families, and local community members and organizations representing multiple varieties of Spanish/English in addition to Khmer/French/Italian/Polish/Bosnian/

Jamaican Creole. They participated in planning and structuring the program's series of projects and culminating art shows in complementary ways.

Together, we explain how this collaboration has built a praxis from drawing on learning theories to inform pedagogical practices, namely (a) exploratory learning to develop critical HL awareness, (b) arts informed by multimodal literacies (Parra, 2013), and (c) wellness (Flores-Hutson et al., 2019; Matthias, 2015; White & Kern, 2018). We use these pedagogies with assistance from readily available technology and describe their tenets in Section 4.1.

As the instructor, Lulu's own critical language awareness developed through study in the courses Theresa taught at the university. Translingual identities (Canagarajah, 2015), translanguaging, third linguistic spaces (Flores & García, 2013), and raciolinguistics (Chaparro, 2019) offered a framework of ideas with which to think about her personal experience as a multilingual teacher and learner. Raising her own critical language awareness revealed the different ways English dominates schooling and how this domination minoritizes, erases, and obscures multilingual students and families. Starting an HL and Arts program held promise to offer students a similar awareness-raising experience in which they could articulate how language use privileges, minoritizes, or obscures different aspects of their ethnolinguistic identities.

As co-author, Theresa provided ongoing dialogues about decision-making and resources for the instructor to consider and to further articulate her perspective about the value and appreciation of all linguistic varieties. Drawing on critical language awareness became a vital conceptual approach to HL teaching that helped students learn how language represents the world and the power relationships among people. Specifically, this construct was useful for Lulu, as the classroom teacher, to develop students' critical awareness of how language can be used for promoting diversity, equity, inclusion, and accessibility (DEIA) exclusion and inclusion, and create relationships that are stratified among diverse language users. Attention to this issue in education shapes beliefs about language and language use (Beaudrie, 2023; Britton & Kraemer, forthcoming).

The integration of arts and wellness emerged as areas responding to students' needs, which we'll explain further in sections that follow. For this reason, the use of technology in our exploratory heritage curriculum was flexibly implemented to attend to students' wellness through developing art and to increase their community participation.

3 What Is the Setting/Context for Developing Our Project?

This project takes place in a Massachusetts under-resourced middle school with a significant high needs, special education, and English language learner population among the predominantly Latiné[1] student body.

This area's demographics include 81.4 per cent of students enrolled in the school identifying as "Hispanic," 14.1 per cent as white, 2.8 per cent as African American, 1.4 per cent as multi-race "non-Hispanic," and 0.3 per cent as Asian. Approximately one-third are designated as having disabilities including attention-deficit/hyperactivity disorder, autism, and language processing and trauma-related symptoms that affect academic and social learning.

In this school district, students also deal with higher poverty levels, with a large percentage (92.8 per cent) designated as "high needs." According to census data, 26 per cent of this city is living in poverty, and 89.3 per cent of enrolled students are designated as from low-income families. There is a generational wealth divide within the city and a lack of investment in public schools that eventually, among other issues, led to Massachusetts state receivership – a governmental takeover of the school district.

However, there are resources that help students become resilient to overcome adversity (Yosso, 2005). In October 2023, students from a local restorative justice youth organization shared their experiences by testifying before their state government in support of a 10-year pilot program for overdose prevention centres. The areas served by the school district have an active arts council, contributing to the community's vibrant music and arts scene. Community members are willing to leverage their positions and volunteer their time to support public school students. The high school theatre program, local media group, restorative justice youth organization, and local community college have contributed to the planning of various course learning goals, activities, and field trips.

---

1. The term "Latiné" is a Spanish language–influenced neologism that refers to populations in the United States that have been called "Hispanics," a Reagan-era term.

The community's current linguistic richness is evidenced by the high level of multilingualism, with census data showing that 42 per cent of persons aged five years and above speak languages other than English at home (between 2018 and 2022).

This district and the state Department of Education faced a lawsuit over long-standing policies, procedures, and actions that denied language access to parents who do not speak English or speak limited English (recently settled, 2020). Implementing an HL program within a Sheltered English middle school setting where 36.6 per cent of enrolled students have a first language other than English and 20 per cent of enrolled students are designated as "English language learners" could serve as a model for how to repair school-community relationships by making multilingual families and students feel seen, welcome, and valued.

3.1 Promising Developments for Transformation of HL Programming

Massachusetts State legislation, passed in 2017, approved the Seal of Biliteracy and ended the exclusion of languages other than English in public schools (Department of Elementary and Secondary Education, 2024). This legislation opened up opportunities for bilingual, dual language programs in school districts throughout the state. While most dual language programs begin with good intentions about building multilingualism and multiliteracies, these programs often have limited enrolment opportunities available to minoritized community members (Cervantes-Soon, 2014; Freire et al., 2021) and often do not fully address HL learner needs. Frequently, HL learners are expected to be linguistic or cultural experts, and their home language fluency is used to support the elective bilingual learners while their dynamic and unique language needs go unaddressed.

During the pandemic, digital technologies afforded teaching and learning opportunities that were more intimately connected to students' home life. Various technologies offered dynamic ways to engage in content and language learning, but at the same time, there was a growing sense of isolation and loss in human-machine interactions. Post-pandemic, the social and emotional well-being of students has drawn much attention. Subsequently, in returning to in-person learning, special spaces became necessary for students to develop their interpersonal skills through sharing representations of their identities and hands-on creative activities.

Given that anti-multilingual legislation was overturned and instruction during the pandemic necessitated using more than English alone, a space opened up for addressing multiple generations' instruction in a language other than English in state public schools. Parents, staff, and teachers, in addition to students, had the opportunity to come to terms with the effect of a 15-year legislation that previously prohibited instruction in other languages in state public schools. Consequently, this legislation opened up a special space for HL users and the actual valuing and use of this space to address what learners understood as heritage languages in order to overcome the legacy of HL suppression. We argue that the way a Spanish heritage speaker interacts with the dominant English language and their home language carries different kinds of ideological power and social identity based on their lived experiences. In our interinstitutional planning, we wanted to address what can be done to repair the disenfranchisement and alienation of our students' multilingual families. Therefore, our programmatic effort required helping shift language ideologies about the value and affirmation of heritage language users' identities in order to build further resources in their communities.

3.2 Collaborative HL Learning: Technology in Art-Making

Our interinstitutional collaborative heritage program began in the fall of 2021 as an after-school initiative to explore identity through art-making. In the spring semester of 2022, a small group of Spanish heritage language students were invited to join a pilot course to further explore identity through language and the arts. In the following 2022–2023 school year, the "HL and Art" program was initiated consisting of one semester-long enrichment course open to all students in the daily middle school schedule. The course was offered in the fall and spring semesters. In this chapter, we report on the different cohorts of students who participated in the 2022–2023 HL and Art program offered over the two semesters. In our planning, we recognized that art-making with technology would allow students to express their thoughts and feelings as they became invested in creatively constructing their representations of their identities. Through the use of technology in art-making, students learned about themselves and each other, including working through the challenges and conflicts that can arise in heterogeneous communities. Using technology to inquire into geography, history, and family stories supported their art-making by providing information to represent their heritage identities and to develop their social emotional learning.

In this chapter, we will report on how students' hands-on learning experiences through art inside and outside the classroom helped them engage with their own and their classmates' HL communities. We describe key assignments and elaborate on the implementation of the culminating project while drawing important comparisons between the first semester and second semester groups. The development of this program is still ongoing, and the non-linear progress of initiating such a program is an important lesson for readers hoping to attempt their own interinstitutional collaboration.

4 How Can Interinstitutional Goals Using Technology Strategically Inform an HL Curriculum?

This report on our collaboration in the ongoing development of a middle school curriculum for the HL and Art program has several major goals. One is to describe how technology supported culturally, linguistically, and neurally diverse student groups in questioning, researching, and expressing their cultures and identities for different audiences. As the different online platforms that were used were not specifically designed for acquisition of a particular language, these technologies served the exploratory language program in building critical language awareness and inspiring students to further develop their literacies (Arendt & Reershemius, 2024).

A second goal involves documenting the concerted effort to revitalize the existing resources by increasing the use of HL resources, both human and machine, by members of the school, community, and universities. Supported by technological affordances and in response to the constraints of a middle school enrichment course, our curriculum planning focused on projects that could promote student agency through art-making informed by multimodal literacies. Students would make choices about what and how to represent their ethnolinguistic identities visually, then articulate their artistic decision-making in an art statement. Families, community members, and school staff served as collaborators and audience members for these projects, enhancing the social emotional learning and articulation of language ideologies that take place in such intergenerational and multilingual social interactions.

In Section 4.1, we begin by identifying the key project and mini-lesson examples in the form of a table to help readers understand how the curricular plan emerged from our theoretical framework. For the purpose of Section 4.1, we also elaborate on the culminating project to demonstrate how a shared understanding of critical HL awareness was built among all participants, and we describe how the plan shifted while attending to student activity. Next, in Section 4.2, we describe the affordances of using technology with an art orientation in a middle school classroom and the need for wellness and social emotional learning in these human-machine interactions. Lastly, in Section 4.3, we illustrate our collaboration's strategic responses to scheduling, student groupings, and other administrative constraints placed upon the developing program.

4.1 Building a Shared Understanding of Critical HL Awareness

To begin, we briefly describe the major curricular activities and projects that emerged from our theoretical framework to show how our collaborative plan to support diverse students in building critical language awareness was implemented in school year (SY) 2022–2023. Critical language awareness through exploratory learning has been instrumental in raising students' awareness of language ideologies (Parra, 2016). This pedagogy has tenets in terms of understanding that language variation is natural as is recognizing the intrinsic value of students' own variety and that of all others. It strives to develop student consciousness of the political, social, and economic power structures that underlie language use, including understanding ideologies concerning prestige and non-prestige varieties in monolingual/bilingual practices. The pedagogy offers students opportunities to exercise agency in making their own decisions about language use and bilingualism. Art-based pedagogies (Matthias, 2015; Parra, 2013), when used with heritage learners, afford communication that's "not merely as an opportunity to speak, but to engage critically with the ideology and substance of speech, writing, and other forms of cultural production" (Giroux, 1991, p. 249). Wellness is a key construct in positive education, which strives to enhance student well-being through personal projects that develop academic growth while promoting student retention and engagement (Coulombe et al., 2020; Little & Gee, 2007; White & Kern, 2018). These pedagogies inform practices included in the program.

Specifically, students completed three major projects throughout the semester: (a) "Baseline Assessment: Heritage Human," (b) "Mid-Unit Assessment: Cultural Symbols Project," and (c) "Final Project: Community Night & Art Show." Each project required a visual representation, an art statement, a presentation to an audience, and a reflection on learning. Between each of the projects, mini-lessons were provided in response to student heritage identities and interests. The major assignments in Table 5.1 outline examples of students' realization of our goals. Table 5.1 illustrates how technology use in both art-making and schema-building affected wellness by tracking the ways in which student identities were empowered and how the projects and mini-lessons provided social emotional learning around healthy relationships.

Students progressed through the exploratory inquiry process with a typical gradual release of guidance so that they could tackle the culminating activity of exhibiting at, planning, and hosting the Community Night & Art Show. Each step utilized technology because it afforded opportunities for language learning through metalinguistic and cross-cultural concepts. Due to space constraints, further discussion in this section will highlight how the Final Project: Community Night & Art Show engaged all participants in building critical HL awareness.

The group's diversity and opportunities for choice in representation with media, imagery, and themes created a lively forum to discuss language, use translanguaging while collaboratively planning, co-create shared projects, and develop skills for building positive relationships. With multiple opportunities to collaborate and present their work to authentic audiences, students built presentational skills that were useful in the planning process and their public exhibition. In a highly diverse learning and teaching setting, certain technologies can jumpstart the need to communicate. Google Classroom, Slides, Docs, and Gmail offered students opportunities to directly communicate with peers and staff members who identified themselves as willing to help with organizing the Community Night & Art Show event. Bilingual staff members offered to support students in translating the art statements so that they would be accessible to Spanish-speaking families, and consequently an intergenerational dialogue of language use was created.

As students engaged in interactions discovering and sharing resources, we learned that students needed guided instructions for participation to

Table 5.1 Heritage Language and Art Curricular Outline, Grades 6–8 (SY 2022–2023)

Assignment	Art and Purpose	Language Modalities	Technology in Classroom Instruction and Community Presentation	Impact on Wellness
Baseline Assessment: Heritage Human	Colouring human outline with coloured pencil and crayon **to represent identity**	**Visual** representation **Writing/ Speaking** explanation	Dry media on paper colouring sheet iPad Applications: 1. Voice Memo 2. Padlet 3. Nearpod	<u>Empowering Student Identities</u>: 1. Self-awareness and questioning attitudes towards their heritages 2. Agency via artistic choices <u>Nurturing Healthy Relationships</u>: 1. Peer feedback 2. Collaboration on exhibition of the project
Mini-Lesson: Building Schema of Heritage	Co-creating an identity word cloud as a **heritage schema-building mini-lesson**	**Speaking/ Listening** in discussion **Reading** survey questions **Writing** survey responses	Websites: 1. Word Cloud iPad Applications: 1. Padlet 2. Google Forms	<u>Empowering Student Identities</u>: 1. Self-awareness and questioning attitudes towards their heritages 2. Naming and affirming students' identities <u>Nurturing Healthy Relationships</u>: 1. Turn & Talk with a peer 2. Building on each other's ideas

(Continued)

Table 5.1 Continued

Assignment	Art and Purpose	Language Modalities	Technology in Classroom Instruction and Community Presentation	Impact on Wellness
Mini-Lesson: Mapping the Language of Family	Language relationship map, family vocabulary, and storytelling as critical **language awareness schema-building mini-lesson**	**Speaking/Listening** in discussion of personal experiences **Reading** multilingual family vocabulary **Writing** Venn diagram of similarities and differences between the classroom heritage languages	YouTube HL Exploration: 1. Multilingual music 2. Language lessons 3. Travel vlogs by multilingual content creators iPad Applications: 1. Google Slides 2. Google Translate with read-aloud 3. Voice Memo (recording discussion of personal experiences)	Empowering Student Identities: 1. Self-awareness of student attitudes and assumptions towards multilingualism 2. Naming and affirming important relationships in students' lives Nurturing Healthy Relationships: 1. Becoming aware of and curious about different languages 2. Acknowledgment of the awkwardness and challenges that arise within multilingual communities 3. Making space to explore the reasons why some students reject their heritage identities
Mid-Unit Assessment: Cultural Symbols Project	Mind mapping of material culture and feelings/attitudes about students' cultural identities	**Visual** representation **Writing/Speaking** explanation	Acrylic and watercolour on canvas board Websites: 1. Google Image search (reference images for mind maps) 2. Scratch coding iPad Applications: 1. Google Slides	Empowering Student Identities: 1. Self-awareness of students' intersectional identities 2. Agency via artistic choices Nurturing Healthy Relationships: 1. Peer feedback 2. Sharing resources, respect, boundaries 3. Learning from work being done in other classes 4. Asking peers for advice and help in achieving their project goals

| Final Project: Community Night & Art Show | Different artistic media were used to plan and produce a final visual art project | **Visual** representation **Writing/Speaking** explanation **Speaking/Listening** to participate in planning the Community Night & Art Show public event | Utilized for Final Projects:
1. Acrylic and/or watercolour on canvas board, stretched canvas, clay sculptures, or cardboard diorama
2. Google Slides presentation with screen recording and voiceover narration
3. iMovie with written captions
4. Scratch coding a game or animation
5. Voice Memo and QR code art statements
Utilized for Community Night & Art Show Communication & Planning:
1. Google Classroom
2. Gmail
3. Google Docs
4. Google Slides
5. Google Translate
6. Canva
7. Google Forms | Empowering Student Identities:
1. Self-awareness of students' nuanced ethnolinguistic identities
2. Agency via artistic choices
Nurturing Healthy Relationships:
1. Peer feedback
2. Sharing resources, respect, boundaries
3. Collaborating towards shared goals
4. Communicating effectively in group projects and event planning
5. Conflict resolution |

facilitate collaboration. Some students formed intense bonds through the shared use of different heritage Spanishes; other students changed their final project partners because of shared cultural backgrounds; and still others chose to work in groups based on a shared interest in a particular media. While the first semester students needed more background knowledge on what heritage means and how they relate to theirs, by the second semester, students new to the course already had an understanding of what heritage means from having socialized with their peers and/or having attended the previous semester's Community Night & Art Show.

Moreover, as students learned to use new technologies, they also taught each other and their instructor. Some introduced new digital tools in creating their final projects. For example, a few students in the first semester took the initiative to code their own animations and games for their final projects using Scratch, a free online coding website. Subsequently, more instruction in the different media options for creating the final projects was provided both by the instructor and by students with expertise in the new media options as a way to build up language awareness and background knowledge about representing culture and identity.

4.2 Technological Affordances

Our project with technology-supported learning provides several lessons for initiating HL programs using technology with an art orientation. In this exploratory project, students' interests drove technology use and critical language to access resources that were relevant and engaging. By examining the students' progress in carrying out their projects, we learned about the need to nurture positive relationships and a sense of belonging in a post-pandemic language class. As well, we noted how everyday digital technologies such as the internet and sharing devices can mediate students' deeper thinking. What became visible were the values informing students' creative decision-making. Furthermore, in the process of examining students using everyday digital technologies to create their projects, additional pedagogical needs were revealed, including those to build shared community values such as how to be respectful, safe, and responsible.

Both the Baseline Assessment: Heritage Human and the Mini-Lesson: Building Schema of Heritage helped the instructor elicit background information about the heritage and abilities represented by the students in each cohort and semester. The use of Google Forms, WordCloud, Nearpod, and Padlet supported student participation through anonymous postings and brought forth discussions of digital citizenship and respect within the HL learning community.

4.3 A Strategic Response to "What the HTTPS Is Going on Here?"

Given an 80 per cent Latiné student population, our heritage program originally intended to focus on Spanish varieties. However, during the SY 2022–2023 implementation, scheduling issues arose that obligated grouping students into cohorts that were not according to their HL. It became important to negotiate adjustments for students enrolled in the first-year HL and Art courses in order to include a wider range of minoritized heritage identities, such as Cambodian, African, French, Bosnian, Lakota, Mexican, vernacular English, Irish, and Italian.

Given this diversity, the project's goal shifted from developing Spanish HL awareness towards understanding diversity, collaboration, and artistic media across multiple heritage languages. This shift afforded (the possibility of) honouring the diverse languages in this school community and bringing them to attention through creative art production.

This approach inspired the classroom teacher, Lulu, to invite diverse groups' culture and their languages into school life. The university professor, Theresa, contributed resources online that could be used in decision-making about representation. This interinstitutional collaborative response to school-based administrative constraints illustrates the non-linear progress of initiating an HL program within the public school system. The theoretical framework of our planning allowed for strategic changes to be made while maintaining the program's goals for building critical language awareness through technology in art-making and attending to the wellness of all students.

5 What Happens When Investigating Technology in an Exploratory HL Program?

Getting students excited about learning takes pedagogies that ignite their curiosity and build critical appraisal of their own learning in order to set further goals. Expeditionary learning is just this type of experience that involves active questioning, researching, and expressing one's own understandings to self and others (Fariño, 2015). As such, this type of learning affords opportunities to use everyday technologies to expand students' knowledge of their cultures and identities in different communities. When this pedagogy is combined with learning heritage languages and literacies, technology becomes a powerful tool and medium in building practices that link heritage learners to their local and diasporic communities. For this reason, while specific online computer-assisted language learning (CALL) platforms exist that are designed for specific language acquisition, we opted for readily available and non-proprietary technologies to serve inquiries in an exploratory language program.

Immediately, there was a need to economically initiate a program that could build critical language awareness and inspire learners to further develop their abilities. A pedagogy-building critical language awareness could draw attention to how language functions to structure social worlds through texts and language use. This approach means language use is a focus not only as a means of representing knowledge but also for its ideological power to influence social identities (Loza & Beaudrie, 2021; Vañó García, 2023). Taking such a focus allowed for challenging bilingualism myths and building new ways to forge agency and creativity.

The following examples of technology use in exploratory learning provide evidence of students becoming powerful communicators through expressing their decision-making and specific deliberations about how they wanted to communicate their message artistically. The constraints that arose in managing resources like internet use, shared devices, and online communication and the classroom teacher's limited security control created sites for learning languages to creatively and collectively solve problems and build activism in the community.

5.1 Facilitating a Positive Learning Community Using Norms

We conceptualize the HL and Art classroom as a safe space and shared resource for exploring intersectional identities. With this approach, students had the choice to work independently or with others on projects and make project decisions facilitated by technology. In SY 2022–2023, students used technology for research, production, and collaboration. Creating norms for technology use allowed learning to extend into online spaces like

Google Classroom or within a shared slides presentation. Management of the class set of iPads required attention in order to bypass the restrictions placed on creating user profiles (i.e., one profile per device rather than per individual user). However, by assigning individual accountability, a sense of personal ownership of these iPads developed.

Other issues around sharing the iPads arose, especially when students' choices or practices conflicted with each other, for example, changing photo features, deleting photos other device users needed, and students completing assignments in the wrong Google accounts. Such conflicts were essential for the co-creation of additional norms and routines. These moments empowered students to suggest accountability ideas for communal tablet use. One suggested that images should be saved at the end of class so that, if anything happened in the photos app, their image bank would still be available in Google Drive. Others also had different suggestions about what to do to ensure security in their accounts. Some students signed in and deleted their school accounts every time they used their assigned device; they wrote procedures on a poster to help others. It was a timely opportunity for students to collaborate and show digital responsibility between different classes. The shared iPads created opportunities for students to see themselves as part of a community larger than their classroom and further develop both empathy and responsibility.

5.2 Teaching Students to Respond to Peer Artwork

The Heritage Human project, assigned early in the semester, provided the instructor with information about students' prior knowledge, abilities to visually represent information, and ability to describe their artistic choices in writing. Each cohort's students were invited to choose where and how their classwork would be publicly displayed in anticipation of the school's open house. Then, students were asked to curate the exhibits as one collective art show and offer observations. This task introduced students to the diversity of culture, thinking, and artistic expression and prepared them for the bigger task of organizing the end-of-semester Community Night & Art Show.

During this early project, students learned to talk about the artwork using sentence frames like "one thing about this art piece that works for me is… because…" and "one thing about this art piece that doesn't work for me is... because..." Using Nearpod, an application combining media, management, and assessment, students were able to view a display, anonymously post responses, and then discuss the posts before moving on to the next display, all without leaving the classroom. Having these boundaries made it easier for students to practise giving and receiving effective feedback. It also illustrated why creating the art statement was important.

The instructor selected one individual Heritage Human project for all cohorts to view and respond to because the student had not completed colouring or decorating her image. During discussion, most peers responded that it was bad because it was blank and that the student did not even try. When they read the corresponding art statement, the student's choices became clear and were quite impactful. The student left her Heritage Human project blank because she did not feel her heritage in her body at all, and this disclosure opened up deeper conversations about identity and self-knowledge. This example also demonstrated the importance of using the sentence frames to structure their responses. From the discussion, students understood how language carries ideological power because the piece judged as "bad" was actually very personal, touching, and well done.

5.3 Practising Collaboration and Leadership Over Time

Having multiple opportunities to practise speaking with each other about artwork with awareness that authors choose how to depict their illustrations was essential for empowering students as communicators.

Before starting their Cultural Symbols Project, a mid-unit assessment focused on symbolically representing their ethnolinguistic identities, students completed a sketch with labels and received feedback from a peer or small group. The peer feedback routine continued as planning progressed, affording students vital lessons. This collaborative learning was most evident in the final projects where students were using techniques newly acquired from their peers. Students also learned more about their shared heritages from more knowledgeable peers. For example, Puerto Rican symbols like the flamboyán, amapola, and coqui, which were represented in some students' Cultural Symbols Projects, began to appear in other students' final projects.

Making dialogues a regular routine throughout the semester gave students ample opportunities to practise speaking and translanguaging with each other about concepts, information, and artwork, improving their confidence. Setting this groundwork at the beginning of the term was important so that they could later effectively work on their final projects, plan the culminating the Community Night & Art Show event, and interact with guests. For example, students took leadership roles in organizing tours and creating a program for visitors. They had the chance to make the connection that it's not enough to assign responsibilities – they also had to ensure individuals understood their role.

5.4 Using Technologies and Working with Neurodiversity

Diversity within the HL and Art courses included neurodiverse students, which necessitated modified interactions with peers and the materials. Particularly in the second semester, when more students had significant reading, writing, and language challenges, technological assistance was particularly supportive. The initial Heritage Human project proved immensely challenging to complete for several sixth graders, who kept restarting their illustrations. Among those who struggled were several students who had previous coding experience using the program Scratch. Accordingly, instruction responded by allowing the students to use their preferred media. Giving students with expertise the chance to teach their classmates and assigning responsibilities to students also supported managing supplies in cohorts where the sometimes chaotic distribution and clean-up of supplies proved overstimulating for some students.

Since there is no wrong way to be artistically creative, the arts orientation helped build up student confidence in taking risks to express their ideas. The hands-on multimodal art projects removed barriers to representing their ideas and met many students' sensory needs. Art-making put students at ease in using and talking about their heritage languages and families, while applications like Flip or Voice Memo supported orally developing art statements, removing limitations faced in composing by writing or typing.

5.5 Exposing Myths of Bilingualism

Outside the HL program, heritage learners have varying opportunities for using their non-English languages. Some students in the course were first generation, and the HL is the primary language used at home. Other students in the class primarily used English in the home, as they were the second-, third-, or fourth-generation speakers in their families or because they had been adopted or were in foster care. While the community and school have Spanish language resources, Spanish has many varieties. When Spanish HL speakers visited the class, metalinguistic discussions came about naturally. Bilingualism myths like "I speak broken Spanish" or "I understand Spanish, but I don't speak Spanish" or "I speak Spanish like a gringa" came to the surface and were questioned, both by Spanish in-group members and by comparing other HL speakers' attitudes towards their heritage languages. Conversations about family language enabled role play and investigations into HL use. For example, some students felt confident and fluent when using their language to correct behaviours, while others uncovered HL traces they did not think they had discussed by talking about Wigilia, the Polish Christmas Eve celebration.

5.6 Embracing Heritage in Many Forms

To inspire students to further develop their HL awareness, the activities we developed embraced heritage in many forms, with an open idea of what it means to speak and learn a home language. We recognized that using visual arts to express what they know and learn about their heritage helped students identify with their heritage, and writing their art statements developed their attitudes and confidence about their heritage identities. Technology was an important tool for combining student interests, islands of competence, and multimodal learning about heritage, language, and community.

The Community Night & Art Show allowed for student leadership and connection with a public audience. Technology was used for publicity, designing the art show program, sharing documents, and for making digital projects accessible. During the event, students used language to explain to visitors how to interact with their projects. The interactions with non-English-speaking visitors gave students first-hand experience in the value of multilingualism and showed them that language use in multilingual communities is varied and dynamic. This family night event affirmed student heritage identities across varying multilingual proficiency levels and inspired them to further their abilities for future opportunities.

5.7 Inspiring Students to Further Develop Their Abilities

Resources in heritage languages other than Spanish were more challenging to find already existing within the school and community. The Community Night & Art Show represented an effort to pool community resources together, as it brought all these diverse heritage communities together and offered students authentic opportunities to use their HL. Since the 2022–2023 implementation, other university partners have further leveraged their language resources in support of the HL and Art course by providing students more opportunities to interact with HL communities.

In both semesters, students' art statements showed greater detail and length of their explanatory prose between projects. For the heritage speakers, translating their art statements using Google Translate also supported more revisions and additional details as students worked between two languages. The eighth graders with high fluency levels in Spanish worked with bilingual staff to edit the art statements, and students learned how to look at the editing notation to make revisions.

In the course feedback surveys, students of all language backgrounds overwhelmingly responded that they wished they had learned more Spanish (and other languages). The classroom teacher conducted small group discussions to find out more about this wish for more language learning as the same students had previously shown resistance to the academic lessons that would have enabled more language learning to take place. Debriefing the course in small groups, students understood that their desire to learn more languages could be achieved through technology since they considered using the iPads to be fun. For example, they named the filters in Flip, a video discussion and sharing application, as a way to make oral language assessments less stressful. Additionally, technology offered neurodiverse students more ways to express themselves, which subsequently encouraged them to participate in discussions.

6 What Are the Big Ideas about Integration of Arts into HL through Technology?

Here we synthesize how the arts approach, HL learning, and technology affected students' conceptualization of heritage identity. Collaborating on the arts integration in HL through technology has taught us to examine not only technologically supported language development but also technology-mediated human relationships. As students carried out their projects, we learned lessons about how language is used in a post-pandemic classroom to enact healthy relationships and productive group work both face to face and digitally. As we can readily see in their engagement with social media in wider society, for middle school students, self-discovery is a high priority in their identity development and social participation. Including in the program a culminating family Community Night & Art Show event created a context within which students could see themselves as members of a face-to-face multilingual community.

Since returning to in-person learning during this post-pandemic time frame, social emotional learning and a sense of belonging have been very challenging for human-machine interactions. Digital technologies, such as the internet, and sharing devices have become significant in engaging students to promote complex abstract thinking via scaffolded concrete activities. Also needed are community-building values such as how to be respectful, safe, and responsible, and these values are not easily learned alone in online environments. In summary, we learned how students became powerful multilingual communicators through guided choices in expressing their message artistically and explained their decision-making orally and/or in writing with technological assistance.

While no specific CALL commercial apps were used in this program, the technologies that were used became media that allowed for discussion and accessibility. Using digital technology to engage students in building schema, creating art media, and building communicative skills all represent CALL innovations that situate language learning in meaningful contexts that reflect student interests and abilities. Moreover, students showed more sustained attention to their projects if they could learn to use popular applications to accomplish the assignments.

Raising language awareness can occur even when HL content is taught and discussed in English. Naming and identifying with the benefits of multilingualism, language ideologies expressed by students and staff began to shift away from the limiting multilingualism myths expressed before the course started. Multilingual staff and community members who visited the classroom and attended the Community Night & Art Show modelled how languages are dynamic and changeable. Students demonstrated a shift towards embracing possibilities of wholeness in their expanding multilingual repertoire through eagerness to further their abilities and through the sudden decline in using derogatory labels like "lingy" for students designated as English language learners.

7 What Are the Takeaways?

In light of this project, one important contribution that technology use has offered this fledgling HL and Art program was to amplify student multilingual choices and consequences. We argue that a shared goal of teaching/learning about our heritage and organizing a productive community night were accomplished through this approach. In general, technology made both concepts and collaboration accessible for students. With regard to traditional media literacies, students were quickly able to make a slideshow or code an animation, which offered an authentic and relevant material context for the complex activity of reading, writing, speaking, and listening in creating an explanatory art statement.

Considering how technology enhanced a rich heritage learning experience, we found evidence that students developed a more critical media literacy. Students showed an understanding of how language awareness includes multimodal representation through images and sound assembled together with language to convey identities and enable communication with a range of community members. As we continue the ongoing interinstitutional collaboration on HL programming, we recognize that furthering relationships with local and global HL communities could sustain students' HL usage and create opportunities for further development.

7.1 Challenges of Dynamic Learning Processes with Emerging Technologies

These advances in shifting language ideology and multilingual use were also accompanied by many authentic technological challenges, which encouraged creative problem solving and validated the importance of human and critical collaboration. We further elaborate with two examples.

7.1.1 Example: Technology Barriers
Managing devices in the middle school classroom encompasses ongoing security issues. This challenge means that teachers need to negotiate with

the administrators who determine security, profile, and application settings. When security decisions are made by outsourcing, as it was in our case, consideration needs to be given as to how these affect the classroom learning experience. Without including staff and students, as the users, inequitable decision-making and device use policies may continue to disrupt learning rather than enhance it.

7.1.2 Example: Placement and Scheduling

In the 2022–2023 year of implementation, all grades participated in an exploratory curriculum, with the goal for sixth grade to remain as an exploratory experience in heritage, identity, and art for a semester. One major challenge that arose consisted of how to work towards students achieving the Seal of Biliteracy in the context of a HL program, which has students who use different languages. This award recognizes levels of biliteracy that would need further development in each of the heritage languages (Department of Elementary and Secondary Education, 2024); then assessments to document this development would also be required. These elements were not included in this exploratory curriculum design. Placing students into HL class sections with the same language for full-year instruction could support more assessment of biliteracy and multilingual development. Unfortunately, limited space and staffing to support smaller cohorts grouped around shared heritage remains an issue in under-resourced schools.

Stratified levels of decision-making, responsibilities, and motivating factors also hindered appropriate scheduling. For example, district leaders wanted students and families to have a choice in enrichment courses and for schools to offer them as electives for seventh and eighth grade. The communication between building administrators and teachers was not sufficient to uphold the district's promise to families. Consequently, there was no opportunity for creative problem solving among all stakeholders.

7.1.3 How to Normalize Heteroglossic Language Perspectives

There is much work still ahead to raise awareness about multilingual identities and how multilingual individuals use languages. Most district administrators and teachers have standards-based, rigid, monolingual ideologies towards language and literacy acquisition that are rooted in white privilege and standard language ideologies. These present obstacles to teaching students to be change agents in accepting their heritages as assets. In general, some teachers and administrators alike have a predominantly fixed mindset about acknowledging and critically examining their own agency to make change in the ways they use language, which leads to the failure of effective advocacy for HL learners and their dynamic, creative, and fluid language practices.

7.2 Technology in Promising Sustainability of Future HL Development within Communities

In retrospect, challenging moments were an underutilized opportunity for language learning as the focus remained on how students or the instructor could work around disruptions to application availability or internet access. In future iterations of this type of exploratory learning, student agency in human-machine interactions could be further empowered if evaluative activities could be included such as composing feedback to the app designers, providing suggestions to district technology administrators, or advising how school-based technology management could include orientations for students about use, maintenance, and safeguards in order to develop student responsibility and critical understanding of cyber security, among other emerging concerns regarding technology use.

HL learning is a lifelong process; technology can make it more authentic to contemporary concerns and connect to social issues in the students' life. Furthermore, accessible technology can be utilized to reach more audiences over time and space. Student documentation of planning and creating can add to future lesson planning, offering future HL students' authentic examples of prior peers' accomplishments. Documenting their progress towards final projects, and the art shows being available to an online audience, could help wider audiences appreciate multilingual community events.

7.3 Impact Beyond the Time Frame of the Project

This chapter focuses on a unique approach to HL education that is not focused on any one HL. Building value around HL and its usage through the heterogeneity of student abilities – language, technology, community building, and sense of belonging – essentially mediated the development of a humanizing pedagogy in face-to-face and human-machine interactions. Multimodal learning made it possible for students to create and share visual art as opportunities for meaningful communication and to expand their linguistic repertoire.

The ongoing interinstitutional planning and non-linear approach to progress in developing and implementing this HL program has had a lasting impact in the school district and community. Former students now use their HL as youth leaders in a local restorative justice community organization. This outcome potentially expands the community organization's influence in future HL program planning. The scheduling challenges and the need to further develop heteroglossic language perspectives among district and school administrators necessitate that project efforts continue to shapeshift to stay afloat. The program's reach is currently limited to a small group of eighth grade students, but developing relationships with community partners continue to further language and digital media learning.

Having the HL and Art program institutionalized as a semester-based enrichment course for one year in the school brought about heritage identity awareness. Beyond the school, heritage languages have been embraced by the Multilingual Education Department within the district with the director overseeing "heritage corner" construction in multiple schools. The Equity Task Force has a growing awareness of the significance of HL and the director of Diversity, Equity, Inclusion, and Family Engagement is eager to learn more about language ideologies. Affinity group work in the district also raised awareness among staff of their own identities as heritage speakers and furthered conversations around raciolinguistics and critical language awareness in the Allies group.

In conclusion, we hope to have contributed to expanding the wider community's resources by opening public space for products created by learners using technology and the arts to build connections to their HL communities and cultures.

About the Authors

Before becoming a teacher, **Lulu Ekiert** worked in health and wellness as an outside provider of mindfulness education in urban public schools. A visual artist and trauma-engaged educator, she is a heritage language learner who believes in salud y bienestar, culturally advancing pedagogy, multilingual education, learner agency, and the interconnected revitalization of heritage communities, public education, and mental/physical health.

A heritage learner herself, **Theresa Austin** uses critical educational sociolinguistics, ethnographies of communication, and critical discourse analysis to respond to the needs of diverse historically underserved communities. She examines multilingual/literacy policies and planning, as well as cross-cultural issues in curriculum, teacher inquiry, technology-assisted learning, assessment, and evaluation on African American English, ESL/EFL, Spanish, Japanese, etc. She serves on several editorial boards, including the boards of *Multicultural Education & Technology Journal* and *Dialogic Education Journal*, among others.

References

Arendt, B., & Reershemius, G. (2024). *Heritage languages in the digital age: The case of autochthonous minority languages in western Europe*. Multilingual Matters. https://doi.org/10.21832/9781800414235

Beaudrie, S. (2023). Developing critical language awareness in the heritage language classroom: Implementation and assessment in diverse educational contexts. *Languages*, *8*(1), 81. https://doi.org/10.3390/languages8010081

Britton, E.R., & Kraemer, A. (forthcoming). Reframing critical language awareness across curricula: A disciplinary-based world language program. *Journal of Multilingual Theories and Practices* (*Special Issue: Reimagining Language Education through Critical Language Awareness*).

Canagarajah, S. (2015). Clarifying the relationship between translingual practice and L2 writing: Addressing learner identities. *Applied Linguistics Review*, *6*(4), 415–440. https://doi.org/10.1515/applirev-2015-0020

Cervantes-Soon, C.G. (2014). A critical look at dual language immersion in the new Latin@ diaspora. *Bilingual Research Journal*, *37*(1), 64–82. https://doi.org/10.1080/15235882.2014.893267

Chaparro, S.E. (2019). *But mom! I'm not a Spanish Boy*: Raciolinguistic socialization in a two-way immersion bilingual program. *Linguistics and Education*, *50*, 1–12. https://doi.org/10.1016/j.linged.2019.01.003

Coulombe, S., Hardy, K., & Goldfarb, R. (2020). Promoting wellbeing through positive education: A critical review and proposed social ecological approach. *Theory and Research in Education*, *18*(3), 295–321. https://doi.org/10.1177/1477878520988432

Department of Elementary and Secondary Education. (2024). *Massachusetts State Seal of Biliteracy*. https://www.doe.mass.edu/scholarships/biliteracy/

Fariño, Y. (2015). *Expeditionary learning: An effective approach for heritage language education*. CASLS InterCom. https://caslsintercom.uoregon.edu/content/20404

Flores, N., & García, O. (2013). Linguistic third spaces in education: Teachers' translanguaging across the bilingual continuum. In D. Little, C. Leung, & P. Van Avermaet (Eds.), *Managing diversity in education: Languages, policies, pedagogies* (pp. 245–258). Multilingual Matters. https://doi.org/10.21832/9781783090815-016

Flores-Hutson, P., Maier, M.I., Carrizal-Dukes, E., Durá, L., & Gonzales, L. (2019). La salud en mis manos: Localizing health and wellness literacies in transnational communities through participatory mindfulness and art-based projects. *Present Tense*, *7*(3), 1–5. https://www.presenttensejournal.org/volume-7/la-salud-en-mis-manos/

Freire, J., Gambrell, J., Kasun, G.S., Dorner, L.M., & Cervantes-Soon, C. (2021). The expropriation of dual language bilingual education: Deconstructing neoliberalism, whitestreaming, and English-hegemony. *International Multilingual Research Journal*, *16*(1), 27–46. https://doi.org/10.1080/19313152.2021.1929762

Giroux, H.A. (1991). Postmodernism as border pedagogy: Redefining the boundaries of race and ethnicity. In H.A. Giroux (Ed.), *Postmodernism, feminism, and cultural politics: Redrawing educational boundaries* (pp. 217–256). State University New York Press.

Little, B.R., & Gee, T.L. (2007). The methodology of personal projects analysis: Four modules and a funnel. In B.R. Little, K. Salmela-Aro, & S.D. Phillips (Eds.), *Personal project pursuit: Goals, action, and human flourishing* (pp. 51–94). Lawrence Erlbaum Associates Publishers. https://doi.org/10.4324/9781315089928

Loza, S., & Beaudrie, S.M. (Eds.). (2021). *Heritage language teaching: Critical language awareness perspectives for research and pedagogy*. Routledge. https://doi.org/10.4324/9781003148227

Matthias, B. (2015). Talking images: Exploring culture through arts-based digital storytelling. In L. Parkes & C.M. Ryan (Eds), *Integrating the arts: Creative thinking about foreign language curricula and language program direction* (pp. 37–56). Cengage Learning.

Parra, M.L. (2013). Expanding language and cultural competence in advanced heritage- and foreign-language learners through community engagement and work with the arts. *Heritage Language Journal*, *10*(2), 253–280. https://doi.org/10.46538/hlj.10.2.7

Parra, M.L. (2016). Critical approaches to heritage language instruction: How to foster students' critical consciousness. In M. Fairclough & S. Beaudrie (Eds.), *Innovative approaches in heritage language teaching: From research to practice* (pp.166–190). Georgetown University Press.

Vañó García, I. (2023). A call for critical and open pedagogies in Spanish heritage language instruction: Students as knowledge producers of Open Educational Resources (OERs). *EuroAmerican Journal of Applied Linguistics and Languages*, *10*(1), 21–38. https://doi.org/10.21283/2376905X.1.10.1.2742

White, M.A., & Kern, M.L. (2018). Positive education: Learning and teaching for wellbeing and academic mastery. *International Journal of Wellbeing*, *8*(1), 1–17. https://doi.org/10.5502/ijw.v8i1.588

Yosso, T.J. (2005). Whose culture has capital? A critical race theory discussion of community cultural wealth. *Race Ethnicity and Education*, *8*(1), 69–91. https://doi.org/10.1080/1361332052000341006

PART TWO
CALL IN/THROUGH LESS COMMONLY TAUGHT LANGUAGES

6 Indigenizing Language Pedagogies with Technology: Entangling Human and Non-Human Affordances for Indigenous Language and Culture Maintenance, Revitalization, and Reclamation

Sabine Siekmann, Joan Parker Webster, and Steven L. Thorne

1 Introduction

This chapter discusses four teacher-researcher inquiry projects designed to support Alaska Native language and cultural maintenance and revitalization efforts in school-based Indigenous language education. These projects, which were part of a series of grants that spanned 10 years, brought together various stakeholders, including university faculty from different institutions, school district personnel, classroom teachers, and tribal organizations, to participate in an interinstitutional collaborative community that focused on developing Indigenous language pedagogies that utilize digital technology as a transformative vehicle (Freire, 2005).

The chapter begins with a broad description of the context of school-based language and culture maintenance and revitalization efforts in Alaska. The literature review, which provides the ethico-onto-epistemological grounding for our work with teachers and language learners in this context, brings together the Western pedagogical framework of multiliteracies (e.g., New London Group, 1996), Vygotskian sociocultural theory, and Indigenous ways of being-knowing-doing. We then present our meta-analysis of four teacher-researcher inquiries, which focuses on the uses of technology and Indigenous ways of being-knowing-doing to disrupt monoglossic and monolingual ideologies. The chapter concludes with a discussion of how these projects make visible relatedness and entanglement among people,

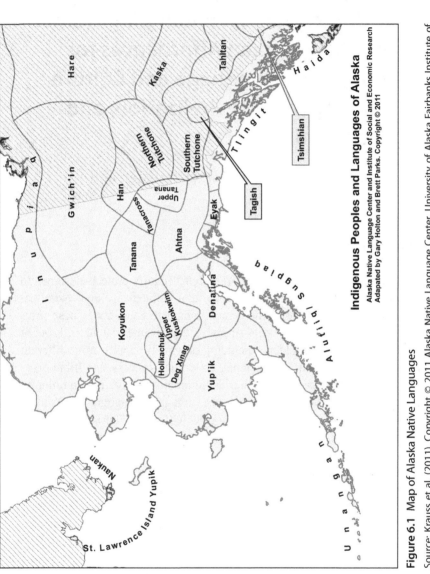

Figure 6.1 Map of Alaska Native Languages

Source: Krauss et al. (2011). Copyright © 2011 Alaska Native Language Center, University of Alaska Fairbanks Institute of Social and Economic Research, University of Alaska Anchorage. This map is licensed under the CC BY NC-ND 3.0 US Licence and published with permission from the Alaska Native Language Center.

language, culture, teaching, and learning that form the foundation for sustainable Indigenous language and culture processes.

2 Context

Alaska has a rich linguistic and cultural landscape, including 20 Alaska Native languages (see Figure 6.1). Language and culture maintenance and revitalization efforts are underway for all of Alaska's Native languages. However, despite significant political advances, such as the 2014 resolution to add all 20 Alaska Native languages as co-official languages for the State of Alaska, the continued language shift to English has interrupted intergenerational transmission of language and cultural knowledge, raising the stakes for school-based language and culture programs.

Schools are often cited as a key factor accelerating language and cultural loss through explicit suppression of Indigenous languages and imposing normative pressure to assimilate and to adopt English and Western ways of knowing and doing (Marlow & Siekmann, 2013). At the same time, schools have increasingly come to be viewed as having the potential to support language maintenance and revitalization efforts by teaching Alaska Native languages through a variety of program types. Some communities, especially in the Yup'ik region, have established programs that deliver instruction through the medium of the local Alaska Native language at the elementary school level (e.g., Yup'ik immersion or Yup'ik/English dual language programs).

In order to address a lack of professional development opportunities specifically for teachers in these programs, a group of stakeholders came together to develop interinstitutional collaborations through a series of grants. Their overarching goals were to

- improve Alaska Native and English education
- enable local leadership in language programming
- foster community-driven research (Marlow & Siekmann, 2013)

Over the course of a 10-year collaboration, stakeholders included university faculty from different institutions, school district personnel, classroom teachers, and tribal organizations. The three authors of this chapter are white university faculty members who taught classes in the graduate programs that were developed as a result of this collaborative work. All authors also served on graduate committees for participating teacher-researchers who conducted teacher action research projects and theses, which we discuss in this chapter. In addition, Siekmann (Linguistics Program, University of Alaska Fairbanks) served as co-director and Parker Webster (School of Education & Center for Cross-Cultural Studies, University of Alaska Fairbanks) was the evaluator on all of the grants, while Thorne (Department of World Languages and Literatures, Portland State University; Department of Applied Linguistics, University of Groningen) was a visiting faculty for two of the grants. The teacher-researchers work in various rural educational settings across the state and represent different linguistic and cultural backgrounds as well as a variety of language education models.

3 Literature Review

In this literature review, we discuss the Western pedagogical framework of multiliteracies (e.g., New London Group, 1996), Vygotskian sociocultural theory, and Indigenous ways of being-knowing-doing. We explain how these Western conceptual frameworks come together with Indigenous ways of being-knowing-doing to provide the ethico-onto-epistemological grounding for our work with teachers and language learners in the context of school-based language maintenance and revitalization efforts.

3.1 Multiliteracies

The projects discussed in this chapter draw on the pedagogical framework of multiliteracies (New London Group, 1996). Members of the New London Group observed that "the world was changing, the communications environment was changing, and it seemed to us to follow that literacy teaching and learning would have to change, as well" (Cope & Kalantzis, 2009, p. 165). According to Kalantzis and Cope (2008), these critical changes were due in part to "a technology revolution, which not only changes the way we work but also the way we participate as citizens" (p. 200). In order to allow full participation of culturally and linguistically diverse citizens in increasingly globalized societies, the New London Group (1996) argued for an expanded view of literacy and literacy pedagogy that values

Table 6.1 The "What" of Multiliteracies: Designs of Meaning

Available designs	Found and findable resources for meaning: culture, context, and purpose-specific patterns and conventions of meaning-making
Designing	The act of meaning: work performed on/with available designs in representing the world, or other's representations of it, to oneself or others
The redesigned	The world transformed, in the form of new available designs, or the meaning designer who, through the very act of designing, has transformed themselves (learning)

Source: Cope & Kalantzis (2009, p. 176).

multilingualism and multiple knowledge systems. This shift means that citizens in today's social, cultural, political, and economic world must be able to negotiate a variety of multimodal texts (Jewitt & Kress, 2008), which are situated within a socio-semiotic resources approach whereby meaning is constructed using multiple sign systems (e.g., images, gestures, music, mathematical symbols, etc.). Therefore, the "new literacies" of a multiliteracies pedagogy do not rely solely on the linguistic sign system to construct meaning (Cope & Kalantzis, 2000; Street, 1995). This concept of multiliteracies, therefore, reflects a dynamic notion of what a *text* is, allowing for meaning-making across multiple sign systems. Rather than ask what a child knows, we can ask how many ways are available for this child to know (Halliday, 1973).

The New London Group (1996) first utilized the design metaphor to explain multimodal and multilingual meaning-making processes of multiliteracies. As learners engage in the design process, they act as active designers of meaning rather than as passive recipients of knowledge. The three elements of the design process, *available designs*, *designing*, and *the redesigned*, are summarized by Cope and Kalantzis (2009) in Table 6.1.

Viewing available designs as discernable patterns situates these resources within observable actions that are always in flux. In addition to the notion of expanded texts that includes visual, oral, written, and multimodal representations, these patterns also include norms and values within various community and cultural activities. Available designs are always situated within sociocultural contexts. In the act of designing, the actor draws from a diverse and complex array of available designs to engage in the action of meaning-making. This act repositions the actor-designer as producing rather than reproducing knowledge, which draws upon an array of meaning-making resources in expressing their voice. Designing, therefore, is an act of transformation, which is the essence of learning. The redesigned is not only the physical-material designs (e.g., new visual, written, oral texts) but also the designer themself. In this way, the act of designing changes representations of meanings available to others and to oneself.

3.2 Sociocultural Theory

The New London Group brought together scholars from various academic disciplines who shared an orientation towards language, literacy, and learning as a socially situated and socially transformative activity, including Vygostkian sociocultural theorists (i.e., Courtney Cazden). Similarly, the authors of this chapter, in assembling our available designs, drew upon Vygotskian sociocultural theory of mind (Vygotsky, 1978b), which views human activity as goal directed, collaborative, and mediated by material and symbolic tools that are shaped and reshaped by the individuals and communities that use them. Tools such as digital technologies transform the way humans act on the world, and the cultures-of-use of tools/technologies evolve as they are used by individuals and communities (Thorne, 2003, 2016). While the appearance and use of digital technologies have been correlated to language shift to English in many traditionally Indigenous communities, a primary emphasis of the technology projects we describe in this chapter appropriate technologies to sustain and expand Native Alaska cultures and languages.

According to Vygotsky, human developmental processes, particularly in the contemporary era, involve technology-rich activity in the zone of proximal development (ZPD), which is described as "the distance between the actual developmental level as determined by independent problem solving and the level of potential development as determined through problem solving under adult guidance or in collaboration with more capable peers" (Vygotsky, 1978a, p. 86). One of Vygotsky's key insights is that collaborative learning, especially in instructional settings, precedes and shapes individual development. Deliberately designed learning environments, such as the use of digital technologies in the Alaska Native language educational settings we describe below, can prompt significant qualitative changes in development (Siekmann & Parker Webster, 2023). In these contexts, the ZPD functions not only as a model of the developmental process but also as a conceptual tool that language educators can utilize to understand, intervene, and amplify students' emerging capacities (i.e., when and how much assistance to provide). In this sense, the ZPD conceptually aligns with the Indigenous Yup'ik pedagogical approach of *upingakuneng* (when they are ready). In this approach, the teacher begins with expert-apprentice modelling of an activity, such as skin sewing. As she is modelling, she begins to talk aloud about what she is thinking, what steps she is taking, and what decisions she is making on how to resolve problems. During this time, students have an opportunity to observe an expert at work and see how her thought processes guide her practices. As each student feels ready, they move to their own work area and begin to do their own work, while the teacher continues working on her own project. If students decide they need help, they can go to the teacher's worktable to observe or ask for help (Lipka et al., 2005). In this model, the agency of when to begin working and when to seek assistance resides with the learner, and the teacher is always available to provide guidance as the more-knowledgeable expert.

Bringing these two Western epistemological and methodological frameworks together allows us to utilize sociocultural and multiliteracies approaches in complementary ways. First, using sociocultural theory and multiliteracies as available designs, together with Indigenous teacher-researchers, we developed an iterative and cyclical design process (first mentioned in Siekmann & Parker Webster, 2023, p. 31). We then explored a range of technology-mediated activities to create an array of available designs (see Figure 6.2). Teachers and learners utilized these available designs to establish multiple ZPDs. It is in this process that an available design can be amended based on its affordances and appropriateness to the goal-directed activity. Both product and process are redesigned as insights, and new understandings emerge interactively over time; subsequently, the redesigned become new available designs for subsequent design cycles.

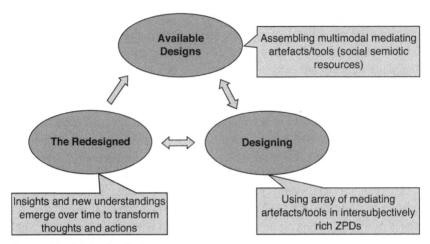

Figure 6.2 The Design Cycle
Source: Based on the design process as described by Cope and Kalantzis (2009, p. 176) and adapted from Siekmann and Parker Webster (2023, p. 31).

Because linguistically and culturally sustaining teaching-learning is the primary activity of our work with teachers and students in Alaska Native communities, we approach this process using a design cycle (Figure 6.2) that resonates with Indigenous ways of being-knowing-doing, which we describe below.

3.3 Indigenous Ways of Being-Knowing-Doing

In addition to the Western academic available designs we have presented, the teacher-researchers whose work is discussed in this chapter also drew on Indigenous ways of being-knowing-doing. While recognizing that there are local differences in the cultural traditions, knowledges, and practices across Indigenous communities, we focus this literature review on the elements of Indigenous ways of being-knowing-doing found in the broader literature by Indigenous scholars. The interrelated elements, which the teacher-researchers utilized as part of their array of available designs for their projects, include relatedness, land, the agentive nature of human and non-human aspects of the world, and traditional stories.

Engman and Hermes (2021) explain that, in the Anishinaabe worldview, "relationality is part of an Indigenous epistemology that organizes land, language, culture, and all living things in relation to each other" (p. 90). Furthermore, according to Watts (2013), Anishinaabe cosmology does not recognize hierarchies of agency. In other words, "relations with non-human agents are approached with no sense of superiority and with a focus on establishing ethical commitments to particular agents and communities of agents" (Rosiek et al., 2020, p. 338). Martin (2008) describes the Aboriginal worldview:

> It is this relatedness to these elements and not the elements in themselves that holds and affords agency. It is this coming to know the world, to understand relatedness to the elements in that world and how one is related to those elements that underscores Aboriginal worldviews. (p. 62)

In the Yup'ik worldview, *yuuyaraq*, this non-hierarchical relatedness is known as *pugtallgutkellriit*, which translates as "those who float together with a purpose" (Siekmann et al., 2019, p. 129). According to Chief Paul John, "this term is based on how a fishing net, like those used in subsistence fishing, is held up by a series of floats. To be efficient and in order to catch fish, all have to be on the same level, floating together" (as cited in Siekmann & Parker Webster, 2023, p. 133).

Another recurring theme in much of the literature on Indigenous knowledge systems is the centrality of the holistic and inseparable relationship between people, knowledge, and the land (McGregor, 2004). According to Battiste and Henderson (2000), "perhaps the closest one can get to describing unity in Indigenous knowledge is that knowledge is the expression of the vibrant relationships between people, their ecosystems, and other living beings and spirits that share their lands" (p. 42). According to Martin (2008), Australian Aboriginal language groups historically existed as nations, each having their own forms of cultural and social expression. Each language group was sustaining its ancestral estate, also referred to as Country:

> Country refers not only to land, but also to the elements within it, including animals, plants, climate, sky, waterways, land, and people ... Although Aboriginal groups are autonomous, most are equally interconnected for the purpose of looking after Country, the elements, and each other. (Martin, 2008, p. 60)

The discussion of land and relatedness by Indigenous scholars situates "living things" as going beyond the Western concept that reflects a human-dominated hierarchy of agency. Such "detailed explications of the relation between particularity, non-human agency, knowledge, thought, place, and being are ubiquitous in contemporary Indigenous studies literature … and is taken as a given" (Rosiek et al., 2020, p. 337). Relatedness, then, implies a relationship not only among human actors but also among humans, the land, and other non-human agents.[1]

Engman and Hermes (2021) explain that "local land is central to ways of knowing and being, thus it is also central to learning" (p. 87). They describe how Ojibwe immersion students learned in partnership with the land on forest walks with Ojibwe Elders, in which students, Elders, and the land actively engaged together in naming requests, relational knowing, and cooperative action.

Another recurring theme in the literature on Indigenous knowledge systems and Indigenous pedagogies is the centrality of stories in passing down cultural knowledge and values. "Stories are not just entertainment but also are ways through which elements (land etc.) express relatedness and identity. Stories represent deep knowledge rather than representation of information" (Martin, 2008, p. 62). Stories are tools that embody Indigenous ways of being-knowing-doing and serve as an intergenerational and relational methodology for teaching and learning language, cultural knowledge, and values. Martin (2008) explains the relatedness of all elements of Indigenous knowledge systems in stories:

---

1. See Rosiek et al. (2020) for a critique of Western new materialist theories. They argue in part: "Agent ontologies in Indigenous studies literature are well developed in many of the places where the new materialist agential realism literature is not. The current literature on agential realism in the Eurocentric canon is most frequently focused on justifying the idea of non-human agency against the grain of presumptions that the objects of our studies passively await our discovery and description. The language and assumptions underlying contemporary Indigenous philosophy, by way of contrast, often presume the existence of pervasive non-human agency. There is, therefore, less need to argue for agent ontologies against more mechanistic ontologies that have characterized Western thought for centuries. A greater portion of Indigenous scholarship focuses on working out specific performative and ethical implications of agent ontologies on their own terms" (p. 336).

"Knowledge occurs in knowing your stories of relatedness (ways of knowing) and respecting these stories (ways of being) and the ways this relatedness is expressed (ways of doing)" (p. 63). Just as land, animals, and other non-human elements have agency, stories are also viewed as living agents by many Indigenous communities (Rosiek et al., 2020). Similarly, Dr. Arevgaq Theresa John articulates the important epistemological-ontological-methodological significance of storytelling for Yup'ik people:

> The oral traditions of pre-contact time, when the earth's crusts were thin, were creation stories, ghost stories, and Shamanism. These teach the interconnectedness between the human and non-humans when they can become one, which is symbolized in the half man-half animal masks. If humans live accordingly by following cultural epistemic values, then they will earn their role to be good hunters. That is why animals reciprocate by giving themselves to the hunters, who earn their role by showing respect to the animal by taking good care of it. These stories, with their morals and lessons that pertain to our culturally systemic values, build the foundation to make us resilient in understanding our historical standpoint and our interconnected world view; so do our language, culture, ceremonies and our family kinship trees. The fundamental concept of being connected requires respect for one another. (as cited in Siekmann & Parker Webster, 2023, p. 117)

In the next section, we analyse four teacher-researcher projects focusing on the redesigned product and process through the lens of land, relatedness, and stories as elements framing technology as a tool for disrupting monoglossic and monolingual ideologies.

4 The Redesigned: Analysing the Relatedness of Technology and Indigenous Ways of Being-Knowing-Doing within the Design Cycle

Each discussion in this section foregrounds the aforementioned elements playing the most central role in the teachers' and students' design processes and how the redesigned (see Figure 6.2) contributes to an Indigenized curriculum for transformational teaching and learning using technology.

4.1 Decentring Monoculturality through Digital Storytelling

Sheila Wallace, a Yup'ik first language speaker and certified teacher, designed a Yup'ik class as an additional language class for middle and high school students in Bethel, the hub community of the Yukon-Kuskokwim Delta region. Sheila focused on developing a year-long multimedia language and culture class to counteract Yup'ik language attrition in students who were entering seventh grade after attending Yup'ik medium schools. The class was based on traditional story genres, including *qanruyutet* (words of wisdom) and *qulirat* (instruction on the traditional knowledge system), as well as songs, chants, and dance that are grounded in Indigenous ways of being-knowing-doing. Throughout the class, Sheila's students created several multimodal projects, including a public service announcement, a multimedia presentation, and digital stories based on research with local Elders.

While Sheila's students created a variety of Yup'ik medium resources throughout the semester, of particular relevance to disrupting English dominance in the public sphere are the public service announcements (PSAs) focusing on traditional Yup'ik knowledge and cultural practices that students produced in collaboration with local Elders. PSAs are important communication systems in rural communities in the Yukon-Kuskokwim Delta. Because of the isolation in rural Alaska, the radio is a lifeline, both for local and regional information. With ongoing language shift, almost all radio programming in Bethel, where Sheila teaches, is produced in English. Creating PSAs in Yup'ik provides meaningful models of language-in-use that are available publicly to the community, which disrupts English dominance in public broadcasting. Sheila is purposeful in designing experiences and outlets for authentic ways to use Western technology, such as the radio, in order to maintain and expand the visibility of Yup'ik language and knowledge in the region:

> I want my students to grow and achieve and be ambassadors for their language, their culture, and their communities ... In our Yukon-Kuskokwim area, the influx of technology through television, radio airwaves, and the internet has greatly influenced the increase in English language use. However, we can instead use the same technology tools used by our youth as a vehicle to promote the Yup'ik language by making them accessible online. (Wallace, 2010, p. 47)

In addition to creating public resources, such as PSAs, Sheila also articulated how the redesigned products would contribute to filling the gap in Yup'ik language materials:

> It is important to note that the Yup'ik multimedia curriculum uses technology as a tool to generate language rather than as a tool that teaches language, such as Rosetta Stone, for example. All final projects will be using technology as a production tool (i.e., iMovie, website, Podcast, etc.) using the Yup'ik language. What I hope results from this curriculum development is that, first, it gives students with proficiency and literacy skills in Yup'ik an opportunity to expand their language learning in an academic environment. I feel that these students have great potential for expanding their Yup'ik fluency through projects that help contribute to the preservation of our language while providing Yup'ik material for other teachers and learners of Yup'ik. (Wallace, 2010, pp. 57–58)

Sheila's use of stories as an integral part of the redesigning processes illustrates the disruption of the monoculturality of much of the Western curriculum in schools. For Sheila, bringing traditional Yup'ik storytelling into her available designs to create her redesign re-places stories at the centre in an Indigenized curriculum:

> Building this curriculum has taught me the important role of Yup'ik storytelling in our daily lives. I have learned how traditional storytelling shapes the lives of people. They teach about how one should conduct themselves in culturally appropriate ways. Fables and customs teach heavily on how animate and inanimate things should be handled, especially during hunting, gathering, and preparation of animals. (Wallace, 2010, p. 56)

4.2 Reclaiming and Retelling Stories using Technological Tools

Candace Branson also used Indigenous storytelling and culturally based activities as a tool for language preservation and revitalization, and as a pedagogical tool to teach language, culture, and values. Due to earlier contact with colonial languages, language shift in the Alutiiq region has severely disrupted intergenerational transmission of the language and traditional stories told in Alutiiq. While many stories, such as *unigkuat*, were lost outright, those that were preserved were often written down in languages other than Alutiiq (e.g., Russian and English). Candace, an adult learner of Alutiiq herself, began her instructional planning by collaborating with fellow language learners and Elders to reclaim the story of *Grouse Girl – Qateryuk* (Golder, 1907; see also Branson, 2015). Candace developed a four-week unit for her beginning Alutiiq language high school students in Kodiak, Alaska, which included an initial Elder-led discussion about the significance of storytelling, a multimodal telling of the story in Alutiiq, meaning and form–focused practice in the use of past tense, and students digitally recording their oral retelling of the story.

Candace started her process of designing from a stance that recognizes the historical role of schools in enforcing hegemonic linguistic and cultural practices aimed at eradicating Alaska Native languages and replacing them with English to assimilate Indigenous communities into Western monoglossic and monolingual ideologies. She describes how "one of our Elders remembers having to write 'I will not speak Alutiiq' on the chalkboard many days after school" (Branson, 2015, p. 3). While looking for traditional Alutiiq stories to use in her high school language class, Candace realized that the non-Alutiiq authors of extant versions of the stories had replaced the core cultural values and meanings based in Alutiiq ways of being-knowing-doing with Western ideologies:

> Golder, the ethnographer who first wrote down this particular story, was not an Alutiiq speaker ... [T]he stories were told in Russian and later translated and written in English from memory ... [which] most likely embellished and altered the story. He may not have included key cultural concepts, rituals, and story themes due to his cultural orientation and audience – the American public. (Branson, 2015, p. 17)

Candace and her fellow Alutiiq language learners, who identify themselves as "language warriors" (Branson, personal communication), committed to reclaiming their stories, not for the sole purpose of teaching language (words and grammar) but because they carried with them the voices of the ancestors passing down their Alutiiq knowledge and values.

> I wanted [my students] to understand why Alutiiq people had stories about animals transforming into a human and that these stories were not just for entertainment, but taught the world view, expectations of the community, social roles, and the difference between right and wrong. (Branson, 2015, p. 21)

By making this reclaimed story available to the public via the internet, Candace reconnected intergenerational lines for passing down this traditional story, which had been interrupted by colonial hegemonic monocultural and monoglossic ideologies and practices:

> Applying technology to the stories can make them available to a broader audience. The lesson unit I created only reaches 20 students a year, but a video of a traditional story can reach thousands in a number of days when shared widely. This can increase the number of authentic materials in Alutiiq in the community, as well as the accessibility of those materials. (Branson, 2015, p. 34)

The redesigned curriculum that Candace and her students developed around this particular story makes visible how Indigenous ways of being-knowing-doing can potentially bring about transformative change, transitioning from a Western-centric curriculum towards a more linguistically and culturally sustaining way of teaching and learning.

> The process and discussion validated that the current educational system is only one way of gaining knowledge and that the rest of our community's knowledge can be learned in other ways, including listening to our Elders, who often did not complete much American schooling ... The end result was the take home message that the participants left with, [which] was that our language, stories, process of mentorship, our family connections, traditional gatherings, ceremonies, competitions, travels and much more were all valid ways of learning. (Branson, 2015, pp. 24–25)

4.3 Reimagining Technology as a Tool for Passing Down Language through Cultural Practices

Sondra Shaginoff-Stuart worked with university students at the Kenai Peninsula College who, like herself, were second language learners of their ancestral language, Ahtna. Recognizing that the historical trauma of not being allowed to use the language in schools prompted her students' hesitancy to speak their ancestral language, she developed an Indigenous pedagogy for language teaching that emphasized healing and well-being. Using the cultural activity of beading, she created a series of language lessons grounded in the connectedness of Indigenous ways of being-knowing-doing. While planning her lessons, Sondra worked with her Elders to develop the language needed to teach the lessons to her students and to create instructional multimedia YouTube videos in Ahtna. These materials provided access to language used in the culturally based activity of beading, not only to language learners in Sondra's class but also to the larger community. Sondra used hands-on activities to teach students vocabulary related to beading and useful phrases to use as each student actively created their own beaded necklace. In a culminating activity, learners recorded their own instructional videos in Ahtna to teach others how to create a beaded necklace.

Colonialist monoglossic and monocultural ideologies have ruptured intergenerational transmission of Ahtna and most other Alaska Native languages. This rupture has resulted not only in language shift to English but also to the more tacit effects of trauma brought by these hegemonic practices, which is experienced by many members of Alaska Native communities. This underlying trauma was expressed by Sondra's students through their hesitancy to speak Ahtna, even in her language classroom. Sondra recognized that her teaching required a foregrounding of healing in order for her students to ready themselves for learning to use the language in the Western context of a university classroom. In her own healing and language learning process, Sondra learned from her Elders about the central role relatedness plays in Ahtna ways of being-knowing-doing, which she explains:

> My Aunt Katie would tell us that everything is alive, from a blade of grass to even a rock. The water, sky, trees and mountains are alive; in fact, the mountains are our people, and we experience them all around us through the environment and stories. (Shaginoff-Stuart, 2016, p. 12)

Sondra describes the connectedness and inseparability of good thoughts, a clear mind, and healing to her process of designing a culturally based language pedagogy:

> During this process of beading and writing, my Elders came to mind, Helen Dick from Lime Village, Jeanie Maxim of Gulkana, and my Aunt Katie, their prayers, discussions and memories to find our natural connections to activities to bring our languages to the sound world, not just to paper. This healing aspect of connection to words, sounds and activity is where the mind opens

to learn and feel safe to speak, and to express and live the culture. Cultural knowledge, such as what my Elders talk about here, is transmitted through these activities by recognizing that everything is alive and has meaning. (Shaginoff-Stuart, 2016, p. 39)

Since Elders are culture bearers and therefore living available designs (Siekmann & Parker Webster 2023), and because of the limited number of Ahtna Elders left who still speak the language, it is essential to preserve their voices and teachings using the language, cultural knowledge, and values so they can be passed down to future generations. As illustrated in Sondra's project, digital technology, such as iMovie, can be used as a tool to bring Elders' voices into the classrooms today and into the future.

The learners also developed the confidence not only to start using Ahtna in the classroom but also to create and record their own videos, which would be available online as examples of language in use or as what Sondra refers to as "living language":

> Students then apply what they learned by developing their own [beading] patterns and sharing the lesson with others in the classroom or outside of the class. This creates a living language that is used and reused, embedded in the items and the action of a living culture and experience. (Shaginoff-Stuart, 2016, p. 18)

Sondra's redesigned illustrates how speaking Indigenous languages within and beyond the classroom through the use of technology can be part of the healing process and adds to the available designs of limited resources in Indigenous languages. Additionally, making Ahtna medium materials available online disrupts the overwhelming prominence of dominant languages on the internet and creates a space for the Ahtna language-culture community.

4.4 Connecting Virtual and Physical Realms of Languages and Cultures through Mobile Augmented Reality Gaming

Natalie Cowley taught fifth/sixth grade English language arts in a dual language school located in the remote community of Kasigluq, where many families still use Yup'ik in everyday life. A non-Native educator, Natalie designed instruction and learning grounded in Yup'ik ways of being-knowing-doing through the cultural activities of storytelling and traditional practices and redesigned her literacy instruction using a mobile augmented reality (AR) game. Using a novel set in the Indigenous lands of the Yup'ik people, *A Raven's Gift* (Rearden, 2013), as the starting point, Natalie immersed her students in a post-apocalyptic world based on the premise that they had to learn how to survive after a strand of the avian flu swept through the Yup'ik region, destroying much of the modern infrastructure. Guided by a narrator in the mobile game, the students completed a series of quests that involved interviewing Elders to gain the necessary skills and knowledge for making shelter and clothing, hunting, and using medicinal plants. These activities also required students to use both Yup'ik and English, and culminated in students creating digital stories based on their experiences with the AR game, which are published online.

Even though students in dual language schools use two languages throughout the school day, the schools are still based on a monolingual ideology, separating each language into discrete instructional periods based on subject. For example, during English time (such as Math, English Language Arts, etc.), the language of instruction is restricted to English, and during Yup'ik time (Science and Yup'ik Language Arts), Yup'ik is the language of instruction. Since teachers on the "English side" are usually monolingual English speakers, but Yup'ik medium teachers are always bilingual in English and Yup'ik, the result is that the English periods are monolingual while in the Yup'ik portions of the curriculum, English is often used in addition to Yup'ik.

Natalie, a native speaker of English, disrupts the dominance of English language and Western knowledge by using Yup'ik language and culture as an explicit available design for students in her English Language Arts classroom. She further disrupts the monoglossic ideology of Standard (Academic) American English (SAE) by including Southwestern Alaska Regional English (often referred to as Village English) as an available design to use during game play.

> The storyline of the game is presented in SAE; however, the videos and audio of Elders are presented in Yugtun [the endonym for Yup'ik]. The students are able to discuss and take notes in Yugtun or in [Village English]. They then interview Elders using Yugtun, but their final journals and digital stories are in SAE with some inclusion of Yugtun. I wanted my project to show them that each language/dialect has a place and use in our classroom. (Cowley, 2015a, p. 7)

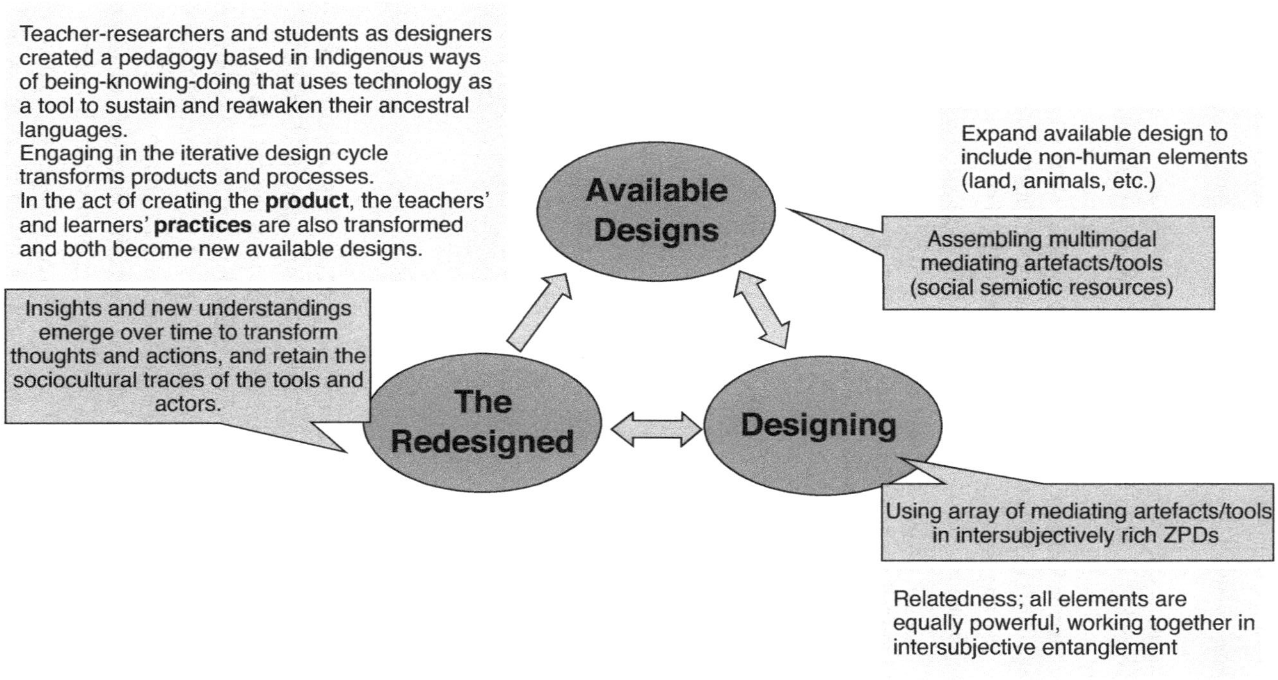

Expand available design to include non-human elements (land, animals, etc.)

Assembling multimodal mediating artefacts/tools (social semiotic resources)

Using array of mediating artefacts/tools in intersubjectively rich ZPDs

Relatedness: all elements are equally powerful, working together in intersubjective entanglement

Available Designs

Designing

The Redesigned

Teacher-researchers and students as designers created a pedagogy based in Indigenous ways of being-knowing-doing that uses technology as a tool to sustain and reawaken their ancestral languages.
Engaging in the iterative design cycle transforms products and processes. In the act of creating the **product**, the teachers' and learners' **practices** are also transformed and both become new available designs.

Insights and new understandings emerge over time to transform thoughts and actions, and retain the sociocultural traces of the tools and actors.

Figure 6.3 Our Redesigned Conceptual Framework

Source: The authors.

The following excerpt from Natalie's lesson plan describes how the students advance through the AR game:

> Have students discuss what they learned from the Elder on how to build a shelter. Then they need to draw a picture of how they would build a shelter using tarp and rope. Once students have taken a picture of their drawing, then have them grab a tarp, rope, and a pair of scissors. They will then go out behind the school to build their own shelter using the supplied materials and materials they find outside of the school. When done, they will record themselves explaining how they made their shelter and why.
>
> Students finish shelter. Then students get on Aris [the AR tool] to get the prompt to journal about how they survived the first week [of the pandemic in the novel] by using knowledge from Elders, so others may learn how to survive from them. (Cowley, 2015b, Teacher Guides section, Week 1)

Natalie designed the use of technology in such a way that Aris, the virtual platform used to build and play the mobile games, acts as a road map, prompting students to advance in their quests. However, the students complete the quests themselves on and in relationship with the land, using the material resources found in the natural world. The mobile device orchestrates her students' designing as they use their full array of available designs, including languages, cultures, and multiple modalities. In this way, technology is reframed as a vehicle and catalyst to engage with the local culture, knowledge, and environment.

5 Conclusion

These four inquiries each foreground Indigenous ways of being-knowing-doing through intergenerational collaborations among Elders, teachers, and students. From this ethico-onto-epistemological (Barad, 2007) grounding, the four featured teacher-researchers utilized Western pedagogical frameworks and technological tools that resonated with and were adapted to Indigenous pedagogies, allowing them to reclaim classrooms for Indigenous language learning. Specific instances of technology integration included the creation of instructional videos by Elders and students, digital storytelling, and a place-based mobile augmented reality game. All of these contribute to creating a living language, which in turn contributes to promoting more equitable conditions more equitable conditions for Indigenous language teachers and their students through capacity-building, decolonizing, and emancipatory practices.

In this chapter, we have discussed a number of available designs, including multiliteracies, sociocultural theory, Indigenous ways of being-knowing-doing, and the teacher-researchers' projects emerging from our work with language teachers who are all committed to supporting language pedagogies that utilize technology for linguistically and culturally sustaining language teaching. Figure 6.3 illustrates our redesigned conceptual framework, which expands Western available designs by drawing on elements from Indigenous ways of being-knowing-doing (relatedness, land, non-human agency, stories).

We expanded the notion of multimodal available designs and tools to include non-human elements. In our model, we articulate designing as constituted by relatedness among all elements (e.g., land, human–non-human, stories). In terms of the redesigned, we focus on how teacher-researchers-as-designers and their students-as-designers can use technology resources for designing instructional practices (such as digital storytelling, mobile augmented reality games, and online Indigenous language resources and teaching materials) that have the potential to transform technology from being a tool of language shift to English into a tool for mediating culturally and linguistically sustaining pedagogy.

About the Authors

Sabine Siekmann is professor of applied linguistics at the University of Alaska Fairbanks. Specializing in language pedagogy, she conducts largely collaborative research in the areas of bilingualism, Indigenous language maintenance and revitalization, second language teaching, computer-assisted language learning, and critical intercultural education. Siekmann's research is informed by cultural historical activity theory, teacher action research, and other critical approaches to language pedagogy and theory.

Joan Parker Webster is a retired associate professor of education at the University of Alaska Fairbanks (UAF), specializing in multiliteracies, critical pedagogy, and cross-cultural education. Currently, she is affiliated assistant professor in the UAF Center for Cross-Cultural Studies, primarily working within the Indigenous studies PhD program. She continues to work with teacher action research collaboratives in STEAM education and to conduct critical ethnographic research with Alaska Native communities and schools.

Steven L. Thorne is professor of second language acquisition in the Department of World Languages and Literatures at Portland State University (United States), with a secondary appointment in the Department of Applied Linguistics at the University of Groningen (Netherlands). His research interests include formative interventions in world languages education contexts, digital media and mobile technologies, Indigenous language reclamation, and investigations that draw upon sequential traditions of language analysis and usage-based approaches to language development.

References

Barad, K. (2007). *Meeting the universe halfway: Quantum physics and the entanglement of matter and meaning*. Duke University Press. https://doi.org/10.2307/j.ctv12101zq

Battiste, M., & Henderson, J.Y. (2000). *Protecting Indigenous knowledge and heritage*. Purich Publishing. https://doi.org/10.59962/9781895830439

Branson, C. (2015). Qulianguanek litnauwilita: Let's teach through stories [Unpublished master's project]. University of Alaska Fairbanks.

Cope, B., & Kalantzis, M. (2000). Designs for social futures. In B. Cope & M. Kalantzis (Eds.), *Multiliteracies: Literacy learning and the design of social futures* (pp. 203–234). Routledge. https://doi.org/10.4324/9780203979402

Cope, B., & Kalantzis, M. (2009). "Multiliteracies": New literacies, new learning. *Pedagogies: An International Journal, 4*(3), 164–195. https://doi.org/10.1080/15544800903076044

Cowley, N. (2015a). *Surviving Alaska* [Unpublished master's project]. University of Alaska Fairbanks.

Cowley, N. (2015b). *Surviving Alaska*. https://nataliecowleyakiuk.wixsite.com/indigenousfuturisms

Engman, M., & Hermes, M. (2021). Land as interlocutor: A study of Ojibwe learner language in interaction on and with naturally occurring "materials." *The Modern Language Journal, 105*(S1), 86–105. https://doi.org/10.1111/modl.12685

Freire, P. (2005). *Pedagogy of the oppressed*. Continuum International Publishing Group.

Golder, F.A. (1907). *Aleutian stories.* Alaska Native Language Archive. https://www.uaf.edu/anla/record.php?identifier=AL950B(B076)1907

Halliday, M.A.K. (1973). *Language as social perspective: Explorations in the functions of language.* Edward Arnold.

Jewitt, C., & Kress, G. (2008). *Multimodal literacy.* Peter Lang.

Kalantzis, M., & Cope, B. (2008). Language education and multiliteracies. In S. May & N. H. Hornberger (Eds.), *Encyclopedia of language and education* (2nd ed., Vol 1, pp. 195–211). Springer. https://doi.org/10.1007/978-0-387-30424-3_15

Krauss, M., Holton, G., Kerr, J., & West, C.T. (2011). Indigenous peoples and languages of Alaska [online map]. Alaska Native Language Center and UAA Institute of Social and Economic Research. https://www.uaf.edu/anla/collections/map/

Lipka, J., Sharp, N., Brenner, B., Yanez, E., & Sharp, F. (2005). The relevance of culturally based curriculum and instruction: The case of Nancy Sharp. *Journal of American Indian Education, 44*(3), 31–54. https://www.jstor.org/stable/24398496

Marlow, P., & Siekmann, S. (2013). *Communities of practice: An Alaska native model for language teaching and learning.* University of Arizona Press.

Martin, K. (2008). The intersection of Aboriginal knowledges, Aboriginal literacies, and new learning pedagogy for Aboriginal students. In A. Healy (Ed.), *Multiliteracies and diversity in education: New pedagogies for expanding landscapes* (pp. 58–81). Oxford University Press.

McGregor, D. (2004). Coming full circle: Indigenous knowledge, environment, and our future. *American Indian Quarterly, 28*(3/4), 385–410. https://doi.org/10.1353/aiq.2004.0101

New London Group. (1996). A pedagogy of multiliteracies: Designing social futures. *Harvard Educational Review, 66*(1), 60–92. https://doi.org/10.17763/haer.66.1.17370n67v22j160u

Rearden, D. (2013). *The raven's gift.* Penguin Books.

Rosiek, J.L., Snyder, J., & Pratt, S.L. (2020). The new materialism and Indigenous theories of non-human agency: Making the case for respectful anti-colonial engagement. *Qualitative Inquiry, 26*(3–4), 331–346. https://doi.org/10.1177/1077800419830135

Shaginoff-Stuart, S. (2016). Łinay'sdułkaas de': Let's start sewing [Unpublished master's project]. University of Alaska Fairbanks.

Siekmann, S., & Parker Webster, J. (2023). *Multiliteracies pedagogy and language teaching: Stories of praxis from Indigenous communities.* Springer. https://doi.org/10.1007/978-3-031-31812-2

Siekmann, S., Parker Webster, J., Samson S.A., Moses, C.K., John-Shields, P.A., & Wallace, S.C. (2019). Pugtallgutkellriit: Developing researcher identities in a participatory action research collaborative. *Journal of American Indian Education, 58*(1–2), 124–145. https://doi.org/10.5749/jamerindieduc.58.1-2.0124

Street, B. (1995). *Social literacies: Critical approaches to literacy in development, ethnography and education.* Routledge. https://doi.org/10.4324/9781315844282

Thorne, S.L. (2003). Artifacts and cultures-of-use in intercultural communication. *Language Learning & Technology, 7*(2), 38–67. https://pdxscholar.library.pdx.edu/wll_fac/19/

Thorne, S.L. (2016). Cultures-of-use and morphologies of communicative action. *Language Learning & Technology, 20*(2), 185–191. https://doi.org/10125/44473

Vygotsky, L.S. (1978a). Internalization of higher psychological functions. In L.S. Vygotsky, *Mind in society: The development of higher psychological processes* (M. Cole, V. John-Steiner, S. Scribner, & E. Souberman, Eds., pp. 52–57). Harvard University Press. https://doi.org/10.2307/j.ctvjf9vz4.9

Vygotsky, L.S. (1978b). *Mind in society: The development of higher psychological processes* (M. Cole, V. John-Steiner, S. Scribner, & E. Souberman, Eds.). Harvard University Press. https://doi.org/10.2307/j.ctvjf9vz4

Wallace, S. (2010). *Multimedia curriculum mapping: A tool for task based authentic second language teaching and learning through technology* [Unpublished master's project]. University of Alaska Fairbanks.

Watts, V. (2013). Indigenous place-thought and agency amongst humans and non-humans (First woman and sky woman go on a European world tour!). *Decolonization: Indigeneity, Education & Society, 2*(1), 20–34. https://jps.library.utoronto.ca/index.php/des/article/view/19145

7 Developing an Interactive AI-Based Spoken Dialogue System for Improving Oral Proficiency in Indonesian and Burmese

Rahmi H. Aoyama, Maw Maw Tun, and Reza Neiriz

1 Introduction

Frequent opportunities to engage in the target language are crucial for improving oral communication skills among language learners (Loewen & Sato, 2018). As the primary goal of language learning is to communicate in real life, promoting speaking skills plays an essential role in language development. Despite its importance, one challenge is the limited interactional opportunities for language learners to practise the language outside the classroom (Pawlak et al., 2011), especially for less commonly taught languages (LCTL) learners. In addition to limited exposure to LCTL speakers, there is a need to have more resources available for learners, as only a limited number of universities across the United States offer LCTL programs. For instance, only three universities offer courses in Burmese, and fewer than 10 universities in the United States offer courses in Indonesian. This scarcity of academic programs, limited resources, and extracurricular interaction opportunities hinders learners' ability to achieve proficiency and fully immerse themselves in the target language outside of class time. Consequently, there is a need for more resources to improve oral proficiency, providing opportunities for learners to practise and interact in their target language outside of the classroom setting.

Minimal resources are available for learners of Indonesian and Burmese, as LCTLs. More importantly, all the available resources, including apps and web-based platforms, focus primarily on vocabulary, useful phrases, script writing, reading, and listening skills. For Indonesian learners, some open web-based resources, such as Ayo Membaca (https://ayomembaca.wisc.edu/), Warung Sinema (http://warungsinema.wisc.edu/), Beginning

Indonesian (https://web.uvic.ca/lancenrd/indonesian/), and Indonesian-Pod101 (https://www.indonesianpod101.com/), concentrate on reading, listening, and vocabulary. Similarly, most Burmese resources are also limited to vocabulary (e.g., the Simply Learn Burmese app and Learn Burmese, https://ilanguages.org/burmese.php) and writing script (e.g., SEAsite, https://seasite.niu.edu/; and Learn to Read Burmese Script on the Asia Pearl website, https://www.asiapearltravels.com/language/lesson33.php). The University of Maryland recently created a mobile-based app named Lectia! (https://nflc.umd.edu/projects/lectia) for several languages, including Indonesian and Burmese. However, all the lessons provided in Lectia! solely focus on reading and listening materials for intermediate and advanced learners. Unfortunately, Indonesian and Burmese language learners have limited spoken technological resources for out-of-class uses. Therefore, the project described here aims to develop the first interactive artificial intelligence (AI)–based spoken dialogue system (SDS) for Indonesian and Burmese learners.

Alongside recent technological developments, SDS has emerged as an alternative tool to address the lack of opportunities for practising learners' spoken skills. The SDS innovation creates the impression of conversing with other language learners and offers opportunities to practise the language repetitively. Previous studies also indicated that learners and teachers believed that automatic speech recognition (ASR)–based learning systems offer different exercises that encourage learners to speak in a low-anxiety environment (Chen, 2011; Timpe-Laughlin et al., 2022). Despite the potential use of SDS to improve language learners' oral skills, there are no SDS oral proficiency development materials for the LCTLs of Indonesian and Burmese. The interinstitutional project featured in this chapter describes the development of interactive AI-based SDS oral proficiency development materials that beginning learners can use to enhance their speaking skills, as well as the results of a pilot study on learners' perception of using SDS when learning Indonesian and Burmese.

With the aim of promoting oral proficiency resources for Indonesian and Burmese language learners, two instructors specializing in languages at Northern Illinois University (NIU) and a linguist from Iowa State University started this collaborative SDS project. After joining the Language Assessment Research Conference (LARC) in Chicago in 2022, Rami Aoyama learned about using AI-based SDS as an assessment tool in many languages. The idea to utilize an AI-based SDS to provide opportunities for language learners to practise, instead of being used as an assessment tool, came up as an alternative to help LCTL learners improve their oral proficiency, as well as to address the need for creating spoken proficiency resources.

As limited resources for LCTLs are a common issue, Aoyama invited Maw Maw Tun, a PhD student in instructional design currently teaching Burmese at NIU, to collaborate. They recognized that collaboration across two languages for developing AI-based spoken resources would be a pioneering effort to strengthen the LCTL and language studies field. In need of an SDS expert, Aoyama contacted Reza Neiriz, one of the presenters during the LARC conference, and discussed the possibilities of creating an AI-based SDS for Indonesian. Neiriz's current research focuses on measuring interactional competence through SDS. Neiriz thought this project was aligned with his vision of promoting AI-based technology in languages, especially for LCTLs. Having the same vision for promoting accessibility and oral proficiency resources for all beginning Indonesian and Burmese learners, the team members see this collaboration as a breakthrough to improve students' language skills and hope other LCTL instructors will use this technology to facilitate oral language development.

1.1 The Use of AI-Based SDS in Language Development

According to sociocultural theory by Vygotsky (1978), language acquisition is not only an individual cognitive process but is also shaped by the social and cultural environment in which it takes place. Vygotsky highlighted that learning is a mediated process, where cultural tools, such as language, are central to cognitive development. Lantolf (2006) elaborated on Vygotsky's ideas, stating that language learning occurs through social interaction and collaboration rather than merely through individual cognitive processes. This perspective shifts the focus from the isolated learner to the dynamic interactions between learners and their social environment. Studies have indicated that interaction plays a crucial role in language development, especially in enhancing oral proficiency skills (Lyster & Saito, 2010; Mackey & Goo, 2007). Despite the importance of interaction in language development, learners of LCTLs face the issue of limited opportunities to engage in the target language outside the classroom.

In order to increase learners' opportunities to practise communication in the target language, the team decided to explore the use of SDS technology. SDS is considered a viable alternative tool to practise language as it allows learners to converse with the system (as if interacting with a speaker of the target language) without limitations, providing accessibility from any location and receiving individualized feedback (Doremalen et al., 2016; Fryer et al., 2019). By utilizing SDS, learners are afforded the opportunity to practise the target language repeatedly, at their convenience and in their chosen environment. This increased access to engaging in the target language can contribute to the improvement of language learning outcomes, as learners acquire language through frequent interactions in various social situations, promoting language development (Lantolf et al., 2015; Vygotsky, 1978).

The use of SDS also has the potential to create a more enjoyable learning environment for learners who suffer from anxiety when speaking. Studies by Anderson et al. (2008), Johnson (2019), and Bashori et al. (2021) have indicated that SDS offers an alternative mode of interaction that lowers anxiety for learners. Bashori et al. (2021) conducted the study on learners' perspective on practising English with SDS. Practising with SDS has been shown to provide a fun and enjoyable learning experience, largely due to the fact that learners feel less worried about making mistakes when conversing with the conversation engine. These systems create a low-pressure environment where learners can practise their speaking skills without fear of judgment or immediate criticism, which is often present in traditional classroom settings. The conversational nature of SDS allows learners to build confidence gradually, making the overall language learning process more effective and enjoyable.

2 Developing an AI-Based SDS

2.1 Dialogue Development

Developing the AI-based SDS for Indonesian and Burmese included three phases: (1) dialogue development, (2) prototype development, and (3) prototype testing. The first phase, dialogue development, involved selecting role-play scenarios for the SDS prototype. During this initial phase, the two researchers, who are also language instructors, brainstormed scenarios targeting Novice Low to Novice High proficiency levels. The rationale for selecting novice levels is based on the observation that novice-level learners often encounter significant challenges in finding opportunities to practise speaking and listening skills, as most resources for speaking and listening are written in higher level language. By focusing on beginners, the SDS aims to provide essential support in building foundational language skills, thereby helping learners gain confidence and advance to higher proficiency levels more effectively.

The current project focused on developing simple daily conversation scenarios: (a) introducing oneself, (b) ordering food at a café, and (c) describing one's place. According to the American Council on the Teaching of Foreign Languages (ACTFL) *Proficiency Guidelines* (ACTFL, 2012), novice learners are able to communicate in highly predictable everyday routines. Therefore, common daily conversations were selected. Following the scenario selection, each instructor crafted a dialogue reflecting real-world conversations and provided feedback on each other's work. The SDS dialogues and strategies were selected and evaluated using the ACTFL guidelines to ensure the level of the text, linguistic features, content, context, and appropriateness for the selected proficiency level.

2.2 Prototype Development

During the second phase, the prototype development, three AI-based SDS prototypes were developed for pilot testing. These prototypes followed a simplified architecture comprising three significant components: ASR, dialogue manager, and text to speech (TTS). All three collaborators started with the coding for each role-play scenario to develop the prototype for the second phase. After the coding was developed and tested in each language, SDS expert collaborator Neiriz created two conversation engines mainly using regular expressions for the Indonesian and Burmese languages. After testing the conversation engines in the browser in written chat form, the conversation engines were converted into two Node.JS back-end models to meet web server application requests. In addition, the Google Cloud Speech-to-Text and TTS application programming interfaces (APIs) were added to the web application. The entire web application was deployed on a virtual private server running a Debian distribution of Linux called Bullseye 11. Linux is an open source operating system that is widely used for server applications. Linux has different variations, called distributions, which are designed for different purposes. Each distribution is identified by a name and a number. Bullseye 11 is the particular version of Linux that the server in this study used.

Node.JS was used to design the back end of this interface. This lightweight, scalable back-end JavaScript framework is especially suitable for small-scale projects. The front end was designed using HTML5, JavaScript, and Bootstrap. The browser's audio API captured and sent the audio to the back end. In the case of the Indonesian language, which had TTS and ASR available, the audio was sent to Google ASR, and the transcript was obtained. The transcript was then run through the back end's regular expression algorithm to choose the appropriate response. Once the appropriate response was chosen, it was sent to Google TTS for an audio file. The audio file was sent to the front end, and the browser immediately played it. An animated face created in Scalable Vector Graphics (SVG) format was played while the response was playing to create the visual impression of speech. All these happened in a fraction of a second. In the case of Burmese, since there was no reliable ASR or TTS, a Wizard of Oz approach was used. This approach sends the audio directly to an instructor interface through WebSocket technology. WebSocket technology allows real-time data exchange between two users that are managed by a server, such as Node.JS, in this case. When the student completed recording the utterance, it was sent to the server, which was immediately forwarded to the instructor's interface. The audio was played immediately, and the instructor chose a response by clicking on a list of available responses. Once the response was clicked, the pre-recorded audio was sent to the student to play. This method had some latency, depending on how fast the instructor chose the response. However, the audio exchange between users happened in a fraction of a second.

It is important to note that, at the second stage, the researchers noticed that Google's ASR for Burmese was extremely inaccurate and could not transcribe even a native speaker's speech accurately. Due to the lack of a viable alternative and the process involved in developing an ASR, the researchers decided to use a Wizard of Oz design. In this design, instead of using an ASR, the instructor received the audio responses from the participants in real time and selected the appropriate responses from a list that was populated based on the original dialogue manager. This method kept everything comparable to a fully automated system. The Wizard of Oz prototype development process will be explained in detail in the next section.

2.3 Prototype Testing

The final phase, prototype testing, involved testing the prototype with Indonesian and Burmese instructors before its launch to students. During each prototype testing session, instructors noted any computer responses that did not align with the role-play situations or any alternative options that could be used as answers. Based on the findings from these tests, the team made necessary adjustments to the prototype, both in terms of responses (for both users and system) and in terms of the interface to make them more user friendly. Initially, the prototypes were designed with the computer system waiting for students' responses before proceeding. However, after testing, a "speak" button was integrated into the interface design to allow students to initiate their responses at their own pace, fostering a more inclusive and flexible interaction model. Adding the speak button accommodates the diverse needs of all users, making it accessible to those who may need additional time, such as students with disabilities or those who process information at different speeds. It also provides flexibility, allowing users to interact with the system in a way that suits their individual needs. The speak button lets students control the pace of their interaction.

After all collaborators were satisfied with the prototypes' dialogue and interface, having conducted extensive tests that confirmed the prototypes met the desired standards of usability and functionality, the developed prototype was shared for testing with two other LCTL instructors who teach Indonesian and Burmese in the United States. Based on the testing process and feedback on the responses and speech comprehension, the team members repeatedly reviewed and edited the tasks to enhance the prototypes.

2.4 Burmese Prototype Development Issues

Since it was not possible to rely on an ASR system to transcribe participant responses in Burmese, a Wizard of Oz system was designed. This system employed two interfaces, one for the participant and the other for the instructor. The participant interface was exactly the same as the ASR-based system. It presented the computer turns produced through the TTS system. However, instead of using ASR to find keywords in the participants' responses in the dialogue manager, the response was routed to the instructor's interface in real time using WebSocket technology. The instructor heard the participants' speech without delay and chose the appropriate response from a list on their interface. All the responses were prewritten based on the dialogue plan to maintain maximum comparability with the ASR-based system. The response played without delay on the participants' interface when the instructor hit the "send" button. The only delay in this approach was the time the instructor spent listening to each participant's speech and choosing and sending responses. This time was almost negligible with the ASR-based system, as the participants' responses were analysed and the appropriate response was produced almost immediately. Nevertheless, the participants might have expected a delay in the Wizard of Oz system due to the processing time required by the computer, which is actually common in everyday voice assistant systems such as Siri or Alexa.

3 Conducting the Pilot Study on the Prototypes

As this project is the first SDS prototype development for LCTLs, it is important to understand learners' experiences with SDS and their perspectives. Therefore, we conducted a pilot study to understand learners' experiences using SDS and to identify its strengths and weaknesses. The initial pilot study focused on two main questions:

1. What were the students' perceptions of using SDS when learning LCTL (Indonesian and Burmese)?
2. What did the students perceive as strengths and limitations of using SDS tasks when practising their oral SDS exercises?

3.1 Participants and Context

Following the initial development phases, a pilot study was conducted on three prototypes with 29 students studying Indonesian and Burmese at NIU. The study included 23 Indonesian students and 6 Burmese students. The smaller number of Burmese language learner participants relates to enrolment trends; enrolment in the Burmese program has declined since the coup in Myanmar, as students with research interests in Myanmar experience travel complications when collecting data there. The World Languages and Cultures program at NIU offers various languages, including Indonesian and Burmese. These five-credit-hour courses involve both face-to-face and virtual meetings weekly. The students are a mix of undergraduate and graduate students, aged 18 to 30. The students include non-heritage learners from diverse departments such as anthropology, political science, history, psychology, education, law, and business. Their reasons for taking Indonesian and Burmese classes are diverse, ranging from personal interest to fulfilling scholarship requirements and fulfilling language requirements for undergraduate studies. Participants were at the beginning and intermediate levels, with limited prior exposure to Indonesian and Burmese. They had limited opportunities to engage in the target language outside of class due to the limited availability of resources and opportunities to practise speaking in Indonesian and Burmese. Therefore, this collaborative project aimed to increase learners' accessibility to oral interaction outside the classroom.

3.2 SDS Tasks

For the current study, three SDS prototypes (introducing yourself, ordering food at a café, and describing your house) were developed. The researchers demonstrated the navigation of the SDS before the students engaged in the tasks. During the data collection phase, participants were situated in a quiet environment. Equipped with headphones and a computer, they engaged in the assigned tasks. Each task took between 5 and 10 minutes. To engage in the task, learners first read the context and communicative objective of the task. For example, when users engaged in Task 2, ordering food at a café, they were given the following instructions: "You are at a café in Indonesia. Order one drink and one food item from the menu given below." The instructions were accompanied by the food menu. This activity required learners to listen and respond to short questions that are characteristic of the highly routinized interaction involved in placing an order at a coffee shop (Figure 7.1).

Once the students started, they could see the avatar, depicted in Figure 7.2, as a simple face, functioning as a human counterpart in the dialogues.

Kopi cita rasa Indonesia

Jenis Kopi	Panas	Dingin
Kopi Tubruk	25k	27k
Kopi Hitam	20k	22k
Kopi Susu	25k	25k
Kopi Jahe	20k	23k
Kopi Luwak	21k	23k
Kopi Tarik	25k	27k

Figure 7.1 Task Description for Ordering Coffee

Test Page for Indonesian Conversation

Click on "Say" button and then say your turn. Once you are done, click "Stop."

Figure 7.2 First Screen of the Indonesian SDS

After students clicked the "Start Conversation" button on the first screen, the computer asked the first question to the student. Users must then respond to the computer on the second screen (Figure 7.3). When ready to answer, students hit the "Say" button and "Stop" when they are finished responding.

The computer repeated the corresponding question three times when students provided incorrect answers. The computer progressed to the subsequent question if students provided incorrect answers three times

Figure 7.3 Second Screen of the Indonesian SDS

consecutively. The computer seamlessly proceeded to the next set of questions in the event of a correct answer. Throughout this process, audio recordings of the students were made. It is important to note that the procedure remained consistent across all three prototypes.

3.3 Procedure

Following ethical research procedures, participants were informed about the research study and recruited voluntarily. After engaging with three SDS tasks, the participants ($n = 29$) completed an online survey, eliciting feedback on their interactions with the SDS. The survey was designed to assess participants' perspectives on the perceived difficulty level, SDS interface, user experience, and language development during their engagements with the SDS avatar. The survey instrument was adapted from Ericsson et al. (2023).

Twelve out of the 29 participants initially volunteered to partake in in-depth interviews, and 8 were later interviewed. These guided interviews were conducted to delve deeper into their experiences using SDS and their perspectives on its strengths and weaknesses. All the interviews were conducted within one week of completing the SDS tasks, with each interview lasting 30 to 40 minutes.

3.4 Data Analysis

In order to explore the students' perceptions of using SDS when learning LCTLs (Indonesian and Burmese) and the strengths and limitations of using SDS tasks when practising their oral SDS exercises, surveys and semi-structured interviews were conducted. The survey data were analysed through descriptive statistics.

The interview transcripts were analysed employing the thematic analysis methodology as outlined by Braun and Clarke (2021). Initially, the two researchers independently identified significant textual segments and generated initial codes. The intercoder reliability across all codes was calculated to be 89 per cent. Subsequently, both researchers collaboratively reviewed and refined the initial codes and subcodes, systematically categorizing them to identify recurring themes and patterns within the data. In relation to research questions, four main themes were developed based on the interview data: learners' perceptions of the SDS interface, user experience, interaction with the SDS, and language development.

4 Research Findings

4.1 Learner Perceptions about SDS-Perceived Task Difficulty, Ease of Use of Interface with an Avatar, and Degree of Language Development

To investigate learners' perception of SDS, survey responses were analysed using descriptive analysis. The survey focused on four parts: the perceived difficulty of the task, SDS interface, user experience, and language development. The initial segment of the survey concentrated on the overall experience of utilizing SDS and the perceived difficulty of tasks within the SDS at the participants' proficiency levels, encompassing five questions. Regarding the difficulty of speaking Indonesian/Burmese with an avatar, the majority expressed ease of use, with 51.7 per cent rating it as easy and 31 per cent finding it very easy (see Table 7.1). There was no significant difference among the three tasks, with the majority

Table 7.1 Learners' Perception of Difficulty (N = 29)

	Percentage (%)				
Item	Very Easy	Easy	Not So Easy	Difficult	Very Difficult
Overall experience	44.8	48.3	6.9	0	0
Rate how challenging/easy it was to speak Indonesian/Burmese with an avatar	31.0	51.7	13.8	3.4	0
Task 1	48.3	51.7	0	0	0
Task 2	44.8	48.3	6.9	0	0
Task 3	41.4	44.8.	13.8	0	0

Table 7.2 Learners' Perception of the SDS Interface (N = 29)

	Percentage (%)				
Item	Very Friendly	Friendly	Neutral	Not So Friendly	Unfriendly
Overall design	65.5	31.0	3.5	0	0
Avatar	55.2	37.9	6.9	0	0
Button	75.9	20.7	3.4	0	0

indicating the tasks as easy to do, whereas only 6.9 per cent rated Task 2 as not so easy.

Regarding the interface, the survey explored learners' perspectives on the overall design, the utilization of the avatar, and the use of simple buttons through three questions utilizing a five-level Likert scale: (1) Very friendly, (2) Friendly, (3) Not so friendly, (4) Difficult, (5) Very difficult. According to the survey results (Table 7.2), the majority of students indicated that the design, encompassing the avatar and buttons, was friendly, with fewer than 7 per cent expressing a neutral opinion.

The learners' user experience was investigated through seven questions, shown in Tables 7.3 and 7.4 below.

Regarding the ease of speaking with an avatar (Table 7.3), the majority reported no difficulties in practising speaking with the SDS, with 55.2 per cent finding it very easy and 41.4 per cent considering it easy. Concerning

Table 7.3 User Experience: Ease of Speaking with an Avatar (N = 29)

Item	Percentage (%)				
	Very Easy	Easy	Not So Easy	Difficult	Very Difficult
How easy is it to speak with an avatar?	55.2	41.4	3.4	0	0
How easy is it to understand an avatar when it speaks the target language with you?	51.7	41.4	6.9	0	0
How easy is it to make yourself understood verbally in Indonesian/Burmese with an avatar?	51.7	48.3	0	0	0

understanding the avatar speaking the target language, 51.7 per cent found it very easy, with a similar percentage for making oneself understood verbally in Indonesian/Burmese.

The comfort level (Table 7.4) was also high, with 86.2 per cent being comfortable speaking with the avatar, while only 3.4 per cent indicated feeling uncomfortable. When comparing online interactions with avatars to classroom conversations, 79.3 per cent of participants indicated they felt equally or more comfortable online. Interestingly, a significant 69 per cent of participants indicated they felt a social relationship with the avatar during conversations, suggesting that the interactions were similar to face-to-face conversations. Lastly, 48.3 per cent indicated that speaking with the avatar was as comfortable as having a conversation with a real human being in a similar situation.

In terms of potential language development (see Table 7.5), 82.8 per cent either totally agreed or agreed that it would help them improve, with only 17.2 per cent expressing neutrality or disagreement. Additionally, when asking about specific language skills, a majority – 58.6 per cent – stated that

Table 7.4 User Experience: Comfort Level (N = 29)

Comfort Level	Percentage (%)		
	Comfortable	Neutral	Uncomfortable
How comfortable (natural) do you feel speaking with the avatar?	86.2	10.3	3.4
How comfortable (natural) do you feel speaking with the avatar online in comparison to speaking with someone in the classroom?	79.3	20.7	0
To what extent do you feel a social relationship with the avatar (when you are in contact with each other) during the conversations?	69.0	31.0	0
To what extent do you experience that speaking with the avatar is like speaking with a real human being in a similar situation?	48.3	41.4	10.3

SDS contributes to the improvement of both speaking and listening skills, while 27.6 per cent expressed total agreement and 51.7 per cent expressed agreement concerning pronunciation.

4.2 Learner Perceptions about SDS Providing Practice Speaking in the Target Language

Regarding the interface design of SDS, all eight interview participants stated that the SDS interface and design were user friendly and intuitive, as only two buttons ("say" and "stop") appeared on the screen. When describing the SDS interface, participants frequently employed terms such as "easy to navigate," "simple and easy," and "user friendly." The straightforward layout facilitated participants' navigation, particularly during their initial use of SDS to practise the target language. The absence of intricate

Table 7.5 Language Development (N = 29)

Item	Percentage (%)				
	Totally Agree	Agree	Neither Agree Nor Disagree	Disagree	Totally Disagree
Indonesian/Burmese language in general	41.4	41.4	17.2	0	0
Speaking skills	58.6	41.4	0	0	0
Listening skills	58.6	41.4	0	0	0
Pronunciation	27.6	51.7	20.7	0	0

features rendered the SDS system more accessible, eliminating potential distractions associated with understanding its functionalities.

Regarding potential improvements for interface design, three participants (ID 01, ID 05, ID 07) recommended incorporating a more human-like avatar, suggesting that such an enhancement could improve the naturalism of conversations. ID 01 articulated her perspective: "A simple avatar works, but, you know, I am a very visual person. Seeing a more human-like avatar would help. It would make me feel like communicating more naturally. It will help people like me" (February 20, 2024). The avatar's appearance warrants careful consideration in developing future SDS tasks.

In terms of using SDS, all interview participants expressed it as a positive experience, using the words "enjoyable" and "fun." The affirmative reactions were primarily rooted in the novel opportunities afforded by SDS for language practice, particularly in the context of the Indonesian and Burmese languages. A participant expressed enthusiasm, stating, "This is really cool. We rarely have a chance to practise Burmese outside the classroom. Engaging in simple conversations helps a lot, especially for beginning-level students" (ID 03, February 22, 2024). All participants seemed to be glad to have viable opportunities to practise the language outside the classroom.

In addition to the positive experience of using SDS, most participants conveyed a sense of engaging in a natural conversation with the avatar, attributing this sense to the system's naturalistic tones and regular pacing. Five participants said they were pleasantly surprised by the responses' naturalistic accuracy and the voice's pacing – neither too fast nor too slow.

However, ID 02 mentioned that it was too quick for her. Most interview participants noted that the voice from the SDS prototype sounded realistic and easy to understand. One participant mentioned, "I was very surprised with the voice. It sounds very realistic and easy to understand" (ID 08, February 28, 2024). ID 07 echoed a similar opinion: "I was surprised that the computer could pick up and respond to everything I said. I felt like having a conversation" (February 26, 2024).

The system's requests to repeat when the participant's speech is unclear and the participant's ability to seek repetition of a question from SDS also seemed more naturalistic for the learners. ID 06 enjoyed the interactive feature of SDS, stating, "I felt like it was a natural conversation; SDS asked me to repeat when it was unclear. That made me feel like it was natural" (February 26, 2024). Similarly, ID 03 expressed, "I like it, especially when I can ask to repeat when I am unclear; it feels like a natural conversation in some way." These instances highlighted participants' perception of a sense of presence while engaging in interactive conversations with SDS, given that SDS could understand and respond similarly to discussions with peers.

4.3 Learner Perception about Potential Increase in Language Development

In terms of language development, the participants expressed positive sentiments about the prototype as a great tool for them to increase their speaking and listening levels. ID 05 mentioned, "I believe if I use this prototype regularly as a homework, my speaking and listening ability will enhance" (February 25, 2024). Similarly, ID 03 articulated her perspective: "This would be such a valuable tool to enhance my speaking skills. It could significantly benefit me in preparation for oral exams." SDS emerges as a viable instrument, offering additional opportunities for oral language practice to enhance proficiency skills for LCTL languages such as Indonesian and Burmese.

In terms of the overall experience, nine out of twelve participants agreed that they had a positive experience without encountering any significant challenges, and they enjoyed using SDS to practise their language skills. The participants uniformly acknowledged the utility of SDS in fostering language improvement, particularly in the domains of listening and speaking. However, three participants also mentioned facing technical challenges, such as SDS crashing, longer processing times, and needing to speak louder for the computer to capture their voices.

5 Discussion

Both survey data and qualitative interview data indicated that most students have had a positive experience using SDS without facing significant content or technical issues. Most students reported that they liked the simple interface, reporting ease of use without confusion or nervousness due to intricate functions. Generally, they expressed that SDS could be a tool that helps improve their speaking and listening skills. The positive attitude of learners towards SDS speaking activities also echoes previous studies (Ericsson et al., 2023; Liao, 2009). Similarly, the current study also indicated that students enjoyed using SDS because they can engage in speaking tasks, allowing them to express themselves and receive immediate feedback, which can be a rare opportunity for LCTL learners outside the classroom.

In terms of the strengths and weaknesses of using SDS for oral proficiency practice, learners expressed diverse opinions. One of the strengths of the current SDS prototype is that learners feel like they are experiencing a semblance of human-like conversation. Contrary to findings in prior studies (Bibauw et al., 2019; Jeon, 2022), which suggested that SDS had limited ability to comprehend learner utterances and lacked negotiation capabilities, resulting in conversations that felt less human-like, the current study reveals that students reported a sense of naturalness in the conversation, encompassing aspects such as voice quality, pacing, and the system's ability to provide accurate responses. This shift in perception is likely attributed to the naturalness of the system speech as well as to the ability of students to seek and receive clarifications during interactions with the SDS. In addition, learners mentioned that SDS can contribute to increased accessibility for practising the language. The results of the current study align with previous studies (Doremalen et al., 2016; Fryer et al., 2019) that found SDS can increase accessibility by providing opportunities for repetitive practice, which helps improve oral proficiency.

Additionally, the findings of the study indicated that learners experienced lower stress levels and were less apprehensive about making mistakes when utilizing SDS, which facilitated the cultivation of confidence in language practice. Because SDS promotes learners' confidence and reduces stress in oral communication, it is considered a viable alternative tool for enhancing learners' oral proficiency. SDS offers significant potential for language learning by providing an interactive platform where learners can practise real-life conversational skills in a simulated environment (Bibauw et al., 2019). This result aligns with previous studies in which learners reported increased motivation and reduced anxiety when using SDS (Bashori et al., 2021; Divekar et al., 2022). The anonymity factor, wherein they are not practising with real humans, might reduce their stress and nervousness during language practice.

In terms of weaknesses, students identified several limitations in this prototype, despite its user-friendly interface, enjoyable nature, and high accuracy. The fact that the prototype lacked internet-based accessibility restricted students to using it solely within school premises and limited flexibility and convenience to utilize it anytime and anywhere. The current prototypes were accessible to students in Indonesian and Burmese classes at NIU, not to the public. Providing public access to the prototypes would require a more reliable user access control mechanism, such as a developed log-in system or purchasing a third-party service like Okta. These were not developed for the current project as they were deemed unnecessary due to their controlled use. Additionally, a robust server infrastructure is necessary, costing around $10 to $20 per month for a single server but potentially hundreds of dollars as the user base grows. Google ASR and TTS services also incur costs with each user utterance sent to the server. In the future, we plan to apply for funding so that all the SDS prototypes can be published online and provide access to anyone who would like to practise in Indonesian and Burmese.

In addition, the prototype's simplistic dialogue and interaction raised expectations among students for more complex conversational scenarios in future iterations. Wilske (2015) also argued that only meaning-focused dialogue could provide learners the opportunity to interact realistically. Accordingly, we also plan to develop more meaning-focused intermediate level SDS tasks in the future. Lastly, as the researcher provided only three prototypes, the students expressed a desire for a broader range of scenarios to practise independently. In our further studies, we aim to broaden our research scope to encompass dialectal or regional linguistic variations. This expansion will involve direct engagement with native speakers to capture diverse linguistic nuances during recording sessions. The resultant corpus of recordings will be used to develop an AI-driven SDS, enhancing its capacity to authentically represent a wider spectrum of language varieties.

The study developed three SDS tasks (introducing yourself, ordering food at a café, and describing your house) for novice Indonesian and Burmese learners to provide more opportunities for practising the target language. The findings of the study indicated that learners enjoy engaging with the SDS and find it helpful for language practice. As language acquisition is facilitated by frequent exposure and the ability to practise in various social situations (Lantolf et al., 2015; Vygotsky, 1978), SDS could be an effective tool for language learners to improve oral proficiency skills in less commonly taught languages such as Indonesian and Burmese.

For LCTLs, SDS could be used to provide increased opportunities to practise the target language and engage in spontaneous conversations, which are essential for language development (Chapelle, 2009). However, the study only used three simple dialogues; incorporating more meaning-focused, complex dialogues will help us understand how SDS can contribute to the development of oral proficiency in the future.

6 Limitations of Building Indonesian and Burmese Prototypes

When developing the AI-based SDS for Indonesian and Burmese, the primary hurdles we faced in developing the initial prototype revolved around the testing phase. Since all collaborators were not proficient in both languages, Indonesian or Burmese, all three team members needed to go over all the problems, such as language-appropriate responses, the social aspects of language use, and fixing the coding issues that arose during testing, which consumed a significant amount of time. Another challenge occurred when issues emerged during the testing phase, such as the computer's inadequate response to questions or overly broad answer options. In such cases, the team needed to decide whether to modify the role-play scenarios to be more controlled or interactive conversations.

There have also been concerns that AI models rely heavily on large datasets for training, and they might need more representation of language varieties with limited online presence or documentation. As the prototypes used in our pilot study are only intended for beginning-level learners with limited language exposure, we had planned to use AI-generated data that represent commonly used language forms. However, in future studies, we also plan to collect data for dialectal or regional variations by contacting the speakers and collecting their recordings to create the AI SDS spoken dialogues representing more language varieties.

7 Future Implications

Though the material primarily focuses on beginning-level students taking Indonesian and Burmese courses at NIU, it will be an open educational resource (OER) in 2025, which all Indonesian and Burmese language learners across the world could use. This OER will be contingent upon the availability of financial resources. Due to the scarcity of resources, most LCTL instructors across the United States are always eager to collaborate for material developments and create quality resources. LCTL instructors regularly meet twice a year to collaborate in creating language learning materials. For the last five years, LCTL instructors under the Southeast Asian Language Council (SEALC) project have worked collaboratively to create oral proficiency guidelines and proficiency-based assessments and to develop reading materials. LCTL instructors come from many institutions and universities, such as Cornell University, University of Wisconsin–Madison, UCLA, Yale University, and the like. In the spirit of interinstitutional collaboration, our team plans to share the prototypes with all Indonesian and Burmese instructors across the world who want to use them; to this end, we will publish the prototype on NIU, SEALC, Consortium for the Teaching of Indonesian (COTI), and the Council of Teachers of Southeast Asian Languages (COTSEAL) websites. Hopefully, this prototype will benefit people who want to learn these languages. This project will also be shared with other LCTL institutions and individual learners who are interested in improving their Indonesian and Burmese speaking skills.

About the Authors

Rahmi H. Aoyama has been an Indonesian language instructor at Northern Illinois University (NIU) since 2013. Her dissertation examined foreign language teachers' technological pedagogical content knowledge (TPACK) in teaching listening and speaking skills in virtual worlds. She is a certified tester for Language Testing International. She developed oral proficiency guidelines for Indonesian based on ACTFL standards. Her current research uses SDS to improve speaking proficiency skills in Indonesian classes.

Maw Maw Tun is working as a teaching assistant for Burmese at Northern Illinois University (NIU). She also has experience teaching Burmese at the Southeast Asian Studies Summer Institute (SEASSI) summer program from 2019 to 2023. She holds a master's degree in teaching English as a second language (TESOL) from NIU. She is currently pursuing her PhD in instructional technology at NIU. Her research interest is integrating technology into language learning.

Reza Neiriz is a PhD candidate in the applied linguistics and technology program at Iowa State University. He specializes in language assessment through technology, focusing on spoken dialogue systems. He is evaluating a spoken dialogue system he has developed for assessing oral communication as part of his dissertation project, which the International Research Foundation for English Language Education funds. He has experience creating interfaces for computer-mediated language learning for two NSF-funded projects.

References

ACTFL (American Council on the Teaching of Foreign Languages). (2012). *ACTFL proficiency guidelines*. https://www.actfl.org/uploads/files/general/ACTFLProficiencyGuidelines2012.pdf

Anderson, J.N., Davidson, N., Morton, H., & Jack, M.A. (2008). Language learning with interactive virtual agent scenarios and speech recognition: Lessons learned. *Computer Animation & Virtual Worlds*, *19*(5), 605–619. https://doi.org/10.1002/cav.265

Bashori, M., van Hout, R., Strik, H., & Cucchiarini, C. (2021). Effects of ASR-based websites on EFL learners' vocabulary, speaking anxiety, and language enjoyment. *System*, *99*, 102496. https://doi.org/10.1016/j.system.2021.102496

Bibauw, S., François, T., & Desmet, P. (2019). Discussing with a computer to practice a foreign language: Research synthesis and conceptual framework of dialogue-based CALL. *Computer Assisted Language Learning*, *32*(8), 827–877. https://doi.org/10.1080/09588221.2018.1535508

Braun, V., & Clarke, V. (2021). One size fits all? What counts as quality practice in (reflexive) thematic analysis? *Qualitative Research in Psychology*, *18*(3), 328–352. https://doi.org/10.1080/14780887.2020.1769238

Chapelle, C.A. (2009). The relationship between second language acquisition theory and computer-assisted language learning. *The Modern Language Journal*, *93*(s1), 741–753. https://doi.org/10.1111/j.1540-4781.2009.00970.x

Chen, H.H.-J. (2011). Developing and evaluating an oral skills training website supported by automatic speech recognition technology. *ReCALL*, *23*(1), 59–78. https://doi.org/10.1017/S0958344010000285

Divekar, R., Drozdal, J., Chabot, S., Zhou, Y., Su, H., Chen, Y., Zhu, H., Hendler, J.A., & Braasch, J. (2022). Foreign language acquisition via artificial intelligence and extended reality: Design and evaluation. *Computer Assisted Language Learning*, *35*(9), 2332–2360. https://doi.org/10.1080/09588221.2021.1879162

Doremalen, J.V., Boves, L., Colpaert, J., Cucchiarini, C., & Strik, H. (2016). Evaluating automatic speech recognition-based language learning systems: A case study. *Computer Assisted Language Learning*, *29*(4), 833–851. https://doi.org/10.1080/09588221.2016.1167090

Ericsson, E., Sofkova Hashemi, S., & Lundin, J. (2023). Fun and frustrating: Students' perspectives on practising speaking English with virtual humans. *Cogent Education*, *10*(1), 2170088. https://doi.org/10.1080/2331186X.2023.2170088

Fryer, L.K., Nakao, K., & Thompson, A. (2019). Chatbot learning partners: Connecting learning experiences, interest and competence. *Computers in Human Behavior*, *93*, 279–289. https://doi.org/10.1016/j.chb.2018.12.023

Jeon, J. (2022). Exploring AI chatbot affordances in the EFL classroom: Young learners' experiences and perspectives. *Computer Assisted Language Learning*, *37*(1–2), 1–26. https://doi.org/10.1080/09588221.2021.2021241

Johnson, W.L. (2019). Data-driven development and evaluation of Enskill English. *International Journal of Artificial Intelligence in Education*, *29*(3), 425–457. https://doi.org/10.1007/s40593-019-00182-2

Lantolf, J.P. (2006). Sociocultural theory and L2: State of the art. *Studies in Second Language Acquisition*, *28*(1), 67–109. https://doi.org/10.1017/S0272263106060037

Lantolf, J.P., Thorne, S.L., & Poehner, M.E. (2015). Sociocultural theory and second language development. In B. VanPatten & J. Williams (Eds.), *Theories in second language acquisition* (pp. 207–226). Routledge. https://doi.org/10.4324/9780203628942

Liao, C.F. (2009). EFL learners' use of contrastive stress supported with automatic speech analysis system [Unpublished master's thesis]. Da-Yeh University.

Loewen, S., & Sato, M. (2018). Interaction and instructed second language acquisition. *Language Teaching*, *51*(3), 285–329. https://doi.org/10.1017/S0261444818000125

Lyster, R., & Saito, K. (2010). Interactional feedback as instructional input: A synthesis of classroom SLA research. *LIA: Language, Interaction and Acquisition*, *1*(2), 276–297. https://doi.org/10.1075/lia.1.2.07lys

Mackey, A., & Goo, J. (2007). Interaction research in SLA: A meta-analysis and research synthesis. In A. Mackey (Ed.), *Conversational interaction in second language acquisition: A collection of empirical studies* (pp. 407–452). Oxford University Press.

Pawlak, M., Waniek-Klimczak, E., & Majer, J. (Eds.). (2011). *Speaking and instructed foreign language acquisition*. Multilingual Matters. https://doi.org/10.21832/9781847694126

Timpe-Laughlin, V., Sydorenko, T., & Daurio, P. (2022). Using spoken dialogue technology for L2 speaking practice: What do teachers think? *Computer Assisted Language Learning*, *35*(5–6), 1194–1217. https://doi.org/10.1080/09588221.2020.1774904

Vygotsky, L.S. (1978). *Mind in society: The development of higher psychological processes* (M. Cole, V. John-Steiner, S. Scribner, & E. Souberman, Eds.). Harvard University Press. https://doi.org/10.2307/j.ctvjf9vz4

Wilske, S. (2015). Form and meaning in dialog-based computer-assisted language learning [Doctoral dissertation]. Saarland University.

PART THREE
CALL IN/THROUGH TEACHER PROFESSIONAL DEVELOPMENT

8 Technology-Enabled Interinstitutional Professional Development for Less Commonly Taught Languages

Emily Heidrich Uebel, Luca Giupponi, Koen Van Gorp, and Thomas Jesús Garza

Providing professional development (PD) opportunities for less commonly taught language (LCTL) instructors is crucial to ensuring that these often under-resourced instructors and programs are prepared for the demands of the current technology-filled workplace. This chapter centres on the importance of PD opportunities for LCTL instructors, in particular focusing on some examples that leverage interinstitutional collaborations to pool the strengths and expertise of a community of practitioners. In order to situate these examples of technology-enabled interinstitutional PD, the author team first gives some background in terms of our professional contexts, the centrality of languages (especially LCTLs) to institutional diversity, equity, inclusion, and accessibility (DEIA) plans, and LCTL course sharing.

1 Background

1.1 Professional Context

We begin with an orientation to the professional context of the authors as it influences the types of interactions and outcomes we are able to achieve, both as individuals and in collaboration with others. The author team has worked in varying capacities on the Less Commonly Taught and Indigenous Languages Partnership (https://lctlpartnership.celta.msu.edu/), an Andrew W. Mellon Foundation grant project housed at the Center for Language Teaching Advancement (CeLTA) at Michigan State University (MSU). CeLTA is not directly housed within any language program and, as such, does not have direct influence over language department policies. The result is that CeLTA's efforts focus on research and PD, and rely heavily on collegial collaboration in its interaction with the language departments. The support that CeLTA provides to the language departments is not only tangible, such as financial support for LCTL courses through grants, but also is evident through incalculable contributions of expertise and time devoted to strategic projects, research, and collaboration. Among its many objectives, the LCTL and Indigenous Languages Partnership (henceforth, LCTL Partnership) has focused on bringing together teams of collaborators across institutions to develop open educational materials and courses as well as helping drive innovative ways to leverage existing processes to support LCTL education. CeLTA also houses the National Less Commonly Taught Languages Resource Center (NLRC; https://nlrc.msu.edu/), a Department of Education/Title VI–funded national language resource centre focused on supporting and developing LCTL education by offering PD, creating open and innovative educational resources, and forging strategic collaborations at the interinstitutional level.

1.2 LCTLs and DEIA

A core belief of those who work with the LCTL Partnership is that instruction in LCTLs[1] strengthens institutional capacity for efforts in DEIA; as such, strengthening LCTL programs should be crucial for any institution with a DEIA plan. As described in Fritzsche et al. (2022), a "diverse world language curriculum with LCTLs and Indigenous languages allows more learners to see themselves as represented, respected, and acknowledged" (p. 46). For example, by offering heritage languages that reflect the linguistic and cultural diversity of the United States, institutions create a more inclusive environment where heritage speakers feel recognized and are able to develop their multilingual and multicultural identities. Many articles have identified heritage as a primary reason for students to enrol in language classes, in addition to an increased level of personal interest in the language

---

1. According to Modern Language Association enrolment reports, LCTLs are any languages outside of the 15 most enrolled languages (see Lusin et al., 2023), whereas the National Council of Less Commonly Taught Languages (NCOLCTL) defines LCTLs as "all languages other than English and the commonly taught European languages of German, French and Spanish" (NCOLCTL, n.d.). These projects use the NCOLCTL definition of LCTLs.

(e.g., Brown, 2009; Lee, 2005; Murphy et al., 2009). For example, a student in an MSU Vietnamese class who was a heritage speaker of Vietnamese mentioned, "[I can] talk a lot more about my heritage just because I've learned Vietnamese and learned more about the culture." There has been no research to date that shows that simply offering a wide variety of LCTLs would affect enrolment patterns in any substantial manner, especially considering the relatively low enrolment in LCTLs and languages overall as compared to college and university enrolment (Lusin et al., 2023). However, as diverse populations on campuses have been shown to have positive benefits (e.g., Chang, 2001; Denson & Chang, 2009; Milem et al., 2005), offering a broad range of languages to appeal to the equally broad range of student backgrounds would be a natural net benefit.

It is not only the representation of diverse learners that is important. The dominance of commonly taught languages like Spanish, French, and German in the educational system in the United States necessarily means that the lens through which students are encountering the world (if, indeed, they are exposed to languages other than English at all) is limited to those worldviews and ways of knowing accessible through those languages, literatures, and cultures, which pales in comparison to the diversity extant in the world; these dominant languages are some of the largest colonial languages in the world, and keeping only these commonly taught languages in institutions will reproduce existing biases instead of challenging them (see Freeland, 2021; Meighan, 2022; Pitawanakwat, 2018; Trask, 1999). If institutions wish to create global citizens who can interact with the world as it is, one of the important jobs of language departments must be to advocate for decolonizing the curriculum and adding as many opportunities for global engagement in as many disciplines as possible. Accomplishing decolonizing is not an easy feat, given that the primary and secondary education system in the United States focuses on few languages, which makes it impossible for most students to be able to begin studies in LCTLs before college and even harder still to achieve high levels of proficiency in their chosen language (see Malone et al., 2005). These may seem like idealized perspectives, but language study can contribute to DEIA goals in tangible ways that administrators may find more influential, such as degree completion rates: Those who study languages have better degree completion rates than those who do not take languages (Bell et al., 2020). Furthermore, students who are interested in languages are more likely to study abroad (Goldstein & Kim,

2006), and "studying abroad increases the probability that a student will complete college efficiently and with a strong GPA, especially for minority and at-risk students" (CASSIE, n.d.).

1.3 Sharing LCTLs

One of the more visible ways that the LCTL Partnership (and now, the NLRC) has been able to support LCTL education is through promotion and innovation regarding course sharing across institutions. Conversations about the sharing of LCTLs across institutions are not new, but there has been a groundswell of initiatives that have brought sharing LCTLs to the forefront in recent years (Charitos et al., 2017, Heidrich Uebel et al., 2024). Technology-enabled course sharing can increase enrolments in LCTL courses by drawing students from multiple institutions at once. When planned strategically, course-sharing initiatives can expand the range of courses available to students, not only in terms of the number of languages but also with regard to how many levels of a given language are available. A variety of sharing models are currently in use, and we aim to create templates that institutions can use to share their own languages or engage in partnerships that can allow students to access additional languages without additional monetary obligations from their institutions (see NLRC, n.d.). There are certainly going to be institutions that will be unable to offer their own suite of LCTLs, so engaging in sharing initiatives that suit their context allows them to broaden their offerings, appealing to students who are interested in languages beyond what is currently offered.

Pushback regarding sharing courses often arises as soon as money enters the conversation; administrations may see an opportunity to cut costs by sharing, which may make instructors nervous regarding job stability. Questions arise as to whether such emphasis on money creates constraints for promoting more equitable conditions for LCTL teachers. While we do not negate such concerns, especially in light of the news of language program cuts (see Anderson, 2023; Palmer, 2024), we offer some arguments for how sharing courses can promote more stability among instructional staff by smoothing out often irregular course offerings and creating predictability that can promote more stable enrolment, as well as foster a more positive classroom experience.

In smaller language programs, there often exist one or two instructors for any given language, and class sizes or teaching loads do not allow for consistent articulation/sequencing of courses over years, which disadvantages both the students and the instructor(s). For example, even if an instructor is hired full time, they often will have an expected teaching load of three courses per semester (which is the case at MSU, but smaller institutions may have different expected teaching loads; see Harris, 2015). This arrangement does not allow for one instructor to teach four levels in any one given semester of a typical language sequence. This problem is often remedied by having a heterogeneous "advanced" course that combines the third and fourth years of study. However, enrolment size can also affect whether instructors can offer upper-level courses at all, given the natural attrition experienced in all languages at upper levels. When instructors do not hit the threshold for enrolment, they are generally either forced to cancel the course or may choose to take students on as independent study students so that they do not lose them. In these instances, students are unable to count on the courses being offered in sequence (or at all), and instructors may feel compelled to work more than contracted (e.g., through independent studies) for no additional compensation in order to keep their programs alive. If instructors need to offer independent studies instead of courses due to cancellations, student scheduling conflicts, and/or similar issues, the additional work would engender labour inequity and also create additional burden on administrative staff, especially if it happens in addition to instructors' regular teaching loads. We must note, however, that independent studies in and of themselves are not a problem; independent studies can allow flexibility for students who have completed a suite of courses and want to continue their studies, or they can accommodate students who may have scheduling conflicts. One Portuguese instructor at MSU offered his independent study students (students who had already completed all of the available 300-level courses) the chance to give presentations on various topics for his 200-level courses, describing it as "a win-win proposition" for both the 200-level students and the independent study students.

Even in languages where extremely low enrolment is not an issue, language courses may be operating at low(er) enrolment levels and could easily accommodate several external students through a technologically mediated sharing schema. If departments can count external students towards institutionally recognized enrolment numbers, it would not only allow courses to continue that would otherwise be cancelled for low enrolment but would also relieve students of the burden of scrambling for last-minute replacements for their cancelled courses. For example, external students enrolled in courses at the University of Minnesota and at MSU that are part of an existing infrastructure of course sharing through the Big Ten Academic Alliance, called CourseShare, are counted in university enrolment numbers, allowing the universities to run courses that might not run based on enrolment from their own internal students.

Even if an institution allows a language course to be offered with minimal levels of enrolment, low numbers of students mean fewer options for conversational partners or group structures in collaborative work during the course. If students engage in shared LCTL courses, they get to learn about their own peers in different parts of the country through the medium of the language, enhancing the otherwise naturally insular experience that would occur with students from the same institution.

Most broadly, all sharing of LCTL courses falls into one of three broad categories, described by Heidrich Uebel et al. (2024):

1. *Bilateral language exchange*: an exchange where one institution shares a language with another institution. In exchange, they receive a language they want. These kinds of arrangements can range from simply sharing for one semester/year to multi-year agreements that cement each language's standing at its respective institution.
2. *Consortium*: multiple institutions come together to create a sharing structure that does not necessarily require direct reciprocity from each institution.
3. *Asymmetrical language exchange*: exchanges where one institution offers the language(s), and the other institution offers something else in exchange, whether it is tuition dollars, sharing salary costs, and so forth. This category of exchange has the broadest amount of variability, and there exist myriad ways to deepen the investment in sharing.

While the purview of this author team and our grant projects is within higher education in the United States, we would be remiss if we did not mention that there are initiatives that encourage sharing of LCTLs in K–12 contexts. For example, Aoki et al. (2024) describe the State of Washington's Languages Without Borders project, which promotes access to all languages, including dual crediting, the Seal of Biliteracy, and legislative initiatives.

Given the background on LCTLs in light of a DEIA strategy and some of the possibilities afforded by course sharing, we turn to the importance of professional development for LCTL instructors and the opportunities for computer-assisted language learning (CALL) to increase and expand its reach.

2 Professional Development

2.1 Importance of Professional Development for LCTLs

While it is generally accepted that PD is valuable for language instructors, it is essential to articulate why specific PD opportunities for LCTL instructors are critical.

LCTLs are often faced with a shortage of high-quality pedagogical resources (Blyth, 2013; Godwin-Jones, 2013), instructor isolation, and inconsistent training (Johnston & Janus, 2003) – put simply, LCTL instructors and programs need support (Brown, 2009). Instructors need training on how to use the (few) resources they have, as well as guidance on pedagogy, since many LCTL educators may have degrees in related fields but not necessarily in language pedagogy or second language education (Johnston & Janus, 2003; Heidrich Uebel & Zulick, in preparation).

As mentioned earlier, it is not uncommon for LCTL courses to have a combined third/fourth year due to instructor workload or enrolment. For example, only three levels of Swahili (beginning, intermediate, and advanced) are offered at MSU, with students being able to take the one advanced Swahili course more than once (LiLaC, n.d.). Even without combined-level courses, Murphy et al. (2009) showed that LCTL classes are more heterogeneous in terms of proficiency levels than other classes may be due to a high number of heritage language students and those who have a personal interest in language study in LCTL courses, necessitating the instructor to adapt their teaching and resources to match student needs.

In addition, the tenuous nature of many LCTL instructor positions means that consistent PD over a course of several years may not be possible, or in the case of adjunct or part-time faculty, funding may simply not be available for PD opportunities. As Giupponi et al. (2025) describe, "LCTL instructors' academic positions are often temporary, part-time, or both. While many LCTL instructors can cobble together full-time work … the majority are not in tenure-track positions and over 50% are on fixed-term, annual, or semester contracts" (see also Johnston & Janus, 2003; Heidrich Uebel & Zulick, in preparation).

While course sharing provides many opportunities for LCTLs, it does add a level of complexity to instruction. For example, if an instructor plans to share a course, they must consider whether they need to address multiple modalities at once, such as a videoconferencing environment with both in-person and remote students. If they plan to have all students in the same mode, such as in an online course, careful attention must be given to the design of the online course to take into account the known best practices. Therefore, LCTL instructors who participate in course-sharing agreements should participate in targeted PD offerings to support this specific teaching modality.

2.2 Technology-Enabled Interinstitutional Professional Development

Historically, course sharing has adopted a variety of distribution modes from paired high-definition videoconferencing rooms (see Kaiser, 2024, concerning the Shared Course Initiative, https://sharedcourseinitiative.lrc.columbia.edu/) to asynchronous, fully online courses (such as the Portuguese courses developed by the LCTL Partnership; see Lima & Goebel, 2024), but by definition it includes components of technology-enabled distance learning. As a consequence, instructors' skill sets need to be expanded to include competencies that are traditionally associated with online instruction, such as online course design, communication and facilitation, time management, and technological competencies (Martin et al., 2019). Each of these topics (course design, time management, etc.) have their own definitions and often robust related research; however, creating robust PD programs to address these topics can be daunting, particularly for LCTL programs, which may regularly struggle for resources. Therefore, technology-mediated interinstitutional PD can be advantageous for LCTLs by consolidating resources, demonstrating best practices, and fostering a community of practice. LCTL programs and language centres can also consider pooling expertise across institutions to give participants access to training, teaching approaches, and mentorship that would not be available locally. (See additional ideas on how language centres can collaborate in Giupponi et al., 2021.)

For LCTL instructors involved in cross-institutional course sharing or teaching distance or technology-mediated courses, participating in technology-mediated PD serves not only as a source of information but also as a model for the dynamics of online learning. It is worth noting that technology-mediated PD can be designed along the continuum of synchronous to asynchronous modalities. Synchronous classes, such as those highlighted in the Shared Course Initiative above, allow for real-time interaction between all participants. Emphasizing asynchronous delivery may be less demanding on instructors' busy schedules and can accommodate participants from different time zones and teaching schedules. Technology facilitates a shift from the conventional one-time presentation or workshop format to a more scaffolded and ongoing form of PD. In this approach, participants engage with the content at their convenience, interact with peers and instructors using synchronous and asynchronous methods as appropriate, and complete tasks and assignments relevant to the course goals. This approach also serves as a model of online learning for participants, which research has shown to have a more significant impact on subsequent instructional practices than the specific topic of the PD initiative itself (Borup & Evmenova, 2019).

Furthermore, technology-mediated PD has the potential to foster communities of practice by bringing together LCTL instructors across institutions within the same learning environment. LCTL instructors typically experience greater isolation compared to their counterparts teaching more commonly taught languages and often find themselves as the sole instructor for their language at their institution (Johnston & Janus, 2003). PD initiatives that facilitate ongoing engagement among participants are more likely to lead to the establishment of a distributed community of inquiry – a group of individuals collaborating in learning and reflection to construct personal understanding and refine mutual comprehension. Research conducted using the community of inquiry framework demonstrates that meaningful outcomes are more readily attained when the learning experience is embedded within a collaborative community of inquiry (even if that community is asynchronous), enabling reflective and critical thinking to be put into practice (Cleveland-Innes et al., 2019).

The Michigan State University Online Language Teaching (OLT) Initiative (https://olt.cal.msu.edu/) is an example of how technology-enabled interinstitutional PD can take shape. The initiative was built on the experience of a first PD course called "Fundamentals of Online Language Teaching," which was initially conceived in 2017 as an internal activity designed to support instructors funded by the LCTL Partnership to develop online courses to be distributed via CourseShare. Interest in the course grew, and the first public section of the course ran in 2019. The COVID-19 pandemic precipitated the need for this kind of PD, with over 100 participants and eight sections of the course offered in summer 2020 alone. Based on participant feedback, the initiative began offering advanced courses, with a roster of courses that continues to expand to this day and goes beyond the online modality to topics related to technology integration in the language classroom. Currently, the course roster of advanced courses is as follows:

- Oral Communicative Tasks in OLT
- Creating Engaging Materials
- Purposeful Technology Integration
- Teaching the Whole Class: Technology for Differentiated Instruction

Thanks to generous support from the NLRC, the courses are completely free for participants. To maintain frequent and meaningful instructor-student and student-student interaction, the courses are capped at 12 participants. Prospective participants submit an application detailing their interest in the course and their commitment to the course workload, and those who are selected to participate are notified on a rolling basis. The courses are open to teachers of all languages, but in line with the NLRC's mission, priority is given to LCTL instructors. While instructors from anywhere in the world can apply, the vast majority of interest we have received so far has been from North American higher education professionals.

To further exemplify the potential of technology-enabled interinstitutional PD, the last two courses from the above list will be discussed in more detail.

2.2.1 Purposeful Technology Integration

"Purposeful Technology Integration" (PTI) is a three-week online course that aims to create a space for post-secondary language instructors to identify technology-enabled practices with transformative potential and design a revised teaching approach informed by evidence and their own experiences.

The course mainly consists of resource exploration, discussion, and task-oriented activities. The course culminates with participants delivering a personal technology integration plan (TIP) that describes in detail the approaches that they intend to implement in their courses. It is important to note that the focus of this plan is largely a consequence of participants' own context and experience, so TIPs differ widely from one participant to the next.

The main goal of the course is to make participants aware of the possibilities of technology-enabled pedagogical transformation, that is, the transformation that happens in an educator's practice when a new technology opens the possibility for the adoption of a different pedagogical approach. While introducing a new technology does not automatically guarantee this transformation, technology can, when implemented well, promote better teaching and learning practices by bringing into focus pedagogical practices that are more student-centred, effective, and/or equitable (Ertmer & Ottenbreit-Leftwich, 2013), for example, by providing the opportunity to work in alternative modalities or spend additional time on specific curricular components outside of class.

One of the models that has been most helpful for framing the transformative potential of technology is the PIC-RAT model (Kimmons et al., 2020). Originally intended for K–12 settings and building on previous approaches to technology integration research, the PIC-RAT (Figure 8.1) attempts to bring together students' and instructors' use of technology in the same model. It analyses each instance of technology integration by asking two questions:

1. How are students using a certain technology? (PIC: passive, interactive, creative)
2. How does the instructor use the technology in relation to traditional practice? (RAT: replace, amplify, transform)

The value of this model lies in the fact that it provides educators with a series of questions to evaluate each instance of technology integration and shows a path towards more student-centred, creative uses of technology.

During the two inaugural sections of the course, offered at the tail end of the pandemic, we collected survey, interview, and course materials data from participants. Results showed that their pandemic experience, coupled with the reflective space afforded by participating in the PTI course, led to

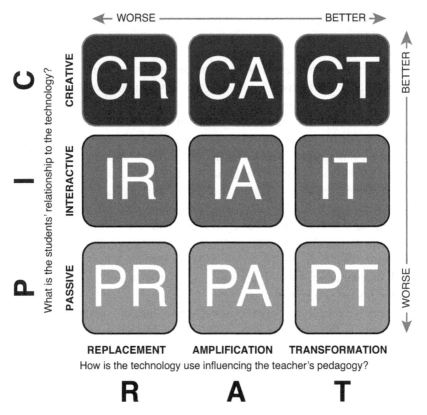

Figure 8.1 The PIC-RAT Matrix

Source: Kimmons et al. (2022), Figure 1. The figure is from the Open Encyclopedia of Educational Technology (https://edtechbooks.org/encyclopedia) and is used under a Creative Commons Attribution 4.0 International Licence.

dramatic transformations in the participants' teaching approaches (Giupponi et al., 2024). Among the most salient findings of the study for the purposes of this chapter is the fact that providing educators with a space for experimentation and reflection on their own practices can open the door to lasting pedagogical change:

> While some language educators have been innovating using technology for a long time, the pandemic seems to have accelerated a deeper integration of technologies in the language classroom and a closer alignment to current, everyday uses of technology involving the coordination of several platforms and

modalities, or what Cappellini and Combe (2022) refer to as "orchestration of environments" (p. 2). From having video calls with native speakers to shopping using online portals, the pandemic finally made it okay to call online activities real life. Indeed, coming to terms with ERT [emergency remote teaching] brought about an epiphany: conducting class online opens a whole new definition of what it means to be engaged in authentic learning. In short, the language classroom became more aligned with the technology-mediated content engagement we all experience in the internet age: a hybrid space that allows individuals to effortlessly switch between modalities based on need. (p. 124)

Additionally, the study found that continued participation in sustained PD activities like the one described above, even or especially during such a stressful time as the pandemic, contributed to developing and refining an innovative mindset among participants, which in turn played a role in the ways they dealt with the challenges and opportunities of the pandemic (Giupponi et al., 2024).

2.2.2 Teaching the Whole Class

"Teaching the Whole Class" (TWC) is a three-week online PD course that leverages technology in both synchronous and asynchronous modalities to facilitate participants' development of differentiated instruction techniques to attain diverse proficiency goals in classes with heterogeneous learners.

Differentiated instruction (DI) describes an approach to teaching that adjusts instruction based on an individual learner's knowledge, approach to learning, interests, and background (Tomlinson, 2004). Contemporary language learners also represent diverse identities in terms of gender, race, ethnicity, sexual orientation, socio-economic background, and (dis)abilities, among other categories. Learner identity is particularly critical in language learning, as representation and articulation of identity is often at the core of motivation (Zhou, 2012). Issues of learner heterogeneity are particularly acute in LCTL programs, where low enrolments often force administrators to merge different proficiency levels into the same course or to include heritage learners in courses designed for non-heritage learners. The TWC course expands on the narrower conceptualizations of classroom heterogeneity by discussing how DI and technology integration together can engender the creation of more effective and inclusive instruction that addresses both the goals of proficiency-oriented instruction and of critical pedagogy for social justice.

TWC is a salient example of technology-enabled interinstitutional PD. The course was built using the existing OLT Initiative distribution infrastructure, while the content expertise came from the fourth author, a faculty member at a different US institution who is also the lead instructor of the course. TWC employs four organizing principles: (a) the use of web-based technologies to select appropriate authentic materials, (b) the design of appropriate, multilevel, learner-oriented tasks, (c) the use of asynchronous online spaces, and (d) the use of performance- and product-based assessment of learning outcomes. Together, these principles can help instructors create a classroom ecology of equitable, inclusive teaching and learning that is attentive to every learner in the class while addressing proficiency benchmarks in the language and culture (Garza, 2021).

The learner-oriented approach of TWC asks participants to consider the individual profiles of learners in their classes and then critically interrogate their existing syllabi, curricula, and materials to determine their efficacy in addressing the learners' needs, levels, and identities. Without exception, participants in TWC have conceded the need to reimagine their courses, materials, and assessment instruments as more differentiated and inclusive. TWC participants learn to use online resources in non-English language web spaces to create an array of proficiency level–appropriate and learner-oriented tasks from a single "source item" of authentic materials. Finally, rather than employing a single omnibus testing instrument for all learners in a course, TWC participants learn how to design and create differentiated task-based assignments for small teams to undertake as capstone projects for assessment. Technology applications are both a means and an end in the TWC course. Various web-based sources and applications are utilized throughout the course, from location realia and authentic materials to workshopping participants' projects online; the final, differentiated, learner-oriented projects that are produced in TWC are then delivered to learners on a wide array of devices and in a variety of application formats.

3 Conclusion

This chapter underscores the critical role of technology-enhanced interinstitutional PD opportunities for LCTL instructors. Rooted in our own professional context and grant work, we explored the close relationship between LCTLs and institutional DEIA strategies, arguing that the inclusion of diverse languages enriches institutional capacities and supports the creation of inclusive environments. In addition, by collaborating across institutions and leveraging the transformative potential of technology-enhanced PD programs, we can address the distinctive needs of LCTL educators, strengthen LCTL programs across the United States, and help create an equitable and inclusive language learning experience for all students and all languages.

We illustrated the transformative power of technology-enhanced PD programs by two course examples. The first example showcased how the course "Purposeful Technology Integration" helped LCTL instructors cope with the challenges and opportunities during and beyond the pandemic and how a community of practice across institutions helped them navigate and apply the learning potential of new technology-enhanced pedagogical practices, building a stronger innovative mindset among LCTL instructors. A second course, "Teaching the Whole Class," illustrated how technology can enhance differentiated and inclusive teaching practices to better suit the wide range of language proficiency levels students bring to a language course. Together, these examples provide an exploration of the intricate connections between LCTLs, DEIA strategies, interinstitutional collaboration, and professional development. They show how technology can be harnessed to empower instructors in adapting to the evolving landscape of language education. Ultimately, the chapter makes a compelling case for the transformative potential of collaborative efforts across institutions and technology-enabled PD, emphasizing their pivotal role in shaping the future of less commonly taught languages in the educational landscape.

About the Authors

Emily Heidrich Uebel is associate executive director of the National LCTL Resource Center and an academic specialist at the Center for Language Teaching Advancement (CeLTA) at Michigan State University. She was lead co-editor on recent volumes on language program vitality in higher education and sharing LCTLs across institutions. Her research interests include language proficiency, educational technology and online instruction, LCTL education, and faculty development.

Luca Giupponi is the head of technology at the National LCTL Resource Center. His work focuses on faculty development, technology integration, and program evaluation. His recent publications include a chapter in a *CALICO* special volume investigating patterns of technology integration in language teachers' classroom practices following the pandemic. He is also the co-editor of a recent volume on sharing LCTLs across higher education institutions.

Koen Van Gorp is assistant professor of applied linguistics and less commonly taught languages (LCTL) coordinator in the Department of Linguistics, Languages, and Cultures at Michigan State University. He also serves as head of research for the National LCTL Resource Center (NLRC). His research interests are task-based language teaching and assessment, and multilingualism. He is founding co-editor of *TASK: Journal on Task-Based Language Teaching and Learning*.

Thomas Jesús Garza is associate professor in Slavic and Eurasian studies at the University of Texas at Austin and director of the Texas Language Center. He has published research on world languages and cultures, and has authored several Russian and EFL textbooks. His current research is on inclusive and accessible language instruction, critical pedagogies of empathy, and marginal masculinities in contemporary Russian and Latino cultures.

References

Anderson, N. (2023, August 18). WVU's plan to cut foreign languages, other programs draws disbelief. *Washington Post*. https://www.washingtonpost.com/education/2023/08/18/west-virginia-university-academic-cuts/

Aoki, M.A., Hugo, R., Trapani-Huebner, V., & Yaden, B. (2024). Languages without borders promoting equitable access to language education. In E. Heidrich Uebel, A. Kraemer, & L. Giupponi (Eds.), *Sharing less commonly taught languages in higher education: Collaboration and innovation* (pp. 218–232). Routledge. https://doi.org/10.4324/9781003349631-21

Bell, A., Bhatt, R., Hodges, L., Rubin, D., & Shiflet, C. (2020). *CASSIE study abroad and world language analyses and infographics*. University System of Georgia. https://www.usg.edu/assets/cassie/documents/National_Sample_CASSIE_Infographic_WLCourseTaking.pdf

Blyth, C. (2013). LCTLs and technology: The promise of open education. *Language Learning & Technology*, *14*(1), 1–6. http://doi.org/10125/24501

Borup, J., & Evmenova, A.S. (2019). The effectiveness of professional development in overcoming obstacles to effective online instruction in a college of education. *Online Learning Journal*, *23*(2), 1–20. https://doi.org/10.24059/olj.v23i2.1468

Brown, A.V. (2009). Less commonly taught language and commonly taught language students: A demographic and academic comparison. *Foreign Language Annals*, *42*(3), 405–423. https://doi.org/10.1111/j.1944-9720.2009.01036.x

Cappellini, M., & Combe, C. (2022). Multiple online environments as complex systems: Toward an orchestration of environments. *Language Learning & Technology*, *26*(1), 1–20. https://hdl.handle.net/10125/73497

CASSIE (The Consortium for Analysis of Student Success through International Education). (n.d.). *Quick information.* https://www.usg.edu/cassie/quick_information

Chang, M.J. (2001). The positive educational effects of racial diversity on campus. In G. Orfield & M. Kurlaender (Eds.), *Diversity challenged: Evidence on the impact of affirmative action* (pp. 175–186). The Civil Rights Project, Harvard University.

Charitos, S., Kaiser, C., & Van Deusen-Scholl, N. (2017). From interinstitutional competition to interinstitutional collaboration. *EuropeNow Journal*, *8*, 1–7. https://www.europenowjournal.org/2017/06/05/from-interinstitutional-competition-to-interinstitutional-collaboration/

Cleveland-Innes, M., Garrison, D.R., & Vaughan, N. (2019). The Community of Inquiry theoretical framework. In M. Grahame Moore & W.C. Diehl (Eds.), *Handbook of distance education* (pp. 67–78). https://doi.org/10.4324/9781315296135-6

Denson, N., & Chang, M.J. (2009). Racial diversity matters: The impact of diversity-related student engagement and institutional context. *American Educational Research Journal*, *46*(2), 322–353. https://doi.org/10.3102/0002831208323278

Ertmer, P.A., & Ottenbreit-Leftwich, A. (2013). Removing obstacles to the pedagogical changes required by Jonassen's vision of authentic technology-enabled learning. *Computers and Education*, *64*, 175–182. https://doi.org/10.1016/j.compedu.2012.10.008

Freeland, M.D. (2021). *Aazheyaadizi: Worldview, language, and the logics of decolonization.* Michigan State University Press. https://doi.org/10.14321/j.ctv16t6n8s

Fritzsche, S., Giupponi, L., Heidrich Uebel, E., Kronenberg, F.A., Long, C.P., & Van Gorp, K. (2022, Winter). Languages as drivers of institutional diversity: The case of less commonly taught languages. *The Language Educator*, 45–47. https://www.thelanguageeducator.org/actfl/winter_2022/MobilePagedArticle.action?articleId=1760118#articleId1760118

Garza, T.J. (2021). Here, there, and elsewhere: Reimagining Russian language and culture courses for social justice. *Russian Language Journal*, *71*(3), 41–64. https://doi.org/10.26067/F8PA-W125

Giupponi, L., Heidrich Uebel, E., Kronenberg, F., & Steider, D. (2025). Supporting less commonly taught and Indigenous languages through technology integration and online language learning. In V. Russell, K. Murphy-Judy, F. Troyan, A. Moeller, & K. Hines-Gaither (Eds.), *The handbook of research on world language instruction*. Routledge.

Giupponi, L., Heidrich Uebel, E., & Van Gorp, K. (2021). Strategies for language centers to support online language. In E. Lavolette & A. Kraemer (Eds.), *Language center handbook 2021* (pp. 61–90). International Association for Language Learning Technology.

Giupponi, L., Zulick, B., & Heidrich Uebel, E. (2024). Post-pandemic language teaching: Language instructors' technology integration practices. In S. Goertler & J. Gleason (Eds.), *Technology-mediated crisis response in language studies* (pp. 114–134). Equinox Publishing.

Godwin-Jones, R. (2013). The technological imperative in teaching and learning less commonly taught languages. *Language Learning & Technology*, *17*(1), 7–19. https://doi.org/10125/24502

Goldstein, S.B., & Kim, R.I. (2006). Predictors of US college students' participation in study abroad programs: A longitudinal study. *International Journal of Intercultural Relations*, *30*(4), 507–521. https://doi.org/10.1016/j.ijintrel.2005.10.001

Harris, M. (2015, May 11). What is the typical teaching load for university faculty? *Higher Ed Professor.* https://higheredprofessor.com/2015/05/11/what-is-the-typical-teaching-load-for-university-faculty/

Heidrich Uebel, E., Kraemer, A. & Giupponi, L. (Eds.). (2024). *Sharing less commonly taught languages in higher education: Collaboration and innovation.* Routledge. https://doi.org/10.4324/9781003349631

Heidrich Uebel, E, & Zulick, B. (in preparation). *Less commonly taught language instructors: An updated look at instructor context and needs* [Manuscript in preparation].

Johnston, B., & Janus, L. (2003). *Teacher professional development for the less commonly taught languages.* https://eric.ed.gov/?id=ED479299

Kaiser, C. (2024). The Shared Course Initiative: Less commonly taught language collaboration at Columbia, Cornell, and Yale. In E. Heidrich Uebel, A. Kraemer, & L. Giupponi (Eds.), *Sharing less commonly taught languages in higher education: Collaboration and innovation* (pp. 39–49). Routledge. https://doi.org/10.4324/9781003349631

Kimmons, R., Draper, D.E., & Backman, J. (2022). PICRAT: The PICRAT technology integration model. *EdTechnica: The Open Encyclopedia of Educational Technology*. https://edtechbooks.org/encyclopedia/picrat

Kimmons, R., Graham, C.R., & West, R.E. (2020). The PIC-RAT model for technology integration in teacher preparation. *Contemporary Issues in Technology and Teacher Education, 20*(1), 176–198. https://citejournal.org/volume-20/issue-1-20/general/the-picrat-model-for-technology-integration-in-teacher-preparation

Lee, J.S. (2005). Through the learners' eyes: Reconceptualizing the heritage and non-heritage learner of the less commonly taught languages. *Foreign Language Annals, 38*(4), 554–563. https://doi.org/10.1111/j.1944-9720.2005.tb02522.x

LiLaC (Department of Linguistics, Languages, and Cultures, Michigan State University). (n.d.). *Swahili.* https://lilac.msu.edu/african-languages/swahili/

Lima, A.M.F., & Goebel, R.C. (2024). The Portuguese language working group: A successful partnership. In E. Heidrich Uebel, A. Kraemer, & L. Giupponi (Eds.), *Sharing less commonly taught languages in higher education: Collaboration and innovation* (pp. 172–184). Routledge. https://doi.org/10.4324/9781003349631

Lusin, N., Peterson, T., Sulewski, C., & Zafer, R. (2023). *Enrollments in languages other than English in US institutions of higher education, Fall 2021.* Modern Language Association of America. https://www.mla.org/content/download/191324/file/Enrollments-in-Languages-Other-Than-English-in-US-Institutions-of-Higher-Education-Fall-2021.pdf

Malone, M.E., Rifkin, B., Christian, D., & Johnson, D.E. (2005). Attaining high levels of proficiency: Challenges for language education in the United States. *CAL Digest.* Center for Applied Linguistics. https://www.cal.org/wp-content/uploads/2022/05/AttainingHighLevelsofProficiency.pdf

Martin, F., Budhrani, K., & Wang, C. (2019). Examining faculty perception of their readiness to teach online. *Online Learning Journal, 23*(3), 97–119. https://doi.org/10.24059/olj.v23i3.1555

Meighan, P.J. (2022). Indigenous language revitalization using *TEK-nology*: How can traditional ecological knowledge (TEK) and technology support intergenerational language transmission? *Journal of Multilingual and Multicultural Development, 45*(8), 3059–3077. https://doi.org/10.1080/01434632.2022.2084548

Milem, J.F., Chang, M.J., & Antonio, A.L. (2005). *Making diversity work on campus: A research-based perspective*. Association American Colleges and Universities.

Murphy, D., Magnan, S., Back, M., & Garrett-Rucks, P. (2009). Reasons students take courses in less commonly taught and more commonly taught languages. *Journal of the National Council of Less Commonly Taught Languages*, 7, 45–80. https://www.ncoltl.org/files/Reasons-Students-Take-Courses-in-Less-Commonly-Taught-and-More-Commonly-Taught-Languages.pdf

NCOLCTL (National Council of Less Commonly Taught Languages). (n.d.). *Frequently asked questions*. https://ncoltl.org/about/frequently-asked-questions/

NLRC (National Less Commonly Taught Languages Resource Center). (n.d.). *Strategic coordination*. https://nlrc.msu.edu/strategic-coordination/

Palmer, K. (2024, May 15). Defense department cuts 13 of its language flagship programs. *Inside Higher Ed*. https://www.insidehighered.com/news/global/study-abroad/2024/05/15/defense-department-cuts-13-its-language-flagship-programs

Pitawanakwat, B. (2018). Strategies and methods for Anishinaabemowin revitalization. *Canadian Modern Language Review*, 74(3), 460–482. https://doi.org/10.3138/cmlr.4058

Tomlinson, C.A. (2004). *Fulfilling the promise of differentiated classroom: Strategies and tools for responsive teaching*. Hawker-Brownlow Education.

Trask, H.K. (1999). *From a native daughter: Colonialism and sovereignty in Hawaii* (Rev. ed.). University of Hawaii Press. https://doi.org/10.1515/9780824847029

Zhou, M. (2012). Language identity as a process and second language learning. In W. Chan, K. Chin, S. Bhatt, & I. Walker (Eds.), *Perspectives on individual characteristics and foreign language education* (pp. 255–272). De Gruyter Mouton. https://doi.org/10.1515/9781614510932.255

9 Interinstitutional and Transnational Language Teacher Professional Development: Teachers' Critical Reflections and Future Directions

An Nguyen Sakach and Trang Phan

Teachers have three loves: love of learning, love of learners, and the love of bringing the first two loves together.

– Scott Hayden

1 Introduction

Professional development (PD) is understood as the ongoing process of refining teaching abilities, pedagogical approaches, and digital literacy in response to the dynamic demands of modern society (Stewart, 2014). PD is believed to be essential for enhancing the skills and knowledge of teachers, leading to improved educational outcomes (Martin & Mulvihill, 2023). In today's rapidly changing world, PD is increasingly important as technology continues to influence lifestyles and create new skill demands. Like many teachers of other subjects, language teachers of this era are required to update not only knowledge or pedagogical approaches but also digital literacy so as to develop professionally. Therefore, information and communication technologies (ICT), which encompass modalities such as virtual communication platforms, online collaboration tools, and digital resources, have been integrated into various facets of the PD projects, enhancing communication, collaboration, and instructional delivery. This chapter explores a language teacher professional development model that incorporates interinstitutional and transnational exchange components and the support of ICT. Specifically, it presents teachers' reflections on their experiences in collaborative professional development projects initiated by the Southeast Asian Language Council (SEALC). These projects involved a reading assessment design workshop (SEALC, 2022) and a reading materials development workshop (SEALC, 2023) for lecturers from multiple institutions in the United States and their counterparts from Southeast Asian (SEA) or European countries. This chapter explores a PD model for a diverse group of teachers who instruct SEA languages including Burmese, Filipino, Indonesian, Javanese, Hmong, Khmer, Lao, Thai, and Vietnamese. Additionally, it investigates telecommunication tools utilized during the training sessions and the hybrid symposia, the telecollaboration tools employed throughout the workshops, as well as the advantages and disadvantages associated with these tools. Data collected from a survey, observational notes, and semi-structured interviews with the SEA language teachers participating in the PD workshops revealed that the teachers' collective wealth of experiences, varied perspectives, and specialized expertise enhanced the collaborative projects, fostering a vibrant exchange of ideas and practices within the global professional learning community.

By examining the exchanges fostered by SEALC, the chapter underscores the critical role of collaborative PD in advancing the field, promoting equity, and addressing global educational challenges. Such initiatives not only help in updating and refining teachers' skills but also build a foundation for a more inclusive and supportive educational environment across different societies and languages. These collaborative efforts can lead to significant improvements in educational practices, ultimately contributing to the global advancement of education.

2 Teacher Collaboration in Professional Development

If you want to go fast, go alone. If you want to go far, go together.
– African Proverb

Research indicates that good-quality PD can help teachers increase their knowledge, skills, and understanding of teaching practices (Bachtiar, 2020; Desimone, 2009). According to Bachtiar (2020), high-quality PD encompasses activities that effectively enhance teachers' knowledge and pedagogical skills, foster collaborative engagement, and are rooted in addressing the practical needs encountered within the classroom setting. On the same note, Desimone (2009) identifies five critical features of PD: content focus, active learning, coherence, duration, and collective participation. The positive impacts of "collective participation," or the collaboration between teachers in PD activities, have been well-documented in literature (Belay et al., 2022; Goddard et al., 2007; Jaipal & Figg, 2011; Kirvalidze & Lobzhanidze, 2023; Lakshmanan et al., 2010; Levin & Rock, 2003; Messiou, 2019; Steyn, 2014; Yilmaz, 2022). However, most reported collaborative PD projects have been based on action research of teachers at a single professional development school (PDS) site (Cochran-Smith & Lytle, 2009). Interinstitutional collaborative action research PD projects, if any, are often confined to PDS sites within a school district (Levin & Rock, 2003) or within the same region or state (Jaipal & Figg, 2011). Although international collaboration among academic institutions has expanded recently – promoting knowledge exchange and idea sharing between partners (Amaratunga et al., 2018) – teacher PD initiatives aimed at fostering collaboration among teachers across institutions and countries are relatively scarce. This scarcity can be attributed, in part, to the considerable investment and commitment required from both organizers and participants to facilitate such endeavours. Therefore, examining a case study of collaborative PD across institutions and borders will provide valuable insights into efficiently and effectively planning such projects.

In the realm of language education, where the teaching of less commonly taught languages (LCTLs) faces unique challenges, collaborative PD efforts are particularly crucial. Limited availability of high-quality and up-to-date teaching materials necessitates increased workload for lesson preparation. Furthermore, single-person LCTL departments often require instructors to cater to diverse student needs across various proficiency levels within the same class. Finally, fluctuating enrolment numbers and limited career advancement opportunities within these departments can lead to feelings of professional stagnation. For LCTL teachers, who often lack access to specialized resources and professional networks (see Chapter 8 by Heidrich Uebel et al., this volume), collaborative PD initiatives offer a pathway to enhance their expertise and address the specific needs of their learners. These initiatives enable the exchange of ideas, resources, and best practices among teachers from diverse backgrounds, enriching the professional learning community and promoting diversity, equity, inclusion, and accessibility (DEIA) in education.

The focus on reading assessment design and reading materials development in the collaborative projects examined in this chapter holds significant importance in language education. Effective reading instruction is vital for language acquisition and literacy development, requiring specialized knowledge and instructional strategies (Smith, 2011). Collaborative PD endeavours in these areas can therefore facilitate the sharing of innovative assessment techniques and instructional approaches while promoting cultural and linguistic diversity in reading materials, thereby fostering inclusive learning environments.

In this context, SEALC acts as a catalyst for interinstitutional and transnational collaboration among language educators. By organizing collaborative PD projects such as reading assessment design and reading materials development workshops, SEALC plays a pivotal role in advancing SEA language teacher professional development and promoting DEIA in language education. Through an exploration of these initiatives, this chapter aims to illuminate the potential benefits and challenges of collaborative PD across institutions and borders, providing insights for future endeavours in the field of language education. By delving into these endeavours, it aims to offer insights for future initiatives in PD for language teachers.

Furthermore, the chapter seeks to provide empirical backing for key learning theories. Adult learning theory (Knowles et al., 2020; Merriam & Baumgartner, 2020) emphasizes the importance of self-directed learning and leveraging prior experiences, which are essential for shaping educators' career paths. Wenger's (1998) concept of communities of practice underscores the significance of collective learning and knowledge sharing among teachers. Vygotsky's (1978) social constructivist theory further demonstrates how social interaction and collaboration can enhance individual learning in professional development settings. These theoretical frameworks not only inform the interpretation of the study's findings but also underscore their practical implications for designing and implementing effective collaborative PD.

3 The Southeast Asian Language Council (SEALC) and PD Projects Investigated

3.1 SEALC and PD for SEA Language Teachers

In the United States, the majority of instructors teaching languages at the higher education level are non-tenure–track faculty members, encompassing teaching professors, lecturers, adjunct faculties, and instructors. PD opportunities for these language instructors commonly comprise workshops, conferences, and training sessions organized by academic institutions, language teaching organizations, and professional associations such as the ACTFL (formerly known as the American Council on the Teaching of Foreign Languages), the National Council of Less Commonly Taught Languages (NCOLCTL), the Center for Advanced Research on Language Acquisition (CARLA), the Center for Educational Resources in Culture, Language and Literacy (CERCLL), and the National Less Commonly Taught Languages Resource Center (NLRC). Most PD activities are designed to bolster pedagogical skills, integrate technology into language instruction, and cultivate cultural competence.

As for SEA languages, the Council of Teachers of Southeast Asian Languages (COTSEAL) and SEALC are the two main professional organizations that promote and coordinate activities in the field of SEA language teaching. The SEA languages commonly taught at institutions in North America, which are referred to in this chapter, include Burmese, Filipino, Indonesian, Javanese, Hmong, Khmer, Lao, Thai, and Vietnamese; all these languages are considered LCTLs in the US educational context. SEALC, based at the University of Wisconsin-Madison, has been funded since 2019 by the Henry Luce Foundation under the award titled "Professional and Materials Development to Strengthen Southeast Asian Language Instruction." SEALC's Oral Proficiency Guideline project, launched in 2019, marked a significant step towards interinstitutional and transnational collaboration among SEA language teachers. In this project, SEA language teachers based in Southeast Asia and the United States gathered together to create specific guidelines for each language based on the ACTFL guidelines. SEALC draws language educators transnationally through its mission to facilitate collaborative PD initiatives that address the specific needs of SEA language instructors. By providing a platform for educators to engage in meaningful exchanges and collaborative projects, SEALC enables teacher participants to collectively work towards shared and open access assessment and teaching materials for SEA languages. Through these initiatives, SEALC contributes to the advancement of language teacher PD and promotes DEIA in language education on a global scale.

The onset of the pandemic prompted a shift towards telecommunication as a means to maintain workflow within SEALC's projects. This transition underscored the pivotal role of ICT in fostering collaboration across institutional and national boundaries. Interestingly, what initially may have been perceived as a temporary modality for PD during the pandemic has revealed new avenues for promoting broader collaboration across institutions and borders.

3.2 SEALC's PD Projects in the Study

The Reading Assessment Design Workshop 2022 (SEALC, 2022) and the Reading Materials Development Workshop 2023 (SEALC, 2023) were selected for this study because they were organized after the beginning of the pandemic, when most people were expected to be more fluent with ICT.

The term "workshop" refers to the whole process that consisted of three main components: initial training session(s), followed by a project phase, and concluding with a symposium where participants presented their work. Teachers teaching the same language group from different institutions were paired or worked in groups of three. The Reading Assessment Design Workshop tasked each group with designing one reading test for both intermediate and advanced proficiency levels in the language they taught. By contrast, the Reading Materials Development Workshop focused on lesson development, with each group creating one reading lesson for both intermediate and advanced learners in their language. The developed works underwent a thorough review and revision process, incorporating feedback from peers and then trainers, before being piloted across the participating institutions. Following the pilot phase, another cycle of collaboration was initiated for further material revisions. Both workshops ended with presenting the revised products of collaboration in a hybrid symposium with SEA-based presenters joining virtually and US-based presenters joining in person. Even though the workshops were free of charge and open to all teachers in non-profit institutions, with accommodation and food provided during immersive training, participants had to apply and express their commitment to the project. Each project was expected to last about six months but actually extended over two semesters or a whole school year, requiring a high level of commitment and sustainable collaboration. The training part offered flexible modalities for participation, including asynchronous courses, in-person sessions, and synchronous lessons. ICT was utilized not only in training but was also in teamwork, enhancing all components of the workshops.

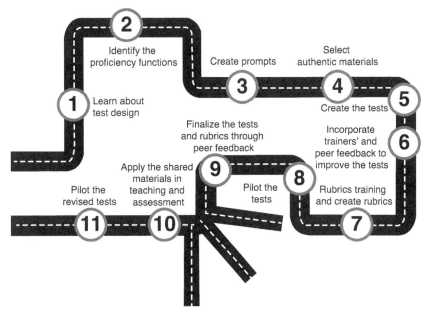

Figure 9.1 Several Phases in the Reading Assessment Design Workshop
Source: Sakach and Dinh (2023).

Figure 9.1 illustrates the different stages of the project, each accomplished through collaborative efforts between pairs/groups of teachers and the collective contributions of the language team. As mentioned, the training component offered diverse learning modalities, all integrating ICT to facilitate seamless collaboration across institutional and national boundaries.

The Reading Assessment Design Workshop, which occurred in 2022, included one four-day in-person cohort in March and one three-day virtual cohort in March. For the in-person cohort, a total of 29 participants were in attendance, among whom were instructors teaching seven different languages (Burmese, Filipino, Hmong, Indonesian, Lao, Thai, and Vietnamese). The virtual cohort, primarily intended for instructors based in Southeast Asia, consisted of 25 participants representing five languages (Burmese, Filipino, Indonesian, Thai, and Vietnamese) from a collective total of 15 institutions. The primary objective of the Reading Assessment Design Workshop was to equip teachers with skills to create effective reading assessments tailored to diverse learner needs. As a result of this collaboration, more than 40 proficiency tests for intermediate and advanced levels in the participating languages were created. These assessments, while not published online, are shared among the teachers for instructional use.

The Reading Materials Development Workshop, occurring in 2023, also consisted of two main cohorts: one three-day SEA-based cohort in March and one three-day US-based cohort in April. The SEA-based cohort met in person at a university in Thailand and included 26 participants representing languages such as Filipino, Indonesian, Thai, and Vietnamese from 10 different academic institutions. The US-based cohort, which met at a university in the Midwest, included 28 educators representing a wider range of eight languages (Burmese, Filipino, Hmong, Khmer, Indonesian, Lao, Thai, and Vietnamese) from 13 institutions across the United States. The primary goal of the workshop was to develop reading materials aimed at enhancing reading proficiency at intermediate and advanced levels. The collaborative effort yielded nearly 50 reading lessons for eight participating languages. These lessons are published online and available to instructors and learners under a Creative Commons licence (https://sealc.wisc.edu/reading-materials-development-workshop/).

Both workshops welcomed participation from teachers of SEA languages, with educators from various institutions across national borders. Specifically, teachers representing the Burmese, Filipino, Indonesian, Thai, and Vietnamese language groups participated in both workshops. Each language group was led by a designated team leader, coordinating the collaborative efforts of participants from different institutions. As authors of this chapter and participants in the workshops, we both serve as Vietnamese language lecturers. One of us took part in both workshops, while the other joined only the reading materials development workshop.

3.3 Data Collection and Data Analysis

Subsequent research associated with this project aimed to investigate the current state of PD for educators from both SEA- and US-based institutions, with a focus on those involved in the 2022 Reading Assessment Design Workshop and the 2023 Reading Materials Development Workshop organized by SEALC. Qualitative data collected include ethnographic observation notes, survey responses ($n = 17$), and interviews ($n = 7$). The survey was sent to the participants after the completion of these PD activities to gather insights into their experiences and perspectives. Those who expressed interest in a follow-up interview were invited for an individual semi-structured interview. For the data analysis, the survey was analysed using descriptive statistics to identify the ICT tools utilized the most and the participants' attitudes towards their integration into different stages and components of the workshop. Additionally, analysis of demographic data collected from the survey offered valuable insights into participants' characteristics, guiding future PD initiatives. The audio of interview recordings was first transcribed and separately coded and themed by the two interviewers to identify recurring patterns and significant insights. The two authors exchanged their coding and had a discussion to decide on the common themes. Interview data provided a comprehensive understanding of the teachers' reflections on their experiences. This thematic analysis enabled the extraction of key insights into the educators' perspectives on this model of PD and the use of ICT tools in this collaborative learning and doing experience.

4 Current Scenario of PD for Teachers of SEA Languages

Both survey responses and interviews reveal that almost every home institution encouraged their teachers to participate in PD, but not all could provide the learning opportunity or financial support. Most SEA-based teachers did not find many resources around them, and thus, they actively sought free PD opportunities offered online. Conversely, US-based teachers reported that their institutions did offer many learning opportunities; yet, those PDs were mainly related to computer-assisted language learning (CALL) or just one-hour webinars with no participation, especially not focused on SEA language pedagogy, which was the area they needed. Vy (all names are pseudonyms), a US-based Vietnamese lecturer leading a Vietnamese program housed in a strong department of East Asian languages and cultures, remarked that, despite having many opportunities for PD from their institution, they were interested in and in need of learning from fellow SEA language teachers. This need is because their Vietnamese program was small compared to other language programs offered at their home institution, and they gained more insights when working with fellow teachers who share similar teaching situations.

Besides limited funding, heavy workloads presented challenges for SEA language teachers' participation in lengthy PD projects. Two US-based lecturers in public universities reported in the interview that limited funding and heavy teaching loads discouraged them from participating in PD. Most SEA language instructors functioned as "single-person departments," running the entire program independently and teaching all levels. Consequently, adding another project to their workload presented a significant challenge. Khanh, a US-based Vietnamese teaching professor, commented that, although she began the job with eagerness and innovative ideas for the program, the demands of teaching four distinct courses totalling 16 credit hours per semester led to her burnout, leaving her "too tired to think or want to do anything related to the job." However, this same instructor shared that she still participated in the PD workshops to refresh herself and regain motivation.

In addition, factors impacting funding for teachers included the size of the program and the faculty position. For example, a tenure-track professor in a Vietnamese program at a European institution noted that their institution provided funding to professors but not to instructors, even though they both shared the Vietnamese classes. By contrast, a tenure-track professor in Vietnam reported that they had nearly zero funding for PD due to the department's modest size. Two US-based career-track professors of Vietnamese mentioned that, while their home institution offered numerous PD online workshops on technology, it provided limited funding for external opportunities, such as workshops or online courses with CARLA or ACTFL. Despite both being non-tenure, the lecturer at a private university had a lighter teaching load and lower enrolment, while the teaching professor at a public university taught up to 16 credit hours per semester. These four teachers of Vietnamese, teaching the same language at four different institutions, had different faculty positions and got different levels of access to institutional support. Remarkably, they all had equal opportunities to participate in the same learning opportunities and contribute to the community through the PD facilitated by SEALC. This equality is particularly notable considering institutional and regional differences. Their shared experiences underscore the importance of providing equitable PD opportunities to all educators, regardless of their institutional status or support, to promote the development and sustainability of language programs. Additionally, in the interviews, the teachers also discussed the impact of these PD opportunities on the personal growth of the teachers. For example, three SEA-based participants reported enhanced confidence in communicating with international colleagues using "available normal Google" (as Khanh described it) for telecollaboration. While telecollaboration has been a staple in language learner curricula for some time, its utilization among teachers in PD projects has only emerged as a notable trend since the onset of the pandemic (see for example, Chapter 10 in this volume). This shift underscores the potential of ICT in facilitating collaboration and overcoming geographical barriers in PD initiatives. With a transnational approach to PD, participants have the opportunity to collaborate with educators from diverse backgrounds and access resources and expertise that may not be available locally. In the following sections, further details of the PD programs will be explored, highlighting their value and specific impacts.

5 Telecommunication and Equitable Conditions for Teachers of SEA Languages

I think this is one of the legacies of the COVID time, that we stay connected.
– Chi, a Vietnamese language teacher

5.1 Utilization of Familiar Telecommunication Tools

SEALC's 2022 Reading Assessment Design Workshop and 2023 Reading Materials Development Workshop successfully connected geographically dispersed participants through a diverse ecosystem of telecommunication tools. This section unpacks what and how specific tools were employed during different stages of the workshops, including the initial training sessions, the project phase, and the symposium.

Prior to the workshops, efforts were made to ensure a common understanding of ACTFL/OPI frameworks among all participants. The Oral Proficiency Interview (OPI) is a framework developed by ACTFL for assessing an individual's speaking proficiency. It evaluates a person's ability to communicate effectively in real-life situations, focusing on linguistic accuracy, fluency, vocabulary usage, and cultural appropriateness. The framework provides a structured method for assessing language proficiency levels, ranging from novice to superior, and is widely used in language education to guide instruction and assessment.

All participants attained a shared understanding of the ACTFL/OPI frameworks through the utilization of a learning management system (LMS) called Schoology, which offered asynchronous training modules accessible to everyone. Schoology is a digital learning management platform that provides a centralized hub for course materials, discussions, assignments, and assessments. By incorporating Schoology into pre-workshop preparation, participants across borders were able to access resources and engage in discussions asynchronously, promoting inclusivity and accommodating different learning preferences. These modules provided foundational knowledge and established a baseline understanding before the commencement of the workshops. Additionally, interactive learning and discussions regarding ACTFL/OPI frameworks were conducted synchronously via Zoom sessions, encouraging active engagement and fostering a shared knowledge base among participants.

Throughout both virtual synchronous and hybrid training sessions or symposia, real-time communication was facilitated via Zoom. Additionally, instant messaging platforms such as WhatsApp, Zalo, and Facebook Messenger, chosen by each language group, played a crucial role in fostering informal communication and connections among participants outside of scheduled sessions. The workshop leaders facilitated this selection process by allowing each group to determine which platform best suited their communication needs and preferences, ensuring effective and personalized interaction throughout the PD activities. Each language group created its own chat group, serving as a space for teachers to send quick reminders, share links and pictures, and socialize virtually.

Meanwhile, official communication, workshop updates, and resource sharing were efficiently managed through email, ensuring that all participants remained informed and connected throughout the program. Moreover, cloud-based collaboration tools like Google Docs and Drive, part of Google Suite (G Suite), empowered participants to collaborate on lesson development tasks seamlessly. These tools facilitated shared document editing and efficient resource sharing, enhancing collaboration and productivity during the workshops. Collaboration on refining lesson materials continued through Google Docs and Drive, enabling participants to provide ongoing feedback and updates on the progress of their work. These platforms ensured that the collaborative efforts initiated during the workshops were sustained, fostering continued engagement and support among participants beyond the workshop sessions.

In investigating the telecommunication tools utilized in the workshops, it is important to note that, apart from Schoology – the LMS used by ACTFL in OPI training – the remaining tools are familiar ones used daily by participants for work or personal communication. Each language team had to decide on their communication channel, and each group in the team also had to establish their own workflow and communication strategy. The selection of Zalo, a Vietnamese messaging application, as an informal communication channel for the Vietnamese team further underscores the interconnected nature of "local" and "international" within the workshops.

5.2 Transformative Impact of Telecommunication Tools in Language Teacher Development

Drawing upon research on interinstitutional and transnational PD models (Fassetta et al., 2020), the SEALC workshops demonstrate the transformative power of telecommunication tools in language teacher development. Interviewed participants highlighted several key advantages, particularly for those in Southeast Asia.

The primary benefit lies in the tools' cost effectiveness and time efficiency. Traditional in-person programs often pose financial and logistical hurdles for SEA-based educators. The teachers expressed that leveraging tools like Zoom, WhatsApp, and Facebook Messenger offered a cost-effective solution. Eliminating travel expenses and enabling participation within existing schedules aligned with research on collaborative language partnerships, which emphasizes the importance of accessibility, particularly for under-resourced regions. Studies by Giupponi et al. (2021) and Castrillo and Sedano (2021) have highlighted the transformative potential of telecollaboration in promoting accessibility to educational opportunities, especially in regions with limited resources. Our findings corroborate these claims, demonstrating how telecollaboration can democratize access to professional development for educators in Southeast Asia, ultimately contributing to the advancement of language education in the region.

As previously mentioned, the survey data revealed that SEA-based educators commonly cited financial constraints and logistical challenges as major barriers to participating in in-person PD programs. Most workshop participants also agreed that the use of telecollaboration tools eliminated the need for travel expenses and accommodation, making participation more feasible and cost effective. Moreover, the flexibility of telecollaboration allowed educators to engage in PD activities within their existing schedules, mitigating time constraints and enhancing accessibility.

Another advantage of telecollaboration tools is their enhanced reach and inclusivity, drawing participants from various transnational locations across Southeast Asia and beyond, such as Indonesia, Laos, the Philippines, Singapore, Thailand, Vietnam, and Italy. By transcending geographical limitations, these tools extended the program's reach to a wider range of SEA and other language teachers, fostering diverse regional representation and enriching learning experiences through varied perspectives. The first training component in the workshop was OPI familiarization, in which participants learned asynchronously on Schoology before meeting the trainer synchronously via Zoom for discussion and clarification. Schoology's features, such as discussion forums and document sharing, allowed participants to collaborate effectively regardless of their physical location or time zone. Notably, the use of Schoology demonstrated adaptability to different learning formats, further promoting inclusivity. In the interviews, both Vietnamese teachers based outside the United States expressed appreciation for the ACTFL training delivered through Schoology, which afforded them the flexibility to learn at their own pace. Phương highlighted the efficiency of the learning model, which combined independent asynchronous interaction within the LMS with synchronous Q&A sessions. This approach allowed her to access what she called "international training," which she described as the same professional training as her international colleagues. Phương also noted that such training with ACTFL would have been prohibitively expensive if pursued individually. Meanwhile, Chi observed that the discussions in the LMS forums served as a gateway for people from both similar and different language groups to connect and exchange ideas, fostering a sense of community. As a teacher, Chi found that listening to questions from both her own team and other language groups provided her with "a deeper understanding of various teaching contexts and the challenges they encountered." This comment aligns with research highlighting the value of online communities in developing language awareness, intercultural competence, and digital literacy (O'Dowd & O'Rourke, 2019). Such communities are known to combat social isolation and empower individuals in under-resourced contexts to overcome barriers (Fassetta et al., 2020; Motteram et al., 2020).

A third advantage of these tools is the open access to quality PD and expert trainers. Telecommunication tools provided unprecedented access for SEA-based teachers to ACTFL trainers, previously unreachable through traditional models. Exposure to leading experts and cutting-edge pedagogical approaches, such as authentic materials and task-based language teaching, significantly enriched the learning experience and empowered participants to update their teaching practices. These experiences not only helped bridge geographical divides but also empowered educators in regions with limited resources to access PD opportunities previously unavailable to them. Our data revealed that many teachers in Southeast Asia reported an enhanced sense of connection to a broader community of practice and that the PD experience has "broadened teacher networking and collaboration" (Chi) and "fostered global partnership" (Sudiman). As for the US-based instructors, to be able to connect with SEA instructors was also a valuable opportunity to exchange expertise and get inspired. The collaborative nature of the workshops proved beneficial for US-based instructors as well. An interview with a SEALC official and workshop facilitator, who was also part of the grant writing team, provided valuable insights into the project's origins. The facilitator, Rosalie, mentioned that the project emphasized collaboration because "LCTL is lonely." The connectivity and engagement align with findings from studies highlighting the transformative impact of online collaboration tools in fostering inclusive and supportive learning environments (Fassetta et al., 2020; Motteram et al., 2020).

5.3 Challenges of Telecommunication

While telecommunication tools offer significant advantages for SEA language teacher development, acknowledging their limitations is crucial for a comprehensive understanding. The SEALC workshops' participants revealed several noteworthy disadvantages.

The primary drawback was related to time differences. Coordinating across diverse time zones presented logistical difficulties. Synchronous sessions scheduled to accommodate US trainers often overlapped with late evenings or early mornings for SEA participants. This time difference led to fatigue, reduced participation, and missed sessions, impacting the overall learning experience. For instance, a 3 p.m. afternoon session in California translated to 1 a.m. early morning the next day in Thailand, significantly hindering engagement for participants juggling personal commitments or facing conflicting timetables.

The second issue revolved around limited internet connectivity. Unequal access to reliable internet infrastructure was a significant hurdle, particularly for teachers in remote areas. For example, Chi, a Vietnamese teacher from a suburban area of Hanoi, often experienced dropped calls and lagging video during Zoom sessions, hindering participating fully. Addressing this issue requires exploring alternative low-bandwidth tools and advocating for improved internet access in under-resourced regions (see Chapter 2 by Hauck, this volume, for further discussion on the use of low-bandwidth tools to promote inclusivity in virtual exchange).

The third challenge pertains to the lack of private space. Conducting Zoom sessions from shared spaces like crowded homes or noisy cafés posed challenges for focused participation. Phương, a teacher living in a multigenerational household, often faced distractions from family activities during sessions. This challenge emphasizes the importance of encouraging participants to secure adequate privacy for optimal engagement in online sessions.

Moreover, a theme that was salient in the interview data is the belief that the age of teachers, rather than their geographic region, posed challenges with technology, particularly for the older generation of educators. Five out of seven interviewees noted generational gaps in technological proficiency. It was also observed that, while younger teachers may naturally navigate towards digital platforms, older educators expressed difficulties navigating these platforms effectively and seemed to need additional support and training to effectively utilize these tools. This finding underscores the importance of considering technological proficiency and accessibility when implementing telecommunication tools in PD initiatives. Moving forward, the challenge lies in bridging the gap to ensure equitable participation across all age groups, emphasizing the need for inclusive approaches to training and support. Proactive measures, such as providing alternative communication channels and creating supportive learning environments, are essential to address these challenges and foster greater inclusivity.

Beyond the previously mentioned challenges, some participants also faced language barriers. While English was the primary language of instruction, not all participants were equally proficient, impacting their ability to fully engage in discussions and activities. Some SEA-based participants asked for closed captioning in Zoom; simple accommodations like captioning could make a significant difference for a diverse multilingual audience participating in the training sessions.

These challenges underscore the importance of ongoing development and refinement of telecommunication-based PD models. Implementing strategies such as flexible scheduling, alternative tools, clear instructions, and enabled accessibility can help create more inclusive and equitable learning experiences for all participants, regardless of geographical location, technological access, or generational background.

6 Telecollaboration: Cultivating Connections beyond Training Sessions

It's fostering global partnerships for knowledge and also mutual support across languages, so I think it collectively contributed to the growth and the development of Indonesian language education worldwide to some extent.

– Sudiman, an Indonesian teacher

6.1 Cultivating Connections and Collaboration

The impact of telecommunication tools in the SEALC workshops extended beyond facilitating asynchronous and synchronous learning and meeting delivery. This section shifts the focus from the tools themselves to how participants actively utilized platforms like WhatsApp, Zalo, G Suite, and Facebook to build support networks and sustain engagement beyond formal training sessions. While Section 5 focused primarily on the use of telecommunication tools during the training sessions, this section delves into the project engagements and collaborative efforts that continued afterward.

Participants utilized platforms such as G Suite to create dynamic environments for collaborative learning and resource sharing. G Suite, with its cloud-based tools such as Google Docs and Drive, eradicated the complexities of traditional methods like email attachments and version control issues. For instance, Uyen from Vietnam and Ly from the United States seamlessly co-created a reading comprehension activity within a shared Google Doc. This collaborative effort not only instilled a sense of collective ownership but also allowed for mutual learning from each other's strengths and perspectives. Furthermore, providing feedback became more efficient through Google Docs' comment feature. For example, in the cross-group feedback, a Thai teacher could offer instant suggestions on a post-reading task in an Indonesian lesson, fostering constructive dialogue and enhancing the tool's effectiveness. Additionally, tracking changes became effortless with Google Drive's detailed version history, enabling participants to monitor progress, revert to previous versions if necessary, and ensure alignment among all contributors. These project engagements highlighted the ongoing collaborative opportunities afforded by telecommunication tools, enriching the learning experience and fostering lasting connections among participants.

6.2 Telecollaboration Strategies

First and foremost, "open and sharing" (as described by the teacher Sudiman) has been a key strategy in telecollaboration. G Suite served as a readily accessible repository of valuable materials for future reference. Lesson plans, assessment templates, and other resources remained readily available for participants after the training sessions, empowering them to later adapt and implement these resources in their own classrooms. Collaboration was not just within teams but across various levels, fostering a rich tapestry of learning and support. As shown in Figure 9.2, peer feedback was not only provided by other groups within the same language team but also by groups from different language teams. There was also collaboration among cross-teams within the language group, where one team could access and contribute to the documents of other teams, fostering cross-pollination of ideas and enriching their projects. Throughout the duration of the project, participants could receive feedback from five sources (see Figure 9.2). This abundance of feedback opportunities was invaluable in overcoming the sense of isolation SEA teachers can experience in their practice. Giving and receiving peer feedback over several rounds significantly deepened the telecollaboration among the participants.

Instant communication was reported by team leaders as an effective way to keep team members up to date with project progress and connected with each other. Informal communicative channels such as WhatsApp or Facebook Messenger were selected by the members of the group and the team leaders. Though the use of these channels may appear to be "unprofessional," the participants were comfortable with using them. One teacher noted, "We feel that we are a family." As stated by Sudiman,

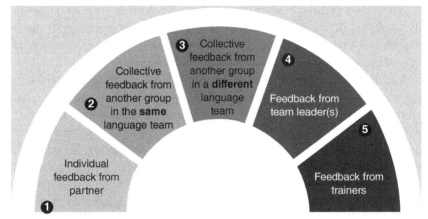

Figure 9.2 Different Types of Feedback One Received in the Workshop
Source: The authors.

his participation in the workshop fostered not only an expansion of his professional network but also the development of friendships among colleagues.

6.3 Challenges of Telecollaboration

While Section 5.3. discussed challenges encountered during the asynchronous or synchronous training sessions, this section delves deeper into the specific obstacles faced by participants in telecollaborative endeavours, which were distinct from the training sessions themselves.

The primary challenge arose from individual digital literacy. Although the SEALC workshops presented an optimistic outlook of connectivity through telecollaboration, the underlying reality revealed numerous obstacles that posed challenges and jeopardized progress for certain participants. It was observed that some young tech-savvy teachers found tools like Zoom and Google Docs to be familiar and intuitive, while older teachers felt as though they were exploring unfamiliar territory. Familiarity with Zoom and G Suite seemed to be perceived by the organizers as a default skill and knowledge of participants. However, participants' struggles with digital literacy extended to specific functionalities within these tools. As reported by a team leader in the interview, one participant even gave up and left a team meeting after failing to figure out how to share screen on Zoom. It was also observed that not being able to locate different versions or copies of the working file was another common issue among the participants. Such experiences underscore the need for tailored support and training to ensure equitable participation across all levels of digital proficiency.

Another challenge stemmed from conflicting commitments. Balancing workshops with existing teaching responsibilities proved an impossible feat for some. Additionally, there were challenges in maintaining enthusiasm. Although the initial training sessions, typically lasting three or four days, sparked enthusiasm and engagement among participants, the subsequent implementation phase, which spanned an entire semester, appeared to lose momentum for some after the initial deadlines passed. One team leader shared an important strategy regarding keeping the flame of motivation burning throughout the workshops for her team. During moments of doubt or hesitation, she encouraged her team to reflect on their personal goals and the larger purpose of their work, emphasizing the impact on their program, language, and cultural heritage. As previously mentioned, teachers needed to apply and be accepted into the program, which can instil motivation from the outset. Planners of a demanding PD project that lasts for days or weeks should explore ways to keep their participants motivated.

7 Recommendations for the Design and Implementation of PD Initiatives

This study underscores the importance of aligning PD initiatives with the practical needs of teachers. The findings of this study align with previous literature, emphasizing that effective PD should prioritize addressing the practical needs of teachers, provide opportunities for active participation and creation, last for a reasonable duration, and crucially, foster collaboration among educators (Desimone, 2009; Jaipal & Figg, 2011). While most participants expressed appreciation for their PD experiences within the project, some teachers voiced a desire for a needs analysis process that would allow them to articulate their current pressing needs. Conducting a needs analysis prior to PD sessions would not only provide teachers with a sense of being heard but also inform organizers about the focal points to address, ensuring that PD sessions are tailored to meet the specific needs of participants.

In addition, it is crucial to consider the duration of PD programs. The extended duration, designed to allow sufficient time for deep engagement and thorough development of skills and materials, was necessary to achieve meaningful and sustainable outcomes. However, teachers' enthusiasm faded as the project prolonged more than one semester, highlighting the need for sustained motivation and support mechanisms to maintain engagement over lengthy PD initiatives. Taking into account that adequate time must be given and that PD should spread over a semester, getting through 20 hours or more contact time (Desimone, 2009), it is recommended that PD programs be two to three months long. This duration allows participants to focus intensively and then apply their newly acquired knowledge immediately afterward. For instance, a PD project could run from June to August, instead of from March to September, enabling participants to apply their learning during the subsequent fall semester. This approach aligns with research indicating that PD should last for a reasonable duration and provide opportunities for application in practice (Desimone, 2009).

Furthermore, collaboration among teachers is commonly categorized into pre-service and in-service, or as mentor and mentee. However, when incorporating ICT into collaboration, it is essential to acknowledge other dimensions such as digital familiarity or generational differences. Providing support tailored to individuals' digital literacy levels and facilitating intergenerational knowledge exchange can enhance the effectiveness of collaborative PD initiatives.

It is crucial to recognize that CALL serves not only as a tool to facilitate language learning for students but also as a domain of learning for teachers themselves. Critically, CALL facilitates equity and inclusion by democratizing access to professional development through online exchanges. This accessibility allows educators from diverse and under-resourced regions to participate in high-quality training and collaborative initiatives that they might otherwise be excluded from, thus addressing systemic disparities in educational resources and opportunities. Interestingly, the research revealed that teachers identified age or generation, rather than regional affiliation or institutional setting, as a primary challenge for both telecommunication and telecollaboration. This finding suggests that collaborative PD can be an effective tool in bridging the generation gap, as younger teachers can provide support to their older colleagues during project implementation.

In the context of PD, engaging with CALL technologies not only enables teachers to enhance their instructional practices but also provides opportunities for ongoing learning and skill development. As educators explore and integrate various CALL tools and methodologies into their teaching, they deepen their understanding of how technology can effectively support language acquisition and pedagogical goals. Moreover, navigating the ever-evolving landscape of CALL necessitates continuous learning and adaptation as new technologies and approaches emerge. Challenges such as lack of digital literacy and limited access to resources can hinder the effective integration of CALL. Addressing these challenges through targeted training and support can enhance teachers' confidence and competence in using CALL. Therefore, acknowledging CALL as both a facilitator of teacher learning and a domain for ongoing professional growth underscores its significance in contemporary language education contexts.

8 Conclusion

This study offers empirical support for foundational principles of adult learning theory (Knowles et al., 2020; Merriam & Baumgartner, 2020), emphasizing the significance of self-directed learning and prior experiences in shaping educators' trajectories. Additionally, it aligns with Wenger's (1998) concept of communities of practice, underlining the importance of collective learning and knowledge sharing among educators. Furthermore, the findings resonate with Vygotsky's (1978) social constructivist perspective, illustrating how social interaction and collaboration facilitate individual learning within professional development contexts.

Our empirical study finds that telecommunication tools such as Zoom, WhatsApp, and G Suite are crucial for facilitating collaboration among geographically dispersed language educators, enhancing instructional practices and fostering global partnerships. However, challenges like time zone differences, limited internet connectivity, and digital literacy disparities necessitate ongoing refinement of these telecommunication-based professional development models.

In the short term, these collaborative initiatives can lead to immediate changes in teachers' instructional approaches as they integrate new techniques and materials into their teaching practices. Over the long term, collaborative initiatives have the potential to open up even further collaboration initiated by teachers themselves. Some of the teachers who participated in the workshop mentioned that they are motivated and inspired to plan their own virtual language tables within the country, develop virtual language exchange programs across countries, or plan for collaborative online international learning projects.

Sustainability in collaborative professional development hinges on institutional support, ongoing mentorship, and community building. Institutional backing ensures resources and infrastructure, while mentorship fosters continuous growth. Community building promotes collaboration and knowledge sharing, sustaining PD initiatives. A holistic approach encompassing these elements maximizes the impact of collaborative PD in language education.

Acknowledging limitations and challenges is crucial for ensuring the credibility and completeness of the study. Potential biases in participant recruitment, such as selection bias, may have influenced the representation of perspectives. Additionally, the study's limited number of participants might have restricted the breadth of insights gathered, potentially overlooking diverse experiences within the language education community. Furthermore, while the findings offer valuable insights into collaborative PD processes, it is essential to recognize the limitations in generalizing the results to broader contexts due to the uniqueness of each educational setting. These considerations contribute to a more nuanced understanding of the study's scope and implications.

While this study investigated the telecommunication tools employed during the workshops and the subsequent telecollaboration, along with their associated benefits and challenges, it did not delve deeply into the social interactions among the participating teachers. Therefore, future research can build upon these findings and enhance professional development initiatives for language educators by exploring these social interactions in greater detail, potentially utilizing relevant theoretical frameworks.

About the Authors

An Nguyen Sakach is an assistant teaching professor of Vietnamese language and culture at Arizona State University (ASU). She has dedicated more than 15 years to teaching and developing materials for Vietnamese learners. With a background in applied linguistics and expertise in computer-assisted language learning as well as curriculum design and materials development, she has successfully obtained several grants for developing learning materials for Vietnamese learners, including a collaborative project on open educational resources tailored for intermediate learners (Michigan State University) and an OURS Mentor Grant to offer research experiences to online students in translation and cultural heritage preservation (ASU). She also co-authored a book on Vietnamese collocations and conceptual metaphors in a book series for Vietnamese children.

Trang Phan, assistant professor in the Department of Asian and North African Studies at Ca' Foscari University of Venice, earned her PhD from the University of Sheffield in 2013, conducted postdoctoral research at Ghent University, 2014–2016, led a state-level project funded by the Vietnam National Foundation for Science & Technology Development (NAFOSTED), 2019–2021, and was a visiting scholar at the Harvard-Yenching Institute, 2020–2021. She has co-edited several volumes on Vietnamese linguistics (John Benjamins, 2019; Springer Nature, 2024) and authored the monograph *The Syntax of Vietnamese Tense, Aspect, and Negation* (Routledge, 2023). Additionally, she co-authored the three trilingual (Vietnamese-English-Italian) textbooks *Vietnamese Vibes 1, 2, 3* (Cafoscarina Press, 2024).

For academic purposes, An Sakach is responsible for Sections 1, 2, 5, 6, and 7, while Trang Phan is responsible for Sections 3 and 4 of this chapter.

References

Amaratunga, D., Liyanage, C., & Haigh, R. (2018). A study into the role of international collaborations in higher education to enhance research capacity for disaster resilience. *Procedia Engineering*, *212*, 1233–1240. https://doi.org/10.1016/j.proeng.2018.01.159

Bachtiar, B. (2020). The characteristics of effective professional development that affect teacher's self-efficacy and teaching practice. *Eduvelop: Journal of English Education and Development*, *3*(2), 131–144. https://doi.org/10.31605/eduvelop.v3i2.624

Belay, S., Melesse, S., & Seifu, A. (2022). Elevating teachers' professional capital: Effects of teachers' engagement in professional learning and job satisfaction, Awi district, Ethiopia. *Sage Open*, *12*(2). https://doi.org/10.1177/21582440221094592

Castrillo, M.D., & Sedano, B. (2021). Joining forces towards social inclusion: Language MOOC design for refugees and migrants through the lens of maker culture. *CALICO Journal*, *38*(1), 79–102. https://doi.org/10.1558/cj.40900

Cochran-Smith, M., & Lytle, S.L. (2009). *Inquiry as stance: Practitioner research for the next generation.* Teachers College Press.

Desimone, L.M. (2009). Improving impact studies of teachers' professional development: Toward better conceptualizations and measures. *Educational Researcher, 38*(3), 181–199. https://doi.org/10.3102/0013189X08331140

Fassetta, G., Al-Masri, N., Attia, M., & Phipps, A. (2020). Gaza teaches Arabic online: Opportunities, challenges and ways forward. In G. Fassetta, N. Al-Masri, M. Attia, & A. Phipps (Eds.), *Multilingual online academic collaborations as resistance: Crossing impassable borders* (pp. 117–130). Multilingual Matters. https://doi.org/10.21832/9781788929608

Giupponi, L., Heidrich Uebel, E., & Van Gorp, K. (2021). Strategies for language centers to support online language instruction. In E. Lavolette & A. Kraemer (Eds.), *Language center handbook 2021* (pp. 61–90). International Association for Language Learning Technology.

Goddard, Y., Goddard, R.D., & Tschannen-Moran, M. (2007). A theoretical and empirical investigation of teacher collaboration for school improvement and student achievement in public elementary schools. *Teachers College Record: The Voice of Scholarship in Education, 109*(4), 877–896. https://doi.org/10.1177/016146810710900401

Jaipal, K., & Figg, C. (2011). Collaborative action research approaches promoting professional development for elementary school teachers. *Educational Action Research, 19*(1), 59–72. https://doi.org/10.1080/09650792.2011.547688

Kirvalidze, M., & Lobzhanidze, S. (2023). Professional development and performance assessment system focused on strengthening teachers' collaboration: The case of Georgia. *Problems of Education in the 21st Century, 81*(1), 66–89. https://doi.org/10.33225/pec/23.81.66

Knowles, M.S., Holton, E.F., III, Swanson, R.A., Swanson, R., & Robinson, P.A. (2020). *The adult learner: The definitive classic in adult education and human resource development* (9th ed.). Routledge. https://doi.org/10.4324/9780429299612

Lakshmanan, A., Heath, B., Perlmutter, A., & Elder, M. (2010). The impact of science content and professional learning communities on science teaching efficacy and standards-based instruction. *Journal of Research in Science Teaching, 48*(5), 534–551. https://doi.org/10.1002/tea.20404

Levin, B.B., & Rock, T.C. (2003). The effects of collaborative action research on preservice and experienced teacher partners in professional development schools. *Journal of Teacher Education, 54*(2), 135–149. https://doi.org/10.1177/0022487102250287

Martin, L., & Mulvihill, T. (2023). Voices in education: Successful professional development for educators: What does it look like and who should be involved?

The Teacher Educator, 58(1), 1–14. https://doi.org/10.1080/08878730.2023.2145716

Merriam, S.B., & Baumgartner, L.M. (2020). *Learning in adulthood: A comprehensive guide* (4th ed.). John Wiley & Sons.

Messiou, K. (2019). Collaborative action research: Facilitating inclusion in schools. *Educational Action Research, 27*(2), 197–209. https://doi.org/10.1080/09650792.2018.1436081

Motteram, G., Dawson, S., & Al-Masri, N. (2020). *WhatsApp* supported language teacher development: A case study in the Zataari refugee camp. *Education and Information Technologies, 25,* 5731–5751. https://doi.org/10.1007/s10639-020-10233-0

O'Dowd, R., & O'Rourke, B. (2019). New developments in virtual exchange in foreign language education. *Language Learning & Technology, 23*(3), 1–7. https://doi.org/10125/44690

Sakach, A., & Dinh, H. (2023, April 20). *A collaborative project: Reading proficiency assessment* [PowerPoint presentation]. Shared LCTL Symposium, Chicago, IL, United States.

SEALC. (2022). *Proficiency-based reading assessment*. The Southeast Asian Language Council. https://sealc.wisc.edu/2021-workshops-2/

SEALC. (2023). *Reading materials development workshop*. The Southeast Asian Language Council. https://sealc.wisc.edu/reading-materials-development-workshop/

Smith, F. (2011). *Understanding reading: A psycholinguistic analysis of reading and learning to read* (6th ed.). Routledge. https://doi.org/10.4324/9780203142165

Stewart, C. (2014). Transforming professional development to professional learning. *Journal of Adult Education, 43*(1), 28–33. https://eric.ed.gov/?id=EJ1047338

Steyn, G.M. (2014). Teacher collaboration and invitational leadership in a South African primary school. *Education and Urban Society, 48*(5), 504–526. https://doi.org/10.1177/0013124514536441

Vygotsky, L.S. (1978). *Mind in society: The development of higher psychological processes* (M. Cole, V. John-Steiner, S. Scribner, & E. Souberman, Eds.). Harvard University Press. https://doi.org/10.2307/j.ctvjf9vz4

Wenger, E. (1998). *Communities of practice: Learning, meaning, and identity*. Cambridge University Press. https://doi.org/10.1017/CBO9780511803932

Yilmaz, K. (2022). Teachers' professional collaboration in Turkey: Current status, barriers, and suggestions. *Ankara Universitesi Egitim Bilimleri Fakultesi Dergisi, 55*(3), 1023–1043. https://doi.org/10.30964/auebfd.1143251

10 Advancing Arabic Language Education: Empowering Teachers and Promoting Critical CALL through the Arabic Teachers' Council

Kamilia Rahmouni

1 Introduction

Arabic instruction in American universities dates back to the seventeenth and eighteenth centuries (Al-Busaidi, 2015). It has traditionally been taught with a focus on scholarly use rather than everyday applications (Mana, 2011). However, beginning in the 1950s, Arabic educators started to gradually move away from grammar-based teaching methods to adopt a more pragmatic and communicative approach (Mana, 2011; Ryding, 1991). This shift was largely precipitated by efforts initiated as early as 1958 and aimed at improving Arabic instruction in the United States (Mana, 2011). In 1958, the Social Science Research Council sponsored a conference of Arabic teachers with the goal of making recommendations specifically related to textbooks and evaluation systems (Al-Busaidi, 2015). This initiative led to the establishment of the American Association of Teachers of Arabic (AATA) in 1963 under the direction of the Modern Language Association (MLA). The goal of the AATA is to foster collaboration among Arabic educators with the aim of advancing the teaching of Arabic and enhancing Arabic programs nationwide. Promptly after its establishment, the AATA started publishing a newsletter, *An-Nashrā*, which later became known as *Al-Arabiyya Journal*, the annual journal of the AATA (Al-Busaidi, 2015).

However, despite this evolution – or, perhaps, because of it – educators continue to face various pedagogical, sociolinguistic, and professional challenges. Issues such as diglossia and the diverse teaching approaches it entails are among the main challenges that Arabic educators have been facing. In essence, while the move towards pragmatism and sociolinguistic authenticity signifies pedagogical progress, it has also introduced new challenges for educators. Beyond these sociolinguistic considerations, Arabic educators have also been grappling with challenges related to limited networking and professional development (PD) opportunities and insufficient resources (Al-Busaidi, 2015).

These challenges highlight the pressing need for innovative approaches to PD and pedagogical training that are not only tailored to specifically address these concerns but also to include, instil, and promote the broader imperatives of diversity, equity, inclusion, and accessibility (DEIA) within the field of Arabic instruction. To address these challenges, this chapter proposes the concept of DEIA-enhanced communities of practice (CoP), which envisions a collaborative space informed by DEIA principles. Within this framework, the District of Columbia Arabic Teachers' Council (DC-ATC) exemplifies a noteworthy instantiation of a CoP effectively responding to the various pedagogical and professional challenges faced by Arabic educators. This chapter identifies workshops organized by the DC-ATC from 2020 to 2023 and illustrates ways in which the council leveraged the transformative potential of technology and online tools in order to improve DEIA outcomes for Arabic language teachers and contribute to the creation of a more effective and inclusive Arabic teaching educational setting.

To achieve this aim, the chapter starts with a brief, yet comprehensive overview of the various challenges faced by Arabic educators, namely diglossia, diverse pedagogical approaches, networking and PD limitations, and resource constraints. It then introduces and explains the DEIA-enhanced CoP framework. The chapter ends with a detailed examination of the practical contributions of the DC-ATC in addressing these challenges and supporting Arabic language educators through the use of online tools, innovative workshops, PD opportunities, and resource-sharing initiatives.

2 Challenges in Arabic Language Instruction: Navigating Diglossia, Pedagogical Diversity, Networking and PD Limitations, and Resource Constraints

Arabic language instructors in the United States continue to face various pedagogical and professional challenges. In addition to diglossia and the diverse teaching approaches Arab language teaching entails, resource constraints and PD limitations remain significant issues for Arabic educational practitioners in the country (Al-Busaidi, 2015). These challenges create a pressing need for collaborative initiatives aimed at supporting Arabic teachers, addressing their needs, and creating a sustainably stronger, more inclusive, and effective environment for teaching and learning Arabic. The following section explores these challenges and their impact on Arabic educators. It begins with an examination of the concept of diglossia and the different sociolinguistic challenges it presents for Arabic educators. It then examines the different pedagogical approaches that have been devised and used to address the issue of diglossia in the Arabic classroom. The section ends with an examination of concerns related to resource access, PD, and networking.

2.1 Diglossia: Navigating Linguistic Varieties and Sociolinguistic Challenges

Coined by American linguist Charles Ferguson in 1959, the term "diglossia" (p. 345) describes a stable language situation that features two linguistic varieties used by a single speech community in different contexts: an informal variety used in everyday speech and a formal, education-acquired version used in writing and formal speech. Ferguson termed these varieties as the low (L) variety and the high (H) variety, respectively. Notably, in his definition, the H and L varieties are genetically related, that is, they originate from the same ancestral language. Fishman (1967) later broadened the concept of diglossia to include the use of genetically unrelated languages, which are distinct languages without a common ancestral origin.

In Arabic, the diglossic situation includes two related varieties: Modern Standard Arabic (MSA, widely known as *Fuṣḥā*) and various regional vernaculars (widely known as *ʕāmiyya*). MSA, the H variety, is the written formal variety that is shared by all Arab communities and used in various areas such as education, literature, journalism, and administration. While MSA is predominantly used in written contexts, it can also be employed in certain formal spoken settings, such as political speeches, news broadcasts, and academic lectures. MSA is generally linked with prestige, although some scholars have challenged this viewpoint (Ibrahim, 1986). Meanwhile, regional vernaculars, which represent the L variety, are often perceived as "corrupted" forms of MSA (Maamouri, 1998, p. 33).

Although these regional varieties are mostly used in everyday informal interactions, they are gradually extending their reach into domains that were previously considered exclusive to MSA. For instance, while MSA remains dominant in formal contexts such as education, literature, and media, regional dialects are now increasingly used and accepted in these formal settings. No spoken Arabic variety has undergone complete codification, which has resulted in numerous spelling variations. Distinctions among these varieties manifest prominently in syntax, lexicon, morphology, phonetics, and semantics (Al-Batal, 1992). The interactions between the H and L varieties also give rise to a spectrum of other linguistic forms.

In order to explore and classify the spectrum of linguistic forms and their interaction with MSA, Badawi (1973) proposed a framework based on five levels of speech. Badawi centred his framework on Egyptian Arabic, which stands out for its extensive usage and influence across the Arabic-speaking world, making it an ideal case study for understanding Arabic language variation. Versteegh (2001) posited that almost everyone in the Arabic-speaking world understands Egyptian Arabic and is able to adapt their speech to it if needed. Badawi's (1973) classification of Egyptian Arabic provides a structured framework to analyse these interactions across various communicative contexts.

The first of the five levels of speech Badawi (1973) delineated is represented by *fuṣḥā at-turāṯ* (Classical Arabic), which includes the language of literary heritage and the Quran. This variety is primarily written but can also occasionally be heard in religious settings. The second level, *fuṣḥā al-ʿaṣr* (Contemporary Classical Arabic or MSA), is a modified form of Classical Arabic. This version is commonly seen in writing and heard in news broadcasts and official speeches. The third level, *ʿāmmiyyat al-muṯaqqafīn* (Educated Spoken Arabic), is a colloquial variety influenced by MSA, which is used in discussions among highly educated people, often on television and in educational settings. The fourth level, *ʿāmmiyyat al-mutanawwarīn* (Enlightened Spoken Arabic), is used in informal contexts by moderately educated people and on television for non-intellectual topics. This variety usually features extensive borrowing from different languages. The fifth level, *ʿāmmiyyat al-ʾummiyyīn* (Illiterate Colloquial Arabic), is used by people with minimal or no education and is, therefore, characterized by the absence of MSA influence and limited foreign borrowing.

The complexity of Arabic language teaching, therefore, stems not only from the two ends of the continuum (H and L varieties) but also from the existence of various intermediate forms. Deciding which variety to teach is intricate. It is a decision that involves political, religious, and national pan-Arab implications that go beyond linguistic or pedagogical considerations. Due to these complications, disagreement persists among instructors regarding the optimal approach to addressing diglossia in the Arabic classroom. In their 2016 study, Snowden et al. revealed that 44 per cent of community college teachers in the United Kingdom recognize that teaching dialects is important for effective communication. Despite this recognition, respondents expressed concerns over their lack of pedagogical skills concerning how to effectively integrate the different varieties into the Arabic classroom. Snowden et al.'s study also revealed that more than half of the teachers surveyed do not recognize the significance of teaching Arabic dialects. These results, the authors argued, indicate that "sociolinguistic awareness must be a fundamental component of teacher training programmes" (p. 6). Even though the study was conducted in the United Kingdom, its findings remain applicable within the US context (Sai, 2017). These challenges have led to diverse approaches in handling Arabic diglossia in language instruction.

2.2 Challenges in Arabic Language Pedagogy: Navigating Diverse Teaching Approaches

This section offers a brief historical overview of the various teaching approaches in Arabic language instruction. This overview's goal is twofold: (1) to trace the evolution of Arabic teaching methodologies over time and (2) to situate present challenges and initiatives within a broader historical context. This perspective helps to better understand the current pedagogical challenges faced by Arabic educators.

2.2.1 The Classical Arabic Approach

The Classical Arabic approach is the oldest approach that originated in response to early demands for using Arabic in biblical and Semitic language studies (McCarus, 1987). Initially, this approach, which focuses on Arabic as a classical language, was introduced in the United States within institutions focused on Oriental and Semitic studies and the study of ancient languages, religions, and civilizations (Abboud, 1971). Instructors adopting this approach focused on decoding classical texts and predominantly used the grammar-translation method with minimal attention to oral proficiency (Abboud, 1971; Al-Batal, 1992). To address these shortcomings, new approaches emerged with the outbreak of the Second World War, which prompted a shift in focus from classical to contemporary Arabic (McCarus, 1987).

2.2.2 The MSA Approach

The MSA approach is based on the exclusive use of MSA as the language of instruction in Arabic classes. This approach is believed to have several advantages. First, it reflects, at least partially, the linguistic reality in the Arabic-speaking world, where MSA is spoken under some circumstances (such as in media and educational institutions). Second, unlike the Classical Arabic approach, the MSA approach has an oral component. Third, proponents of this approach emphasize the uniformity of MSA and its pedagogical advantages, and argue that learning to speak MSA first will facilitate students' learning of vernaculars, rather than starting with dialect instruction first (Alosh, 1992).

However, MSA is not entirely uniform across the Arabic-speaking world. It exhibits regional variations that are influenced by local dialects and non-Arabic languages such as French and English (Gibson, 2002). Additionally, contrary to the belief that MSA serves as a conversational bridge language, Arabs do not resort to MSA to overcome communication barriers. Instead, they often adapt their own dialects in order to facilitate understanding. These shortcomings are especially pronounced for ethnographers who wish to do fieldwork in an Arabic-speaking country. Additionally, critics argue that, by emphasizing written language development over oral proficiency and solely relying on MSA, this approach neglects Arabic dialect diversity and fails to prepare students for authentic real-life conversations (Al-Batal, 2007; Younes, 2006). In response to these shortcomings, there were calls for alternative approaches that prioritize conversational Arabic proficiency and prepare students for real-life interactions.

2.2.3 The Colloquial Approach

Like the MSA approach, the colloquial approach emerged in the United States post–Second World War due to governmental interest in training professionals who are able to effectively communicate with Arabic speakers (Al-Batal, 2007). This approach focuses on teaching specific regional varieties and avoids MSA and the Arabic script by using Roman transliteration in textbooks. This approach has been heavily criticized for its inability to achieve proficient educated speakers who are able to read the Arabic alphabet and for its non-transferability of language knowledge to MSA or other dialects (Alosh 1992). Additionally, the colloquial approach primarily caters to those interested solely in conversational Arabic, which might lead to the selection of varieties unintelligible to speakers of other dialects (Alosh, 1992). Al-Batal (1992) reinforced these criticisms by arguing that the colloquial approach fails to meet the needs of the majority of students who seek overall proficiency rather than just oral communicative skills. Aiming for a more balanced solution, a new approach was introduced in order to address these challenges.

2.2.4 The Middle Language Approach

The middle language approach centres on teaching an intermediate variety of Arabic, commonly referred to as Educated Spoken Arabic or by other terms such as *al-Lugha al-Wusta* (Middle Language), *al-Lugha al-Mushtaraka* (Common Language), and *al-Lugha al-Thalitha* (Third Language; Al-Batal, 2007). Educated Spoken Arabic's unclear characteristics and significant variations pose numerous challenges for both teachers and learners (Al-Batal, 2007). Moreover, relying solely on this approach can negatively impact students' oral proficiency by limiting their ability to navigate and effectively switch between different Arabic variations as needed in different social contexts. Consequently, due to the shortcomings of the middle language approach, an alternative approach was introduced to integrate both MSA and regional variations.

2.2.5 The Simultaneous Approach

In the simultaneous approach, students simultaneously learn MSA and an Arabic regional variety within a single program. Arabic programs following this approach intend to replicate the native speaker experience where individuals acquire a regional dialect at home and subsequently learn MSA in formal educational settings. In order to do that, they start with a regional dialect before gradually incorporating MSA in their Arabic education (Al-Batal, 2007). Despite initial promise, the simultaneous approach has faced several criticisms. Al-Batal (2007) criticized its emphasis on structural dialogues over oral proficiency, an approach that reflects a heavy audio-lingual orientation. Alosh (1992) added that the attempt to turn learners into proficient speakers is unnatural and fails to consider first language (L1) and second language (L2) development and learning differences. Amid criticisms, Al-Batal (2007) contended that, while modifications are needed for broader applicability, the simultaneous approach lays the groundwork for a new and more effective teaching approach and should not be entirely dismissed.

2.2.6 The Integrated Approach

The integrated approach, supported by numerous Arabic pedagogists, sociolinguists, and scholars (Al-Batal, 1992; Al-Batal & Belnap, 2006; Fakhri, 1995; Wahba, 2006; Younes, 2006, 2014), aims to merge the instruction of MSA and a spoken dialect within the same classroom setting. The core of this approach, as outlined by Younes (2014), is to present *Fuṣḥā* and the *ʕāmiyya* variety in the same classroom session. Al-Batal (1992) proposed a modified version of the simultaneous approach to "reflect, in the classroom, the diglossic situation (with its different varieties) as it exists in the Arab world today" by introducing MSA mainly as a written variety alongside a spoken dialect for communication (p. 298). As in the simultaneous approach, the dialect variety can be a specific dialect (e.g., Algerian, Moroccan, Tunisian) or a dialectal group (e.g., Gulf, Levantine, North African). However, while introducing these varieties, teachers should not treat them as separate entities but rather as "components of one integrated linguistic system" where each variety is linked to specific contexts and situations (Al-Batal, 1992, p. 298). Additionally, instructors following the integrated approach need to introduce their students to a third variety, which is a mixture of MSA and a dialect, that is, what Badawi (1973) referred to as Educated Spoken Arabic. Wahba (2006) argued that "both varieties of the language should be taught together, as occurs in natural speech context" (p. 139).

Al-Batal (1992) gives examples in order to illustrate the implementation of this approach. He proposed that, if teachers are to introduce students to the situation of checking into a hotel, then they should introduce the two varieties: MSA for filling out the forms and the dialect for talking to the desk assistant at the hotel. However, if teachers are to introduce students to the situation of talking to a shopkeeper and bargaining, then they should introduce only the dialect. Al-Batal argued that the proportions of each variety would depend on the level: more dialectal elements at low levels and more MSA elements at high levels.

Despite its various benefits, such as sociolinguistic authenticity and emphasis on enhancing communicative skills, the integrated approach still suffers from several shortcomings. The interference from one variety into the other, the problem of testing proficiency, the religious importance of Classical Arabic, the different learning motivations for heritage and non-heritage learners, and the choice of which dialect to teach are among the main issues that arise from integrating MSA and dialects (De Felice et al., 2019). Palmer (2007) characterized this dialectal selection as a "boiling point for heated debate among Arabic teaching professionals" (p. 115), which is heightened by the absence of a standardized or codified regional variety. Overall, despite the increasing recognition of integrating MSA and spoken varieties into Arabic curricula, disputes still persist regarding which varieties to teach and how to incorporate them.

This substantial variation both in the language itself and in pedagogical approaches necessitates a greater need for connectedness and dialogue among Arabic teachers across K–16 levels. The need for collaboration and communication can be most effectively addressed through technologically mediated means such as online forums, virtual workshops, and digital resource-sharing platforms. These online means help facilitate connectedness and address the various needs and challenges that Arabic educators face, including insufficient professional development, lack of training and networking opportunities, and limited access to resources (Al-Busaidi, 2015; De Felice et al., 2019).

2.3 Challenges Related to Networking, PD, and Resource Access

A significant challenge faced by Arabic language educators in the United States is the lack of networking opportunities, which often leads to feelings of isolation and solitude. These feelings are particularly pronounced among educators who serve as the sole Arabic instructor in their institutions (Berbeco, 2019). In addition to feelings of isolation, these instructors also suffer from "unshared language-specific challenges" (Soliman & Khalil, 2022, p. 7), which are exacerbated by the lack of inter-program coordination and the absence of clearly defined objectives within Arabic language education programs across the United States (Abboud, 1995; Al-Busaidi, 2015).

An additional challenge that Arabic educators face is scarcity of materials and resources (Al-Batal, 2007; Al-Busaidi, 2015; Soliman & Khalil,

2022; Versteegh, 2001). Al-Busaidi (2015) argued that, despite efforts to create materials and resources for Arabic instruction in certain programs, teachers still express significant concern about the inadequacy and insufficiency of available resources, particularly in terms of supplemental online resources, dialectal educational resources, and cultural materials (see also Wahba, 2006).

Another substantive challenge in Arabic language education is the lack of professional training (De Felice et al., 2019; Mana, 2011; Nash, 2010; Soliman & Khalil, 2022). Mana (2011) argued that "the field does not have a complete picture of what Arabic teachers feel they need in terms of professional development of knowledge and skills" (p. 1). Similarly, Nash (2010) argued that the continuous shortage of qualified Arabic teachers, particularly those with formal training, represents an ongoing challenge in the field of Arabic education in the United States. These observations call for targeted teacher development programs, specifically focused on teacher certification and on improving teachers' understanding and application of the diverse pedagogic approaches to Arabic diglossic language teaching. The collective impact of these challenges necessitates a holistic approach that addresses not only pedagogical gaps but also social dynamics and systemic professional deficiencies in the field of Arabic language teaching.

Various initiatives have been launched to achieve these objectives such as STARTALK, which was founded in 2006 and is funded by the National Security Agency. By funding teacher training and student programs, STARTALK aims to increase proficiency in less commonly taught languages, particularly critical languages such as Arabic and Chinese (Mana, 2011). Initiatives like STARTALK provide guidance and intensive training for instructors; however, as Mana (2011) stated, many of these training workshops focus on generic principles of teaching, with instruction delivered in English to trainees whose L1 is Arabic. Additionally, published research on the professional development needs of Arabic language educators is still limited (De Felice et al., 2019). Furthermore, a discernible gap still exists between higher education institutions and K–12 schools in the context of Arabic teaching. These collective challenges highlight the pressing need for innovative approaches to professional development, tailored not only to address these specific concerns but also to include the broader imperatives of DEIA in the field of Arabic language instruction.

3 DEIA-Enhanced Communities of Practice

In response to these needs, this chapter proposes the DEIA-enhanced communities of practice framework, which builds upon the concept of communities of practice (CoP). Coined by Lave and Wenger (1991) during their study of apprenticeship as a learning model, the term "communities of practice" refers to the community that "acts as a living curriculum for the apprentice" (Wenger-Trayner & Wenger-Trayner, 2015, p. 4). Wenger (1998) expanded on this concept by arguing that these communities form out of necessity to accomplish tasks, essentially through mutual engagement in a shared endeavour. Through continuous mutual engagement, members of the CoP develop common repertoires such as routines, vocabulary, and ways of interacting. In essence, CoPs are "groups of people who share a concern or a passion for something they do and learn how to do it better as they interact regularly" (Wenger-Trayner & Wenger-Trayner, 2015, p. 2).

Similarly, Liedtka (1999) described communities of practice as "individuals united in action" (p. 5). As such, a CoP is a group of people who share a common interest, profession, or goal and who work together to advance and achieve this goal through collaboration and regular interaction. This organizational and operative structure enables the development of an efficient interactive learning model that can be otherwise challenging to achieve through traditional methods. To support this point, Johnson (2001) argued that a primary reason for the growing interest in CoPs is the "dissatisfaction with traditional learning methods and arenas" (p. 48). In a similar vein, Mortier (2018) asserted that the CoP framework offers an alternative to top-down approaches, allows space for trust and uncertainty, bridges the gap between theory and practice, and minimizes power imbalances.

This chapter expands on the CoP framework to introduce the DEIA-enhanced CoP framework, which emphasizes the need to embed DEIA principles into the community's structure, goals, and activities and ensures that these principles are central elements in the collaborative learning and knowledge-sharing process of the CoP. In the context of this chapter, the DEIA-enhanced Arabic CoP is committed to creating a sustainably supportive and inclusive space for Arabic educators by addressing the challenges they face and establishing an inclusive and accessible collaborative environment where they have equitable access to essential resources,

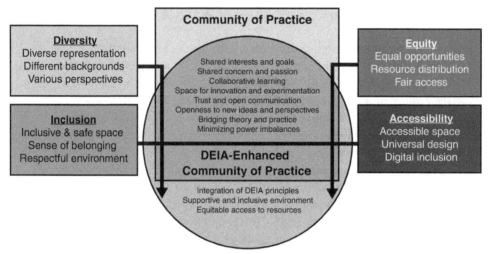

Figure 10.1 DEIA-Enhanced CoP Framework
Source: The author.

professional training, and networking opportunities. These goals manifest through regular PD workshops, online forums for resource sharing, and networking events that connect educators from diverse backgrounds. In pursuit of these goals, the CoP aims to cultivate an environment that embodies the principles of DEIA in the realm of Arabic language education.

Figure 10.1 illustrates the DEIA-enhanced CoP framework, which integrates the principles of DEIA into the traditional CoP model. The DEIA-enhanced CoP expands on the initial framework by explicitly focusing on creating and maintaining accessible, inclusive, and equitable environments for Arabic language educators. To implement these principles, program developers and workshop organizers and presenters design and offer – usually with the help of technology – workshops and programs that ensure inclusivity, accessibility, and fair resource distribution while encouraging attendees from different backgrounds to participate. A DEIA-enhanced approach is particularly important in Arabic language teaching to address the challenges of diglossia, pedagogical diversity, feelings of isolation, and resource limitations.

Within the framework of the DEIA-enhanced CoP, the DC-ATC, which is supported by the Qatar Foundation International (QFI), stands as a notable example of a CoP effectively responding to the complex challenges prevalent in the field of Arabic language education. QFI is an organization dedicated to enhancing and expanding Arabic language education globally by supporting innovative and research-based programs and Arabic language initiatives in state-funded schools. QFI's mission, as stated on its website, is to support "the entire Arabic learning ecosystem" (Qatar Foundation International, n.d.). To accomplish this mission, it facilitated the creation of Arabic Teacher Councils (ATCs) in the United States and beyond, and granted each council funds for teacher training and Arabic language promotion. One of these councils is the DC-ATC, a collaborative group comprising university, community college, and K–12 Arabic educators in the District of Columbia, Maryland, and Virginia region. The DC-ATC was established in September 2019 and is committed to enhancing Arabic language education through

- creating opportunities for teachers of Arabic at all grade levels to meet, network, share resources and ideas
- supporting schools that want to start or increase Arabic language teaching
- sponsoring community-based events that elevate the teaching of Arabic language and culture (DC Arabic Teachers' Council, n.d.)

As evidenced by its mission, the DC-ATC not only offers funding and professional development opportunities but also serves as a valuable platform for Arabic teachers to connect, network, and exchange resources and ideas. By emphasizing this collaborative approach, the DC-ATC aims at creating and maintaining a supportive and inclusive environment for the teaching of Arabic. The following section examines how the DC-ATC uses technology to organize and offer workshops aimed at addressing the challenges that Arabic educators face and alleviating DEIA concerns within the field of Arabic instruction.

4 Navigating Challenges: The DC-ATC's Contribution to Supporting Arabic Teachers

By involving teachers from universities, community colleges, and K–12 schools, the DC-ATC plays an important role in bridging the gap between higher education institutions and primary and secondary schools. According to Soliman and Khalil (2022), the key to advancing Arabic teaching and learning as a communal language lies in the collaboration between universities and schools. They argue:

> Although the type of learners in schools (children) are diverse and have different learning needs from those in HE [higher education], the collaboration between schools and universities would help in creating a more homogenous Arabic teaching community in which universities can benefit from the hands-on experience of school teachers while schools can benefit from university research findings. (p. 10)

Although Soliman and Khalil's (2022) advocacy for interinstitutional collaboration is situated within the context of Arabic teaching in the United Kingdom, their argument is equally applicable to the US educational context. Building on the importance of collaboration, the DC-ATC has organized multiple workshops that align with its mission to create and maintain a vibrant community of Arabic language educators with different institutional affiliations and from various geographical locations. In order to create this community, the DC-ATC emphasized networking and resource sharing within its organized workshops. This emphasis reflects the DC-ATC's commitment to building strong professional connections among teachers that would allow them to easily and effectively collaborate and share resources and expertise. The Appendix presents a comprehensive list of workshops organized by the DC-ATC spanning from January 2020 to December 2023. A total of 30 workshops were organized during that period. Of these, 24 workshops (80 per cent) were conducted online, 4 workshops (13 per cent) were conducted in a hybrid format, and 2 (7 per cent) were conducted in person. It is important to note that, before the COVID-19 pandemic, all workshops were conducted in person. The pandemic-induced mass migration towards remote instruction has indeed had unanticipated benefits in connecting Arabic language instructors by providing them with greater connectedness, flexibility, and access to PD opportunities. The flexibility and connectivity provided by online formats have encouraged the members of the DC-ATC to continue with remote workshops beyond 2023.

The 2020–2023 workshops covered different topics such as innovative teaching practices, technology integration, computer-assisted language learning (CALL), cultural competence, assessment strategies, diglossia, and heritage students' instruction. The diversity of these workshops, along with the predominantly virtual format, helped address the diverse needs of Arabic language educators and allowed teachers from various locations to participate.

Active participation in the workshops was fostered through various methods, including breakout rooms for small group discussions, collaborative activities, and interactive presentations. Diglossia came up as an ongoing concern among participants, even when the workshop topic did not specifically focus on that topic. During the workshops, participants continuously engaged with each other and with the presenter(s) to explore the latest approaches to teaching Arabic dialects and to discuss the practical applications of diglossic pedagogies. For instance, workshops like "Project-Based Learning: A Workshop for Arabic Educators" and "Engaging Heritage Learners through Creative Activities in the Arabic Language Classroom" included extensive discussions on diglossia and diglossic teaching strategies. During these discussions, educators shared their experiences and exchanged insights and practical approaches to address the challenges of diglossia such as contextual learning, cultural immersion, use of authentic materials, assessment diversity, and strategies for effective code-switching.

Another central topic in the DC-ATC workshops was CALL and the integration of technology in language teaching. For example, the "Teaching a Language in a Hybrid Format" workshop explored communication-based and culturally relevant tasks designed for both in-person and online settings. During this workshop, participants were introduced to various educational online tools and given specific steps and examples on how to implement these online tools aimed at engaging students and supporting tasks across interpretive, interpersonal, and presentational communication modes. Tools such as Screencast-o-Matic, the Digital Language Lab, Pear Deck, EdPuzzle, Flip, Padlet, and Booklet were among those presented.

In addition to workshops addressing general CALL applications, several workshops focused on introducing participants to educational online tools that are designed specifically for teaching and learning Arabic. For example, the workshop titled "Using Technology to Support Arabic Literacy" introduced participants to the free, teacher-created resource *Read, Learn and Play Arabic: K–16 Online Interactive Arabic Reading Materials* (RLP; https://campuspress.yale.edu/readlearnplayarabic/). RLP features American Council on the Teaching of Foreign Languages (ACTFL) standards–aligned, levelled texts and virtual practice activities tailored for elementary through university students. During the workshop, attendees were offered the opportunity to engage in hands-on exploration of the presented materials and to learn how to integrate RLP into their courses.

Similarly, the workshop titled "Anamel: A Collaborative Online Anthology of Arabic Modules" introduced participants to an innovative platform for teaching and learning Arabic. The workshop facilitators presented Anamel, a WordPress site that was created by students from Duke University and the University of North Carolina to showcase capstone modules in Arabic. The facilitators discussed the benefits of Anamel for the global Arabic language instructional community and examined the challenges of implementing project-based learning, especially in advanced Arabic classes.

Another significant challenge for Arabic instructors has been the creation and delivery of fully online courses. The COVID-19 pandemic has exacerbated this challenge and prompted Arabic teachers to adapt and find new ways to cope rapidly and effectively. In order to discuss the lessons learned from the pandemic, the DC-ATC offered a workshop titled "How to Design an Online Arabic Course." As its name indicates, the workshop introduced participants to innovative and practical strategies to assist them in designing an effective online class by guiding them through the creation of modules, quizzes, and assignments in the Canvas learning management system, as well as grade management.

In addition to covering CALL applications and Arabic online educational tools, the DC-ATC workshops addressed other concerns in the field of Arabic instruction, such as teaching culture, providing study abroad opportunities, and organizing extracurricular activities. Addressing Al-Busaidi's (2015) argument that "the challenges that face Arabic programmes can also be attributed to the lack of a systematic approach to the integration of Arabic culture as an important factor for language competence" (p. 714), the DC-ATC offered workshops that focused specifically on integrating culture into the Arabic teaching curricular. Workshops such as "Using Ramadan in the Arabic Classroom" and "Teaching Arabic Language & Culture through Food" upheld a dual focus on language and culture by emphasizing the design and dissemination of various cultural materials that represent the diversity of the Arabic-speaking world.

Focusing on addressing the challenges faced by Arabic educators and promoting the principles of DEIA, the DC-ATC's workshop presenters endeavoured to create an accessible and inclusive environment that catered to the different needs of the attendees and their students. In order to alleviate linguistic barriers, several presenters used presentation slides in Arabic and code-switched between Arabic and English. In the same vein, workshop facilitators encouraged attendees to participate and ask questions in the language they were most comfortable with. This linguistic flexibility created a supportive environment that facilitated communication and knowledge sharing among attendees.

In addition to addressing linguistic barriers, the DC-ATC workshops endeavoured to comprehensively address DEIA concerns, including those related to physical abilities and digital inclusivity. When delivering workshops, organizers and facilitators leveraged technology in order to create an inclusive and accessible environment that encouraged and supported open communication and resource sharing. The use of closed captions and chat features during online sessions and the sharing of presentation slides in accessible formats provided attendees with the opportunity to participate in workshop discussions and to enhance their understanding of and engagement with the workshop content. Furthermore, technology played a crucial role in overcoming geographical barriers by allowing educators from different locations to participate in the workshops without needing to be physically present.

However, despite its numerous benefits, the use of technology has also presented some challenges for both attendees and presenters. Issues such as varying levels of digital literacy and inconsistent access to high-speed internet negatively impacted some attendees' ability to participate and fully engage in workshops. Additionally, presenters sometimes experienced occasional connectivity issues that caused temporary disruptions in the flow of the sessions. Another challenge that faced both presenters and attendees was the incompatibility of the Arabic script with some online tools, which sometimes resulted in improperly connected or completely disconnected letters. These issues highlight the need for providing more workshops aimed at enhancing participants' digital literacy and for organizing more trial runs and practice sessions for presenters.

5 Conclusion

This chapter attempted to provide an overview of the Arabic instruction landscape in the United States. To achieve this aim, it started by discussing the various challenges that Arabic educational practitioners have been facing, namely issues related to diglossia, diverse teaching methods, resource constraints, and PD limitations. Despite these continued challenges, Al-Busaidi (2015) argued, the field has managed to make significant strides that have improved the educational experiences for both instructors and learners. The DEIA-enhanced CoP framework, proposed in this chapter and exemplified by the DC-ATC, demonstrates the impact of such communities in mitigating challenges and addressing teachers' concerns. By organizing various workshops, integrating DEIA principles, and leveraging technology, the DC-ATC has worked towards creating and maintaining a supportive, inclusive, and accessible environment for Arabic instructors. The chapter examined the council's organizational and operative structure, explored the workshops it organized between 2020 and 2023, and discussed the impact of these workshops in mitigating the challenges faced by Arabic educators.

Some of these challenges are, indeed, not unique to the Arabic language. It is therefore hoped that the field of language education globally could benefit from adopting the DEIA-enhanced CoP. By fostering collaborative communities, leveraging technology, and integrating DEIA principles, other language education fields can replicate the DC-ATC's efforts to overcome their unique challenges and improve the overall educational experience for both teachers and students.

About the Author

Kamilia Rahmouni is an associate professor at the School of World Studies at Virginia Commonwealth University. Her interdisciplinary research interests include applied linguistics, the use of AI in education, Arabic sociolinguistics, and discourse analysis.

References

Abboud, P.F. (1971). Arabic language instruction. *Middle East Studies Association Bulletin, 5*(2), 1–23. https://doi.org/10.1017/S0026318400052779

Abboud, P.F. (1995). The teaching of Arabic in the United States: Whence and whither? In M. Al-Batal (Ed.), *The teaching of Arabic as a foreign language: Issues and directions* (pp. 13–34). Georgetown University Press.

Al-Batal, M. (1992). Diglossia and proficiency: The need for an alternative approach to teaching. In A. Rouchdy (Ed.), *The Arabic language in America* (pp. 284–304). Wayne State University Press.

Al-Batal, M. (2007). Arabic and national language educational policy. *Modern Language Journal*, *91*(2), 268–271. https://doi.org/10.1111/j.1540-4781.2007.00543_10.x

Al-Batal, M., & Belnap, R.K. (2006). The teaching and learning of Arabic in the United States: Realities, needs, and future directions. In K.M. Wahba, Z.A. Taha, & L. England (Eds.), *Handbook for Arabic language teaching professionals in the 21st century* (pp. 389–399). Routledge. https://doi.org/10.4324/9780203824757

Al-Busaidi, F. (2015). Arabic in foreign language programmes: Difficulties and challenges. *Journal of Educational and Psychological Studies*, *9*(4), 701–717. https://doi.org/10.53543/jeps.vol9iss4pp701-717

Alosh, M.M. (1992). Designing a proficiency-oriented syllabus for Modern Standard Arabic as a foreign language. In A. Rouchdy (Ed.), *The Arabic language in America: Al-Luġat Al-'arabīyat Fī 'Amrīkā* (pp. 251–283). Wayne State University Press.

Badawi, S.M. (1973). *Mustawayaat al-'arabiyyah al-mu'aaSirah fi Misr* [Levels of Contemporary Arabic in Egypt]. Dar al-Ma'arif.

Berbeco, S. (2019). *Case method and the Arabic teacher: A practical guide*. Lehigh University Press.

DC Arabic Teachers' Council. (n.d.). DC Arabic Teachers' Council. Institute for Middle East Studies, George Washington University. Archived at https://web.archive.org/web/20240707142902/https://blogs.gwu.edu/elliott-imes/publichumanities/arabic-teacher-council/

De Felice, D., Lanier, A., & Winke, P. (2019). Serving the less-commonly-trained teacher: Perspectives from Arabic instructors. *The Qualitative Report*, *24*(9), 2309–2327. https://doi.org/10.46743/2160-3715/2019.3277

Fakhri, A. (1995). Arabic as a foreign language: Bringing diglossia into the classroom. In M. Haggstrom, L. Morgan, & J. Wieczorek (Eds.), *The foreign language classroom: Bridging theory and practice* (pp. 135–147). Routledge. https://doi.org/10.4324/9780203820858-9

Ferguson, C.A. (1959). Diglossia. *Word*, *15*(2), 325–340. https://doi.org/10.1080/00437956.1959.11659702

Fishman, J.A. (1967). Bilingualism with and without diglossia; Diglossia with and without bilingualism. *Journal of Social Issues*, *23*(2), 29–38. https://doi.org/10.1111/j.1540-4560.1967.tb00573.x

Gibson, M. (2002). Dialect levelling in Tunisian Arabic: Towards a new spoken standard. In A. Rouchdy (Ed.), *Language contact and language conflict in Arabic: Variations on a sociolinguistic theme* (pp. 24–40). Routledge. https://doi.org/10.4324/9780203037218-8

Ibrahim, M. (1986). Standard and prestige language: A problem in Arabic sociolinguistics. *Anthropological Linguistics*, *28*(1), 115–126. https://www.jstor.org/stable/30027950

Johnson, C.M. (2001). A survey of current research on online communities of practice. *The Internet and Higher Education*, *4*(1), 45–60. https://doi.org/10.1016/S1096-7516(01)00047-1

Lave, J., & Wenger, E. (1991). *Situated learning: Legitimate peripheral participation*. Cambridge University Press. https://doi.org/10.1017/CBO9780511815355

Liedtka, J. (1999). Linking competitive advantage with communities of practice. *Journal of Management Inquiry*, *8*(1), 5–16. https://doi.org/10.1177/105649269981002

Maamouri, M. (1998, September 3–6). *Language education and human development: Arabic diglossia and its impact on the quality of education in the Arab region* [Paper presentation]. Mediterranean Development Forum, Marrakech, Morocco. https://www.scribd.com/document/85028998/Arabic-Diglossia-and-its-Impact-on-the-Quality-of-Education-in-the-Arab-Region

Mana, M. (2011). Arabic-teacher training and professional development: A view from STARTALK. *Al-'Arabiyya*, *44/45*, 87–101. https://www.jstor.org/stable/43208725

McCarus, E.N. (1987). The study of Arabic in the United States: A history of its development. *Al-Arabiyya*, *20*, 13–27. http://www.jstor.org/stable/43191685

Mortier, K. (2018). Communities of practice: A conceptual framework for inclusion of students with significant disabilities. *International Journal of Inclusive Education*, *24*(3), 329–340. https://doi.org/10.1080/13603116.2018.1461261

Nash, A. (2010) Critical issues of Arabic learning and teaching: An interview with Michael Cooperson. *Issues in Applied Linguistics*, *18*(1), 125–139. https://doi.org/10.5070/L4181005126

Palmer, J. (2007). Arabic diglossia: Teaching only the standard variety is a disservice to students. *Arizona Working Papers in SLA & Teaching*, *14*, 111–122. https://journals.uair.arizona.edu/index.php/AZSLAT/article/view/21267

Qatar Foundation International. (n.d.). *About*. Qatar Foundation International. https://www.qfi.org/about/

Ryding, K.C. (1991). Proficiency despite diglossia: A new approach for Arabic. *Modern Language Journal*, *75*(2), 212–218. https://doi.org/10.1111/j.1540-4781.1991.tb05352.x

Sai, Y. (2017). "Arabic is not my language...": Debates over teaching of Arabic in Irish Muslim schools. *Journal of Muslim Minority Affairs, 37*(4), 442–453. https://doi.org/10.1080/13602004.2017.1399602

Snowden, E., Soliman, R., & Towler, M. (2016). *Teaching Arabic as a foreign language in the UK – Strand 1 Research: How Arabic is being taught in schools*. British Council.

Soliman, R., & Khalil, S. (2022). The teaching of Arabic as a community language in the UK. *International Journal of Bilingual Education and Bilingualism, 27*(9), 1246–1257. https://doi.org/10.1080/13670050.2022.2063686

Versteegh, K. (2001). *The Arabic language*. Edinburgh University Press.

Wahba, K. (2006). Arabic language use and the educated language user. In K. Wahba, Z. Taha, & L. England (Eds.), *Handbook for Arabic language teaching professionals in the 21st century* (pp. 139–155). Routledge. https://doi.org/10.4324/9780203824757

Wenger, E. (1998). *Communities of practice: Learning, meaning, and identity*. Cambridge University Press. https://doi.org/10.1017/CBO9780511803932

Wenger-Trayner, E., & Wenger-Trayner, B. (2015). *Introduction to communities of practice: A brief overview of the concept and its uses*. https://www.wenger-trayner.com/introduction-to-communities-of-practice

Younes, M. (2006). Integrating the colloquial with fuṣḥā in the Arabic-as-a-foreign-language classroom. In K.M. Wahba, Z.A. Taha, & L. England (Eds.), *Handbook for Arabic language teaching professionals in the 21st century* (pp. 157–166). Routledge. https://doi.org/10.4324/9780203824757

Younes, M. (2014). *The integrated approach to Arabic instruction*. Routledge. https://doi.org/10.4324/9781315740614

Appendix: List of Workshops Organized by the DC-ATC

Date	Workshop Title	Type
JAN 2020	Interpersonal Communication: A Workshop for Arabic Instructors	Online
FEB 2020	Project-Based Learning: A Workshop for Arabic Educators	Online
APR 2020	Asserting Identity in Children and Youth Literature	Online
MAY 2020	Student-Centered Activities in the Arabic Classroom	Online
NOV 2020	Social Impact Media Awards (SIMA) Studios and Using Film in the Arabic Classroom	Online
DEC 2020	From Morocco to Dubai: Engagement and Immersion with Virtual Reality	Online
JAN 2021	Social Justice and Foreign Language	Online
MAR 2021	Beyond the Boxes: Increasing Student Engagement in Remote Learning	Online
MAY 2021	MovieTalk in the Classroom	Online
JUL 2021	K–5 Arabic Teachers' Resource Exchange and Social Hour	Online
AUG 2021	Anamel: A Collaborative Online Anthology of Arabic Modules	Online
SEP 2021	Arabic Teacher Workshop on Teaching Arabic Language & Culture through Food	Online
DEC 2021	Engaging Heritage Learners through Creative Activities in the Arabic Language Classroom	Online
JAN 2022	Assessing Language Learning with LinguaGrow	Online
FEB 2022	Project-Based Learning II	Online
MAR 2022	Teaching a Language in a Hybrid Format	Online
APR 2022	Useful and Practical Assessment in the Arabic Language Classroom	Online
JUN 2022	How to Design an Online Arabic Course	Online
JUN 2022	Geography in Arabic Literature: Space, Place, and Mapping	In person
OCT 2022	Generating Arabic Buy-in: Getting Students and Families on Board	Online

Date	Workshop Title	Type
DEC 2022	Universal Design: Inclusivity in the Classroom	Online
JAN 2023	Opportunities for Arabic Learners beyond the Classroom	Online
FEB 2023	Using Ramadan in the Arabic Classroom	Hybrid
APR 2023	Resource Sharing for Arabic Middle & High School Teachers	Hybrid
MAY 2023	Resource Sharing for Primary School Arabic Teachers	Hybrid
MAY 2023	Using Technology to Support Arabic Literacy	Hybrid
JUN 2023	Poetry, Literature, and Song in the Arabic Classroom	In person
OCT 2023	Exploring Food Sustainability: Building Global Citizens	Online
NOV 2023	Reading Current Events in the Arabic Classroom	Online
DEC 2023	How to Read the Room: A Storyteller's Approach to Connecting with Students	Online

Index

Note: The letter *f* following a page number denotes a figure; the letter *t*, a table; the letter *m*, a map.

accommodations (for learning), 61–2, 64, 151, 175, 179, 202, 207
ACTFL, 149, 166, 195, 200–5, 231
agency, 113, 127; critical agency, 47; in Indigenous thought,129–31, 141; learner agency in artmaking, 96–7, 99–101*t*; of learners, 39, 41, 43–4, 47
Ahtna, 122*f*, 135–7
Alaska, 9–10, 14, 120–1*m*, 123, 126–8, 132, 138
Alutiiq, 122*f*, 133–5
Anishinaabe, 128–9
anxiety (for language learning), 60–1, 146, 148, 163
Arabic language teaching approaches: Classical Arabic approach, 221; colloquial approach, 222; integrated approach, 224; Middle language approach, 223; MSA approach, 222; simultaneous approach, 223
art, 90–3*t*, 95–8, 99–114*t*
artmaking, 8, 105–7, 135–6
assessment, 165; of learning outcomes, 12, 57, 184; oral language, 109; reading assessment, 18, 191–8, 201–2; SDS as an assessment tool, 146–7; Seal of Biliteracy, for the, 112
asynchronous: teacher professional development, 14, 178–9, 183–4, 196–7, 202, 204, 207, 209; virtual exchange designs, 6, 44, 46, 62, 69
augmented reality (AR), 17, 136–40
authentic materials, 46, 132, 135, 184, 197*f*, 205, 231
automatic speech recognition, 146, 149–52, 163
available design, 26–8*t*, 125*t*, 133, 137, 139–41*t*
avatar, 17, 153, 155–6, 157*t*, 158*t*, 159*t*, 160

beading, 135–7
being-knowing-doing, 124, 128, 130–2, 134–7, 140–41, 139*f*
biases, 41, 43, 82–3, 173, 213
Big Ten Academic Alliance, 176
bilingual, 7, 40, 76, 94, 97–8, 104, 107–9, 138
blended learning, 57, 61

case study, 75, 193, 220
CASSIE, 174
CeLTA, 171–2
centrality of stories, 130
coding, 100–2*t*, 107, 149, 164, 199
Collaborative Online International Learning (COIL), 7, 75–81, 83, 87
colonial hegemonic monocultural and monoglossic ideologies and practices, 133, 136
colonialism and colonial languages, 9–10, 42, 133, 135–6, 173
commodification of technology, 1–2
commonly taught languages, 3, 9–11, 172–3, 179
communities of practice (CoP): DEIA-enhanced CoP, 218, 227; for LCTL teachers, 12, 18–19, 179, 194, 205, 212
community building, 5, 113, 204, 213
community of inquiry, 179
CourseShare, 174
course-sharing models, 11–12, 18, 174, 178
COVID-19: online teaching, 4, 8; and student mobility rates, 68; teacher professional development, 180, 201, 230, 232; and virtual exchange, 33, 57
crisis, 8, 13, 86
critical CALL, 1–4, 13, 15–16, 31, 34, 39–41, 43, 46–8
critical citizenry, 41
critical digital literacy (CDL), 15, 31, 39–41, 43, 46, 48
critical language awareness, 16, 90, 92, 96–7, 100*t*, 103–4, 114
critical literacy, 30, 43
critical media literacy, 111
critical pedagogy, 3, 33, 183
curriculum planning, 96

decolonizing approaches to education, 10, 141, 173
designing, 125–6*t*
differentiated instruction, 180, 183
digital literacy, 15, 191, 204, 233; critical digital literacy, 29, 31, 39, 41; generational gaps, 13, 209, 211–12
digital stories, 137–8; storytelling, 17, 39, 40, 42, 132, 140–41
digital technology, 1, 75, 77, 94, 110, 132, 134; broad reach, 30, 32; inequitable uses, 35; for transformation and social justice, 41, 46, 102, 121, 126–7, 137
diglossia, 18–19, 217–19, 221, 224, 226, 228, 230–1, 234
discrimination, 1, 3, 47, 59, 63, 78–9, 81; narratives, 16, 75, 77, 82–7
diversity, equity, inclusion, and accessibility (DEIA), 2, 4–5, 8, 10, 12, 17, 19, 35, 47, 56–8, 63, 69–70, 92, 172; DEIA-enhanced communities of practice, 218, 226–7, 228*f*, 229, 232–4; and LCTLs, 171–3, 177, 185, 192–5
dual crediting, 177
dual language program, 10, 94, 123, 137–8

Elders, 130, 132, 135–9
emergency remote teaching, 4–5, 183
empathy, 3, 15, 63–4, 68, 77, 81, 105
epistemology, 43, 121, 124, 127–8, 131, 140
e-portfolio, 45, 64–5*t*
ESL (English as a second language), 76–9, 82, 83*t*, 86–7
e-tandem, 7–8, 40
ethico-onto-epistemological grounding, 121, 124

exploratory, 16, 90, 92, 96–8, 102–4, 112–13

global citizen(ry), 3, 15, 30–1, 41, 45, 75–6, 173, 239
global citizenship education, 15, 30–1, 34, 41–3, 45

heritage identities, 96, 98, 100*t*, 103, 108–9, 114
heritage language, 103–4, 107–9, 114, 172; learners, 90, 95, 177
humanistic goals, 2, 3, 19, 77
human-machine interaction, 2, 20, 94, 97, 110, 113

identities: ethnolinguistic identities, 92, 96, 101*t*, 106; of learners, 94–6, 98, 99*t*, 100*t*, 103–4, 108–9, 110–12
ideology, 39, 42, 134
independent study, 175
Indigenous peoples, 127, 130, 138; communities, 126, 128, 131, 134; Indigenous Languages Partnership, 171–2; knowledge, 129; languages, 9–10, 14, 16–17, 121, 123, 137, 140–41, 172; pedagogies, 127, 131, 133, 135, 140; storytelling, 133; ways of being-knowing-doing, 16, 121, 124, 128–32, 135, 140–41
inequities, 1–2, 4–5, 41, 112, 175
information and communication technologies, 4, 191, 196–7, 199, 201, 211
intercultural communication, 2, 8, 29, 65*f*, 67, 77
intercultural competence: in study abroad, 55–8; in virtual exchange, 2, 45–6, 48, 64, 70–1;
intercultural experience, 15, 59, 68, 87

intercultural interaction, 31–2, 56, 59, 64–5
interculturality, 13, 57, 70
intercultural learning, 7–8, 56–8, 61–3, 69–70
intergenerational, 135; collaboration, 140, 211; interaction, 96, 98; teaching methods, 130; transmission of language, 123, 133, 136
interinstitutional goals, 91, 96
interinstitutional partnership/ collaboration, 3, 12, 47, 90, 96, 111, 123, 195; community, 121
interinstitutional planning, 95, 114
interinstitutional professional development, 12–13, 17–18, 123, 171, 177–8, 185, 191, 193–4, 203, 211–13, 228–9
international education, 56–60, 69
internationalization at home (IaH), 33–4, 37, 41, 47–8, 68
internationalization of the curriculum, 56–7
internationalization strategies, 58, 70
internet, 135, 137, 183; limited connectivity, 4–5, 13, 18, 34–6*t*, 40, 60, 102, 104, 110, 113, 132, 163, 206, 212, 233
intersectionality, 84, 100*t*, 104

K–12, 10, 14, 19, 32, 176, 181, 226, 229

labour inequity, 175
language ideology: awareness and shift, 95–7, 110–12, 114; of dominance, 9–10, 17, 40, 90, 121, 131, 134–8
language maintenance and revitalization, 10, 16–17, 121, 123–4, 132–3, 138
language warriors, 134

less commonly taught languages (LCTLs), 9–12, 193, 195, 205; and DEIA, 171–4; learners, 145–7, 156, 161–2, 164–5; sharing, 176–80
linguicism, 76
linguistic variation, 18, 97, 163–5, 220, 222–3, 225
low-bandwidth technologies, 6, 37*f*, 38*f*, 206

media, 69; for learning, 98, 99*t*, 101*t*, 102–3, 106–7, 110–11, 114; media and information literacy, 33, 48
middle school, 16, 90–1, 93–7, 110–1
Modern Language Association, 9, 172n1, 217
monoglossic ideologies, 17, 121, 131, 134–8
monolingual ideologies, 10, 17, 40, 112, 121, 131, 134, 138
motivation: of learners, 10, 56, 59–61, 67, 70, 163, 183, 225; of teachers, 200, 210–11
multilingual, 29; families and communities, 6, 91, 94–6, 100*t*; learners, 7–8, 10, 40, 41, 91–2, 108, 110–14, 172, 207; resources, 44
multilingualism, 7, 38, 94, 125
multiliteracies, 16, 94, 121, 124–5, 125*t*, 127, 141
multimedia, 132–3, 136
multimodal(ity), 29, 38–40, 43–5, 111, 134, 141; artefacts, 8, 76, 107–8, 125, 128*f*, 132, 139*f*; communicative competence, 38; learning, 108, 113, 126; literacies, 92, 96

National Less Commonly Taught Languages Resource Center, 172
neurodiverse, 91, 107, 109

New London Group, 121, 124–6
non-hierarchical relatedness, 129

ontology, 43, 130–1
open educational resource, 145, 165
oral proficiency, 145–7, 162–6
Oral Proficiency Interview (OPI), 201–4

passive, interactive, creative – replace, amplify, transform (PIC-RAT), 181, 182*f*
power and inequality, 40, 46
pragmatism, 217
pre-mobility, 15, 55, 57–8, 63–4, 68, 71
professional development (PD), 177
public engagement, 35, 37–8, 46
public service announcement (PSA), 132–3
pugtallgutkellriit, 129

qanruyutet, 132
qulirat, 132

raciolinguistics, 92, 114
redesigned 125–7*t*, 126*f*, 131, 133, 135, 137–8, 141
reflexivity, 30, 41, 45
relationship between people, knowledge, and the land, 129; relatedness, 130–1, 139*f*, 141; relational knowing, 130
repertoires, 7, 16, 38, 40, 90, 111, 114, 227

Seal of Biliteracy, 177
Shared Course Initiative, 178
social emotional learning, 96–8, 110
social isolation, 4, 94, 132; for LCTL teachers, 12, 177, 179, 204, 208, 225, 228
social justice, 13, 31–2, 36, 41, 58, 78–9, 82, 238*t*

social media, 14, 5–6, 110
sociocultural theory, 16, 121, 124, 126–7, 141, 147, 194, 212
Southeast Asian Language Council (SEALC), 165, 191–6, 198–9, 201, 203
spoken dialogue system (SDS), 17, 146–9, 151–3, 154*f*, 155*f*, 156, 157*t*, 159–67
State of Washington's Languages Without Borders project, 176
storytelling, 131, 133–4, 137, 140–41
student mobility, 33, 56, 57, 59–62, 67, 68
study abroad, 15, 33, 48, 57–62, 64, 67–8, 70–1; experience, 8, 55
sustainability, 33, 42–5, 47, 59–60, 67, 239
Sustainable Development Goal (UN), 37*f*, 38*f*, 41, 43, 45, 48, 78–9, 81
synchronous: teacher professional development, 14, 179, 183, 196–7, 202, 204–5, 207; virtual exchange, 6, 44, 46, 62, 69

target language, 2–3, 145, 147–8, 153, 158–9*t*, 164
task-based language teaching, 205
teacher education, 30, 44, 62, 67
teacher-researcher inquiry, 121
technology integration plan (TIP), 181
telecollaboration, 12, 32, 62, 201, 203–4, 207–11, 213
TESOL (Teaching English to Speakers of Other Languages), 76

text to speech, 149–50, 152, 163
three-way collaboration/exchange, 6, 15–16, 75, 79, 90–1
time zone differences, 18, 29, 179, 204–5, 212
translanguaging, 7, 37, 38*f*, 40, 45, 92, 98, 106
transliteration, 223
transnational partnership, 2–3, 47, 191, 194, 201
tribal organizations, 121, 123

under-resourced settings, 3–4, 6, 93, 112, 171, 203–4, 206, 211

videoconferencing, 6, 11–12, 14, 18, 69, 178
virtual exchange (VE), 6, 14–15, 30–2, 57–8, 62, 75–81, 87–8; critical VE, 7, 14, 31, 34, 37–8, 43–8; hegemonic VE, 42–3; lingua franca approach to VE, 7–8, 15, 39, 44, 46, 64, 76; non-hegemonic VE, 41–3, 45

wellness, 6, 16, 90–3, 97–8, 99–100*t*, 103

Yukon-Kuskokwim Delta, 132
Yup'ik, 122*f*, 123, 127, 129, 131–3, 137–8
yuuyaraq, 129

zone of proximal development (ZPD), 126–7, 128*f*, 139*f*